ΓermΓerm-time opening hours:

All in the Mind

WITHDRAWN

For my mother, Lorna Goodwin, who first introduced me to the subject.

All in the Mind: The Essence of Psychology

Adrian Furnham

Whurr Publishers Ltd
London

© 1996 Whurr Publishers Ltd

First published 1996 by
Whurr Publishers Ltd
19b Compton Terrace, London N1 2UN, England

British Library Cataloguing in Publication Data
A catalogue record for this book is available from the
British Library.

ISBN 1-897635-49-4

Printed and bound in the UK by Athenaeum Press Ltd,
Gateshead, Tyne & Wear

Contents

viii   Preface

1   Chapter 1.
Common-Sense Views and Misconceptions about Psychology

57   Chapter 2.
The Background to Modern Psychology

77   Chapter 3.
Is Psychology a Science?

113   Chapter 4.
That Man Called Freud

127   Chapter 5.
Psychology at Work

153   Chapter 6.
Current Controversies in Psychology

201   Chapter 7.
The Psychology of Everyday Life

242   Chapter 8.
The State of the Art in Psychology

255   References

259   Index

There is something wrong with a society in which parents are afraid to speak to their children without first consulting a psychologist. *(Balaam)*

Anyone who goes to a psychiatrist ought to have his head examined. *(Sam Goldwyn)*

Many who go into the profession (psychoanalysis) do so in order to overcome their own neurosis. *(Professor Ernest Jones)*

Because Professor Feynman answered an Army psychiatrist's questions truthfully he was thought to be insane. *(Stuart Sutherland)*

The business of psychology is to tell us what actually goes on in the mind. It cannot possibly tell us whether the beliefs are true or false. *(Hastings Rashdall)*

Psychiatry's chief contribution to philosophy is the discovery that the toilet is the seat of the soul. *(Alexander Chase)*

Plagued by anxiety, troubled by worry, the psychological individual of our decade seeks only 'peace of mind.' It appears to represent the best way of coping with life's tensions. There is a pathological need to fill the hollow of our inner being. As we do not have a sufficient sense of selfhood, there must be a constant reaffirmation of our existence by seeing ourselves in others. *(Sambar Cohen)*

Fads run their course through the mob like the measles....One of the latest is psychoanalysis. *(Frank Crane)*

A large part of the popularity and persuasiveness of psychology comes from its being a sublimated spiritualism: a secular, ostensibly scientific way of affirming the primacy of 'spirit' over matter. *(Susan Sontag)*

There is no psychology; there is only biography and autobiography. *(Thomas Szasz)*

Psychiatrists are the new monks, their offices the secular monasteries against whose walls come to wail, while seeking to be shriven, the guilt-ridden, the sinner, the troubled-in-mind. *(Alexander Theroux)*

I do not have a psychiatrist and I do not want one, for the simple reason that if he listened to me long enough, he might become disturbed. *(James Thurber)*

Psychotherapy, unlike castor oil, which will work no matter how you get it down, is useless when forced on an uncooperative patient. *(Abigail Van Buren)*

Trying to define yourself is like trying to bite your own teeth. *(Alan Watts)*

psychiatrist (n.) a person who owns a couch and charges you for lying on it. *(Edwin Brock)*

psychiatry (n.) spending $50 an hour to squeal on your mother. *(Mike Connolly)*

psychoanalysis (n.) the disease it purports to cure. *(Karl Kraus)*

psychologist (n.) a man who, when a good-looking girl enters the room, looks at everyone else. *(anon)*

psychopath (n.) someone who lives in an ivory tower and dribbles over the battlements.

Preface

What is Psychology all about?

Psychology is everywhere in today's society. No reporting of a world event or disaster, no television chat show, no medical consultation is complete without the introduction of a psychological angle, from amateurs or professionals. The design of your car, your house, the defence of the realm, they way you raise your children, the computer on which this book is word-processed, all have been influenced by recent psychological research. Psychological theories pepper crime fiction and TV documentaries alike, and psychology has an accepted role in management, in sports and in consumer marketing.

But what exactly is psychology? And what is the difference between psychology and psychiatry? In spite of the ubiquity of the topic, its definition and scope are surprisingly inaccessible to the layperson. Psychology sections of bookshops are often crammed with 'self-help' books which give both a narrow and a wrong impression of the scope of the subject. We are all, of course, psychologists because we are observers of our own behaviour and develop personal theories to account for it. But as an academic subject, psychology is rarely taught in schools and thus few adults are exposed to its systematic study. Evening classes, management courses and the like may provide some limited insight into some aspects of the subject, but given the relative prevalence of 'pop' psychology versus its academic, serious and scientific cousin, it is not surprising that myths about psychology and psychologists abound and there is considerable confusion as to what the discipline does and does not purport to cover.

This book aims to plug that gap and to provide an overview of the scope of the subject for the general reader. I would like you, the reader, to be an educated consumer of the psychological theories and 'evidence' with which you are daily bombarded, to be able to discern the useful from the bogus and to have the critical tools with which to judge the 'ologists' who populate the TV screens and the airwaves. I hope to dispel a few myths, correct a few erroneous beliefs and inform you about one of the most important and exciting sciences.

This is not a textbook, but a guide to some of the issues discussed by ordinary people. It does not cover all of psychology by any means but is mainly concerned with controversial issues and those discussed by the layman and woman. I hope it will leave you better informed about some of the facts and fables surrounding the subject.

Psychology is now one of the most popular subjects to study at university and its popularity has been increasing over the years. It is also one of the most commonly discussed topics in the media. Why is this?

1. As a new science, barely 100 years old, psychology is constantly undergoing development and change. Its birth date is 1879 in Leipzig, Germany. More importantly, new discoveries are constantly being made. Human behaviour is the 'last frontier' for science and psychology is 'Queen of the social sciences'. Anyone comparing a psychology textbook written even 20 years ago with a recent one will immediately see how far the science has developed and, no doubt, how far it still has to go.

2. Psychology is both a pure and an applied science. It aims to understand behaviour and the basic mechanisms and processes that influence ideas, feelings and thoughts. But it also tries to solve human problems and apply the theoretical knowledge gained. In hospitals, factories, schools, prisons, mental hospitals, the government, the military and even the secret service, psychologists have attempted to improve the quality of life by testing and applying their theories.

3. Psychology is multidisciplinary, having close connections with many other subjects including anatomy, medicine, psychiatry and sociology as well as economics, mathematics and zoology. This means that psychology researchers are exposed to a wide variety of ideas, concepts and methods used in other disciplines. It influences and is influenced by many other fields. But psychology is also a core discipline with its own ideas and concepts. It has built up a significant body of knowledge, has its own theories, methods and schools of thought.

4.   Psychology is about all aspects of human behaviour. Newcomers to the subject of psychology are often surprised by the range of things that psychologists study – from dreaming to drug addiction; computer phobia to the causes of cancer; memory to social mobility; attitude formation to alcoholism. Psychologists tend to specialise later on in their careers and take a particular interest in certain psychological processes or groups (i.e. children, mental patients), but many continue to share very wide interests in the nature of human behaviour.

It is no wonder, then, that so many people express a considerable interest in, and a desire to study, psychology. While psychologists are frequently asked to comment on everyday occurrences in the media, and are sometimes portrayed in fictional stories, it is very difficult to get a balanced and informed view of what the discipline is all about. Psychology is the favourite media 'ology' but a two-minute sound-bite does not allow the full intricacy and complexity of issues to be discussed.

As a result many students are surprised – usually pleasantly but not always – to discover what is studied in psychology. Not all are familiar with the scope of psychology and the ways in which it is taught. But a very large number say they wish to continue their studies after graduating: surely a testament to the intrinsically interesting nature of the subject.

I have enjoyed writing this book which was done on three continents: it was started on Christmas Eve (1994) in Cairns, Australia; continued mostly in central London; but finished on a humid summer's day in the Crown Colony of Hong Kong. Parts of the book (sections 1.2, 1.4, 1.5, 1.6, 2.1, 2.2, 3.3 and 3.5) are similar to those found in *Why Psychology?* published by University College Press, London, and written by me. I have drawn on many different books in writing this one and have enjoyed the experience. For me, writing is a sort of therapy; indeed I find I can understand issues more clearly when I write, rather than talk, about them. Of course I should add, as all authors are bound to do, that any errors of omission and commission, *faux pas*, and misjudgements must be mine alone.

Adrian Furnham
Hong Kong, 1995

Chapter 1: Common-Sense Views and Misconceptions about Psychology

1.1 Introduction

Psychology is a new science, barely 100 years old. The subject is constantly undergoing development and change. With new discoveries, we are understanding more and more about such things as how the brain operates, why people behave the way they do and the causes of human unhappiness.

What people who study psychology often say is that it gives you an 'aha' experience. This concept is based on the distinction between trial-and-error learning, which involves trying out theories or hypotheses until the 'correct' answer is found as opposed to just 'fiddling about' with the problem in the hope that the solution presents itself. 'Aha' is the expression of surprised happiness that comes with insight. 'Aha' experiences often occur when psychology can offer explanations for seemingly bizarre or irrational behaviour: why people spend money when depressed or why anorexics starve themselves.

Perhaps more importantly and usefully, psychology teaches people a rich vocabulary through which they can describe and explain behaviour. Just as going to an art gallery with an art historian (or even better, a tape recording of his or her comments) can bring paintings to life because they are able to point out and describe minor details of major significance, so psychology teaches the student the language of behavioural description. There is a joke about 'psychobabble', which is the mis- or over-use of psychological language and concepts, but this usually occurs only in the popular press and by non-psychologists. It is said that because Eskimos have about 50 different words for snow they can distinguish between many different types of snow that we cannot. In this sense psychologists can see more than those who do not have the conceptual language to describe different types of behaviour. Thus they distinguish between different types of depression as well as describing many personality traits.

Some psychological theories are counterintuitive – that is, a number of the theories are not what common sense suggests. Some theories are pretty commonsensical but there are also a number that are not. Nevertheless, many sceptics and some cynics have continued to maintain that all the findings in psychology really are only a form of common sense. Surely, they argue, human nature dictates what people are really like and there certainly is no shortage of opinions from philosophers on the topic of human nature.

One way to discover the real nature of human nature is, according to most psychologists, through scientific experimentation and observation, but lay people do not use scientific evidence when forming their ideas about their fellows. Many believe in superstitions and old wives' tales that have been perpetuated, but never tested, over the generations.

1.2   Superstition vs science

There has been considerable interest in the knowledge, beliefs and superstitions that students bring to psychology courses. In 1925 Nixon sought to demonstrate that his students arrived at the beginning of his psychology classes with a variety of erroneous beliefs about human behaviour, but that these changed as a result of his teaching. Many have attempted to do likewise; most have failed. He gave more than 350 students a 30-item True–False test containing items such as 'Many eminent men have been feeble minded as children', 'A square jaw is a sign of willpower' and 'The marriage of cousins is practically certain to result in children of inferior intelligence'. Over half of this sample believed: 'Intelligence can be increased with training'; 'The study of mathematics is valuable because it gives one a logical mind'; 'Man is superior because his conduct is very largely guided by reason'; 'Adults sometimes become feeble-minded from over-study' and 'You can estimate an individual's intelligence pretty closely by just looking at his face'.

Twenty-five years later Levitt (1952) replicated this study on superstition; a questionnaire was administered to 100 men and the results were compared with those of Nixon. There was overall a significant decline in superstitious beliefs. Some superstitions like those concerning phrenology and physiognomy (determining a person's character by examining bumps on their skull or from the appearance of their face) he believed had become extinct, although he noted that others which had declined, such as those concerning magic, would probably find modern replacements. He concluded that superstitions (or cognitive distortions) must be important to the individual (otherwise they would not be held), ambiguous (because the true facts are lacking or concealed) and related to certain personality factors (insecure, anxious, neurotically prone).

Over 30 years later Tupper and Williams (1986) replicated the study in Australia and found the level of superstition back up to 21% compared with Nixon (1925) at 30.4% and Levitt (1952) at 6.5%. Thus instead of seeing a steady decline in superstitious beliefs over time, the results are moderately consistent between 1925 and 1983. These results do show a modest decline but not as much as predicted by Nixon and indeed an increase on Levitt. Of course, it may well be that methodological artefacts account for these results: for example, Levitt only had male students; Tupper and Williams' (1986) study was done in Australia; subjects from all three groups were not comparable in terms of education and so on. On the other hand, it may well be that superstitious, non-scientific beliefs regarding human nature have only marginally decreased over time. Many researchers believe that although these superstitious beliefs may be culturally relative and changeable following fashions, they are unlikely to decline greatly as they fulfil an important psychological function, namely the reduction of anxiety.

In another example Gregory (1975) replicated a study by Conklin (1919) on genuine superstitions in college students such as unlucky symbols (black cats, the number 13, broken mirrors). The results showed that superstitious beliefs and practices have changed rather than declined over time. For instance, carrying lucky rabbits' feet or avoiding cracks in the pavement were no longer practised, whereas saving certain coins and finding horseshoes were thought to be even more lucky than was thought in the past.

But how superstitious are you? Nearly 50 years ago an American psychologist called Ralya gave the following test to medical students. Read each question and decide whether it is true or false.

Test 1: Beliefs About Human Nature

		True	False
1.	The position of the stars at the time of a man's birth determines, in part, his character.	T	F
2.	The ancient Greeks were born with better intellects than people are endowed with today.	T	F
3.	Man is biologically descended from a species of existing apes.	T	F
4.	Apes have been known to solve problems that the average three-year-old child could not solve.	T	F
5.	Some of the higher apes are as intelligent as the average man.	T	F
6.	Animals depend to a greater extent on inherited ways of doing things than does man.	T	F
7.	The conscience is part of man's natural equipment at birth.	T	F
8.	Mothers instinctively know the best ways of caring for their children.	T	F
9.	Most children are born bad.	T	F
10.	Most children are born good.	T	F
11.	Human nature cannot be changed as it is based upon instincts.	T	F
12.	All people reach physical maturity by the age of eighteen.	T	F
14.	All traits present in a child at birth are inherited traits.	T	F
15.	All traits appearing in a child after birth are the results of environmental influence.	T	F
16.	With the exception of identical twins, it is extremely unlikely that any two people have exactly the same heredity.	T	F
17.	Voodooism is in the blood of the Negro.	T	F
18.	An English-speaking person with German ancestors finds it easier to learn German than an		

English-speaking person with French ancestors.   T   F

19. If the tails are cut off of generation after generation
     of rats, there will eventually be born rats without
     tails.   T   F

20. An average child of the cave-man of 10 000 years
     ago, if brought up in an American home of today,
     would in all probability become an ordinary
     American adult.   T   F

21. Human progress is due to increased native
     intelligence from age to age.   T   F

22. All men are born with equal powers.   T   F

23. The average white man is born superior,
     intellectually, to the average man of any other race.   T   F

24. Primitive people are born with keener
     senses than the more highly civilised.   T   F

25. Men are, on average, born superior
     intellectually to women.   T   F

26. People cannot be sharply differentiated
     into blondes and brunettes in many cases.   T   F

27. If we knew all about a person's heredity we
     could predict his success in the world.   T   F

28. Any child, if carefully trained from birth,
     could be made into a successful doctor,
     lawyer, engineer or journalist.   T   F

29. Geniuses are always successful, whatever the
     handicaps of their environment.   T   F

30. Most great men have been born of poor but
     honest parents.   T   F

31. On average the strongest men physically
     are the weakest mentally.   T   F

32. Homely women are born with more
     intelligence than beautiful women.   T   F

33. Brilliant children are more subject to brain fever
     than children of average or sub-normal intelligence.   T   F

34. No defect of body or mind can hold us back
    if we have willpower enough.   T   F

35. Faith alone can heal a broken leg.   T   F

36. Intelligence plays a larger role in human
    happiness than does emotion.   T   F

37. We are more likely to become fatigued
    from work that does not interest us than
    from work that does interest us.   T   F

38. A person who is fatigued invariably does
    poorer work than the same person fully
    rested.   T   F

39. Two individuals of the same intelligence
    will give almost identical testimony
    concerning an accident which they have
    both witnessed.   T   F

40. All of man's actions are determined by his
    desire to seek pleasure and avoid pain.   T   F

41. A man's character can be read by noting the
    size and location of certain developments on
    his head.   T   F

42. Certain lines on a person's hand are
    indicative of his future.   T   F

43. People with long fingers are likely to be
    artistic.   T   F

45. Red-headed people are likely to be
    temperamental.   T   F

46. Large-mouthed people are likely to be
    generous.   T   F

47. Green-eyed people are likely to be more
    jealous than blue-eyed people.   T   F

48. Brunettes are more trustworthy than
    blondes.   T   F

49. Cold hands are a sign of warm heart.   T   F

50. A person who holds his thumbs in his hands
    is a coward.   T   F

51. A person may be a coward in one situation
    and not in another.   T   F
52. Illegible handwriting is a sign of superior
    intelligence in the educated adult.   T   F

53. If your ears burn it is a sign that someone is
    talking about you.   T   F

54. It is unlucky to have anything to do with the
    number 13.   T   F

55. Beginning an undertaking on Friday is
    almost sure to bring bad luck.   T   F

Items 4, 6, 16, 20, 26, 37 and 51 are probably true, the rest are false.
If you got more than 48 correct, well done. Most people score
between 30 and 40 which shows they remain incorrect about much
of psychology; worse scores than this and they are superstitious or
racist!

Jahoda (1971) tabulated some of these findings (see Table 1.1).

Jahoda (1971) looked at large studies done in England and Germany
in the 1950s. The results, as do more current studies, show a surprising amount of superstition. Consider the four topics he isolated.

N.B. The abbreviation 'N' refers to the number in the sample, 'N.A.'
means 'no answer' and 'D.K.' means 'don't know'; in the case of
England, 'Q' denotes questionnaire results and 'F' those derived
from the field survey. What all the findings show clearly is that extent
to which ordinary people believe in superstition.

1. GHOSTS

England: Do you believe in ghosts?
Q. ($N = 4983$)
Yes 17%
No 58%
Uncertain 23%
N.A. 2%

If you believe in ghosts, have you ever seen a ghost?
Q. ($N = 841$)
Yes 42%
No 22%
Uncertain 35%
N.A. 1%

TABLE 1.1: Percentages of superstitious responses in student samples

	Nixon (1925) (N = 403)	Ralya (1945) (N = 110)	Levitt (1952) (N = 141)	Warburton (1956) (N = 143)	Jahoda (1956) (N = 121)
People born under the influence of certain planets show the influence in their character	15	6			
The position of the stars at the time of a man's birth determines, in part, his character			18	6	
Certain lines on a person's hand are indicative of (foretell) his future	8	2	20	6	
Beginning an undertaking on Friday is sure to bring bad luck	1	1	1	1	
You can make a person turn around if you stare long enough at his back					32
A dog can sense impending disaster better than a man	36	10			51
It's unlucky to have anything to do with the number 13	40	3	1	1	
An English-speaking person with German blood will find it easier to learn the German language than an English-speaking person with French blood			34	38	21
Voodooism is in the blood of the Negro			36	51	
People with long fingers are likely to be artistic	42	6	47	29	36
Red-headed people are likely to be temperamental			40	23	
A large mouth is a sign of generosity			28	16	4
A man's character can be read by noting the sizes and locations of certain developments on his head	40	3	18	15	

N refers to the number of people completing the questionnaire.

Reprinted from G.Jahoda (1971) *The Psychology of Superstition*. Harmondsworth: Penguin.

2. FORTUNE-TELLING

England: Have you ever been to a fortune-teller?
Q. ($N = 4983$)   F. ($N = 1780$)
Yes 44%   Yes 28%
No 53%   No 71%
N.A. 3%   N.A. 1%

If yes, how often have you been?
Q. ($N = 2179$)   F. ($N = 491$)
Once 45%   Once 51%
Twice 24%   Twice 21%
Several times 31%   Several times 25%
N.A. –   N.A. 3%

Did any of it come true?
Q. ($N = 2179$)   F. ($N = 491$)
Yes 30%   Yes 29%
Yes all 2%   Yes all 3%
Yes some 15%   Yes some 14%
No nothing 35%   No nothing 43%
D.K. 11%   D.K. 11%
N.A. 7%   N.A. –

3. LUCK

England: Have you a specially lucky or unlucky day?
Q. ($N = 4983$)   F. ($N = 1760$)
Lucky 9%   Lucky: Unlucky:
Unlucky 5%   Yes 9%   Yes 7%
Both 3%   No 90%   No 91%
Neither 83%   N.A. 1%   N.A. 2%

England: Have you a specially lucky or unlucky number?
Q. ($N = 4983$)
Lucky number 18%
Unlucky number 3%
Both 3%
Neither 76%

England: Do you have a lucky mascot?
Q. ($N = 4983$)   F. ($N = 1760$)
Yes 15%   Yes 12%
No 82%   No 87%
N.A. 3%   N.A. 1%

Germany: Do you find that you have in your life runs of good and bad luck, or have you not noticed anything like that?
($N = 1000$)

Runs of good and bad luck	54%
Not noticed	27%
Cannot say	19%

Germany: Even if you yourself are not superstitious, what numbers, signs or other things predict good or bad fortune for you?
Q. ($N = 1802$)

Concrete indications	46%
Nothing predicts	50%
No indications	4%

4. ASTROLOGY

England: Do you read 'Lyndoe' in the *People*?
Q. ($N = 4983$)
Regularly 50%
Occasionally 39%
Never 10%
N.A. 1%

Do you ever read the horoscope in any other paper or magazine?

Q. ($N = 4983$)	F. ($N = 1760$)
Regularly 35%	Regularly 42%
Occasionally 45%	Occasionally 29%
Never 17%	Never 29%
N.A. 3%	N.A. –

Do you follow the advice in the horoscope columns you read?

Q. ($N = 4983$)	F. ($N = 1249$: only regular or occasional readers)
Regularly 3%	Regularly 5%
Occasionally 22%	Occasionally 18%
Never 70%	Never 76%
N.A. 5%	N.A. 1%

Do you think there is something in horoscopes?

Q. ($N = 4983$)	F. ($N = 1760$)
Yes 20%	Yes 17%
No 44%	No 60%
Uncertain 33%	Uncertain 15%
N.A. 3%	N.A. 8%

Germany: Do you believe in a connection between human fate and the stars?
(N = 2052)
Yes 29%
No 58%
Undecided 13%

Do you happen to have read the past few months your daily or weekly horoscope in a newspaper or magazine?
(N = 2137)
Yes, frequently 34%
Yes, occasionally 27%
No 39%

Do you happen to know if your horoscope at present is favourable or unfavourable?
(N = 1000)
Know the answer 25%
Don't know just now 34%
Never bother about horoscopes 41%

1.3   Myths in Psychology

Psychologists spend a great deal of time and effort attempting to re-educate people who hold erroneous ideas about the subject. From one source or another many lay people come to believe in certain psychological theories that are patently untrue. And because of self-fulfilling prophecies it becomes extremely difficult to dislodge those ideas. Let us consider myths in three areas: the causes of happiness; addiction to alcohol and the nature of crime.

Happiness

Psychologists do not study health; they study illness. They do not study happiness; they study depression. They do not study marriage; they study divorce. It had long been thought that one best understands how a normal process works when it goes wrong. That is, one understands how the clock in the kitchen works only when one has to fix it. But recently psychologists have given up this rather bleak approach and have dared to research such things as health and happiness. In doing so they have exposed various myths (Eysenck, 1990).

- 'Happiness depends on the quality and quantity of pleasurable events that happen to one.' Alas their effect is often transient; worse, they make subsequent, only moderately pleasurable events appear uninteresting in comparison. A person enjoys pleasures because he or she is happy, not vice versa. Happiness is not the result of ever more vivid jabs of excitement. It can be the result of extremely humdrum activities such as stamp collecting or bird watching.

- 'Modern stressful living has made people less happy than in previous times.' This is not 20:20 hindsight but rather rose-tinted spectacles which selectively forget poverty, disease and primitive technology. People in advanced (and supposedly stressed) western developed societies are generally happier than those in under-developed countries. It is the way you live, not your standard of living, that counts most, however.

- 'Those with serious physical disability are less happy than other people.' Whilst sudden or creeping (acute vs chronic) disability does induce depression, studies on quadriplegics have shown that the level of happiness soon recovers and that disability is no handicapper of happiness. Great beauty, physical strength or robust health are not themselves causes of happiness.

- 'Young people in their prime of life with few responsibilities are happier than older people.' In fact, contentment and satisfaction tend to increase with age. The young have stronger levels of positive and negative affect (emotion) but the balance is the same. Young people ride on a more daring rollercoaster of emotion upon which many thrive. They tend to call the flat sections 'boring'.

- 'People who experience great happiness also experience great unhappiness.' This is a popular over-simplification. Being neurotic tends to lead to great highs and lows but for the most part people do not swing widely between the two extremes. And you certainly do not have to 'pay' for happiness with periods of unhappiness.

- 'Intelligent people are happier than unintelligent people.' As an academic, I can confidently confirm that this is completely untrue; indeed the opposite may even be the case. More intelligent people tend to have higher (and more difficult to achieve) aspirations and to worry about things (the arms race, the meaning of life) over which they have no control. Ordinary, 'boring' people do not agonise over 'the meaning of life questions' and may be all the better for it.

- 'Children usually add significantly to the happiness of a married couple.' Again, the opposite is true, particularly for married women. We can be pretty certain that the presence of children reduces happiness because most married couples become happier again as soon as all of their children have left the nest But there is a strong biological need to procreate which can withstand the years of parenting.

- 'Winning a fortune ensures happiness.' Studies of pools winners show that for many the disruption causes the opposite. Loss of friends through jealousy, consistent begging letters and so on can often lead to despair. People soon adapt to their wealth and move in new circles where, by comparison, they are not rich at all. Curiously, most working people who adjust best to their fortune are not those who 'spend, spend, spend' but those who invest it and continue much as before. As with illness and disability, levels of happiness after winning a large sum of money soon return to earlier levels. There are happy and unhappy millionaires.

- 'Men are happier than women because it is a man's world.' In fact, there is precious little difference between them although young women tend to be slightly unhappier than young men, and the opposite is true from middle age onwards. Again, the so-called benefits of being a man do not and cannot ensure happiness.

- 'Pursuing happiness directly is the surest way to lose it – it occurs in a natural way and cannot be produced to order by thinking about it.' Indeed the opposite again is true – anything can be done more effectively and achieved more rapidly when we possess the relevant knowledge. At least knowing what does *not* cause happiness prevents us pursuing it pointlessly.

- 'Happiness is a superficial goal to pursue.' For some who belong to the muscular Christianity school of chin up and buckle down, happiness *per se* is a fruitless goal. They argue it is better to strive for solid work achievements. Also, happiness is linked with physical health and predictive of longevity. As unhappiness can kill you it can hardly be seen as a trivial aim.

- 'Happiness is a fleeting experience; an ephemeral state.' But we know from longitudinal research that the degree of happiness is stable over time. It is linked to personality which,

despite some misconceptions, changes relatively little over
time. Happiness can be attained by adopting an outlook and
lifestyle and can be permanent.

- 'Marriage tends to reduce happiness.' Again, the opposite is
  true, particularly for men. Despite the high divorce rate the
  figures are very clear. Overall, married people are much
  happier than unmarried people.

To many people, the stars of the media, the sports field and the
conference table appear not only extremely well adapted, but also
very happy. Their press agents and hagiographic autobiographies
often strive to create the same impression. And this leads ordinary
people to believe that money, good looks, power and physical
prowess are the key ingredients of happiness. They are wrong. Popular idols and figures also have their problems. They are neither ecsta-
tically happy nor maudlinly depressed. Indeed the trappings of
wealth, power and fame are just that: 'traps and prisons', not
nirvanas. The fact is that ordinary folk are just as happy.

Alcohol

How does one become an alcoholic?

Most people are very familiar with the concept of addiction, be it to
alcohol or drugs, food or nicotine, stimulants or depressants. Many
admit to being addicted to some substance or at least know others
who are. As a consequence they often hold strong, complex beliefs
about both the causes of, and the cures for, addiction.

As the drinking of alcohol in nearly all societies is, and has been, a
frequent occurrence, people are very familiar with the consequences
of alcoholism. However, they remain surprisingly ignorant about the
effects of alcohol and the causes of, or cures for, alcoholism.

Table 1.2 shows 17 common misconceptions about alcohol. A
surprising number of people would endorse these items as true
despite the fact that all are demonstrably false. If their knowledge is
so patchy, if not downright wrong, it is perhaps, therefore, not
surprising that their explanations of, or theories for, alcoholism are
simple or misguided.

Within the social sciences, explicit theories of addiction fall
roughly into three main categories. Biological models or theories
often tend to emphasise the pharmacological properties of the addic-
tive substance (alcohol, nicotine, LSD, etc.) and its effect on the

---

TABLE 1.2: Some common misconceptions about alcohol and alcoholism

1. Alcohol is a stimulant
2. Alcohol is essential to the treatment of certain diseases
3. You can always detect alcohol on the breath of a person who has been drinking
4. One ounce of 86 proof liquor contains more alcohol than a 12-ounce can of beer
5. Body size has little or nothing to do with how much liquor a person can hold
6. Drinking several cups of coffee can counteract the effects of alcohol and enable the drinker to 'sober up'
7. Alcohol can help a person sleep more soundly
8. Impaired judgement does not occur before there are obvious signs of intoxication
9. The individual will get more intoxicated by 'mixing' liquors than by taking comparable amounts of one kind, e.g. Bourbon, Scotch or Vodka
10. Exercise or a cold shower helps speed up the metabolism of alcohol
11. People with 'strong wills' need not be concerned about becoming alcoholics
12. Alcohol cannot produce a true addiction in the same sense that heroin does
13. One cannot become an alcoholic by drinking just beer
14. Alcohol is far less dangerous than marijuana
15. In a heavy drinker, damage to the liver shows up long before brain damage appears
16. The physiological withdrawal reaction from heroin is more dangerous than is withdrawal from alcohol
17. Most alcoholics who have successfully completed treatment can safely resume social drinking

Source: R.Carson and J. Butcher (1992). *Abnormal Psychology and Modern Life*. London: Harper Collins.

---

central nervous system. This approach tends to see the addict as someone who is biologically predisposed to developing physiological dependence. Psychological theories, on the other hand, tend to assume that addicts share personality traits, beliefs and values, and/or maladaptively learned behaviour patterns which make them particularly vulnerable or predisposed to develop addiction. Third, sociocultural or structural models point to class, regional or other macro-sociological differences in addiction and tend to explain addiction as a means of coping with structurally induced stress or inequality. Clare (1979) has subdivided these approaches yet further. Biological causes include ideas concerned with metabolic defects, neurotransmitter alterations and genetic factors. Psychological causes include approaches from psychoanalysis (the alcoholic as dependant), personality theorists (identifying alcoholic traits) and behavioural (learning history) theorists. Sociocultural theories emphasise occupational factors, ethnic factors, familial factors, or more simply the availability of alcohol. However, progressively fewer researchers and reviewers are zealously partisan regarding one or other approach, preferring to be more benevolently eclectic. Interestingly, the popular description of alcoholism as a 'disease' is nowhere featured in any of the scientific explanations.

Crime and Punishment

What determines whether one will be a criminal or not?

Nicholson and Lucas (1984) argue that most people have fairly strong opinions as to the causes of crime; some believe that an individual's upbringing decides whether that person becomes a criminal or not; some believe that it is the situation in which a person finds him/herself; still others believe that criminals are 'born not made' and that 'once a criminal, always a criminal'. This last belief suggests that the criminal 'type' will never change. Which of these views is the more accurate? This question is not only of interest to psychologists; it is crucial to our decisions about how to reduce crime.

Are the following True or False?

		True	False
1.	The elderly run the greatest risk of being attacked	T	F
2.	Psychopaths are typically withdrawn and controlled	T	F
3.	Most victims of rape know their assailants	T	F
4.	Your chances of being robbed are lower than your chances of being admitted to hospital as a mental patient	T	F
5.	Most rapists are armed	T	F
6.	The typical householder must expect to be burgled every couple of years	T	F
7.	Young offenders under 17 in Britain are responsible for less than 20% of all crime	T	F
8.	Most crimes are reported	T	F
9.	Anti-shoplifting signs increase shoplifting	T	F
10.	Once he's married, a man is likely to turn his back on crime	T	F

Answers

1.   False: old people are the least frequent victims of violent crime; the most frequent victims are young men.
2.   False: the psychopath is characteristically outgoing, impulsive and uncontrolled.
3.   True.
4.   True.
5.   False: 30% are armed.
6.   False: houses are burgled less often than they catch fire.
7.   False: the true figure is 36%.
8.   True.
9.   True.
10. True and false: a tricky one, this. Getting married reduces criminality among men in their twenties, but those men who do continue their criminal activities after marrying actually commit more crimes than before.

The punishment for adult crimes may or not be capital punishment. But what of corporal punishment as a way of controlling and educating young people? There are moral questions, but also more simply, and perhaps more importantly, there are questions about efficacy. Essentially the arguments are as follows.

Pro Corporal Punishment

1.   In Britain in 1987 the House of Commons voted in favour of abolishing corporal punishment in state schools, while the European Court of Human Rights ruled in 1982 that parents should be given the right to decide whether their children should be caned. An earlier Bill was rejected by the House of Lords because it would have been unfair, dividing pupils into 'beatable' and 'unbeatable'. Subsequently, however, the Lords passed a new clause in the Education Bill which proposed complete abolition. That this legislation took so long to implement, and then by such a narrow margin, shows the extent to which virtually half of British parliamentarians who are, at least in the Commons, democratically elected and it is hoped representative doubted its wisdom.
2.   Corporal punishment for certain offences is most effective, because it is prompt and feared by nearly all. It combines the elements of the remedial, the deterrent and the day of reckoning. It teaches the schoolchild or the convict that the doing of

wrong is followed by the suffering of pain.

3.   When inflicted justly and without anger, corporal punishment does not brutalise the giver. In most schools where it still occurs, it is resorted to only as a final punishment.

4.   It accustoms the pupil to the hardships of real life and the consequences of misbehaviour. No bitterness is left after chastisement if it has been administered for good reason.

5.   It is impossible always to 'make the punishment fit the crime'. Yet the amount and quality of corporal punishment can be adjusted to suit the gravity of the misdemeanour.

6.   It is better than other punishments, such as forms of 'imprisonment' which are deadening to mind and body. Schools that dispense with corporal punishment, especially for young children, often substitute other methods which are tantamount to torture.

7.   Impositions and detentions are harmful because they increase the number of hours a schoolchild is compelled to spend indoors in physical inactivity. Their natural restlessness is increased by the enforced restraint, so leading to further offences against discipline.

8.   Judicial corporal punishment should be reintroduced for criminals convicted of violence. It would let them know the effect of their crimes on their victims and, as bullies are generally the greatest cowards, be of the utmost value as a deterrent from such crimes in future.

Against Corporal Punishment

1.   Britain, as a signatory to the European Convention on Human Rights, was compelled to comply with the Strasbourg court's 1982 ruling. That the government delayed for more than four years before doing so is a reflection partly of its difficulties in placating its own reactionary backbenchers, who represent a minority view.

2.   It is degrading and otherwise harmful to the victim, while no deterrent to the hardened culprit/criminal who often boasts about it to friends and colleagues as though it were a battle honour.

3.   Its brutalising effect is seen when we observe that those times when parents and teachers resorted to it most were the most brutal in other respects. It appeals to the strain of cruelty that exists somewhere in everyone.

4.   Children and adolescents resent injustice coupled with indignity. Were it true that corporal punishment accustoms them to life's hardships, then every child – but especially the good children and adolescents – ought to receive its benefits daily.

5.   It is often just an excuse for laziness and inefficiency in teachers. By using terror instead of discipline, a bad teacher can continue his/her work when otherwise the impatience of the pupils would force a change in either the methods or the staff.

6.   Impositions and detentions are more effective because they encroach on the leisure time of the person misbehaving (which usually worries him/her far more than physical hurt) and may even give an opportunity for reflection.

7.   In modern schools, there is plenty of opportunity for physical exercise, and it is nonsense to imply that depriving children of this for a few hours is physically harmful. Letting off steam immediately afterwards will always be tempered by a desire to avoid repetition of the punishment.

8.   The infliction of corporal punishment on an already antisocial person who regards violence as a legitimate means of achieving his/her ends is not likely to have any corrective action; on the contrary, past experience indicates that it is more likel to lead to a deeper feeling of enmity towards authority and society.

These debating positions are frequently reiterated. Curiously, the academic debate is not very different and although marginally more sophisticated and filled with jargon, much the same points are made. Since the Second World War in Britain various groups have commissioned reports from working parties on corporal punishment. Most have attempted to define corporal punishment and then ascertain its prevalence. Many have also attempted to review the salient literature and canvass other groups.

In 1979 the British Psychological Society itself commissioned such a report from a working party. Its review covered the effectiveness of punishment with respect to laboratory animals; social, cultural and educational uses of corporal punishment; psychopathology and corporal punishment and attitudes to punishment. The BPS canvassed various bodies, as well as reviewing the salient literature. For instance, it noted that the Association for Behavioural Modification with Children had this to say:

Corporal punishment is only one form of punitive management and it is suggested that it needs to be considered in a broader context. The prevailing view in this Association is that, in general, corporal punishment can and should be avoided. The following broad reasons have been put forward by members to justify this view:

1. It is generally ineffective. More than one commentator has emphasised the way in which school punishment books show the same small band of pupils being caned regularly throughout their school careers. Though the majority of school pupils may behave acceptably under a system which includes corporal punishment, it is felt that they would be equally amenable to milder approaches. It is doubtful whether it significantly improves the overall behaviour of those for whom it is most commonly felt to be necessary.
2. It is unnecessary. There are many countries in the world where corporal punishment in schools is either banned, or simply not used, without apparent ensuing chaos. It could be helpful to the debate in this country to be able to consider the general alternative approach to transgression in school in those countries. Commentators have, moreover, paid tribute to schools in this country where the staff have rejected corporal punishment and have achieved excellent morale.
3. Corporal punishment is a bad example. There is evidence that children imitate the actions of their elders, and that methods of child-rearing depending heavily on punishment of a physically aggressive kind produce children who themselves behave in a physically violent fashion. Children who are beaten tend in turn to beat and bully.
4. It may contribute to poor teacher–pupil relationships. Pupils who are punished physically may develop feelings of resentment or revenge that lead to anti-teacher behaviour which, in turn, may provoke more hostility from the teacher. Better-behaved pupils may also be alienated by such behaviour in the teacher, so that they sympathise with and support the disrupter rather than influencing him/her to behave acceptably. Alternatively, they may become afraid of the teacher.

5. It can exacerbate difficult behaviour. The individual members of any teaching group need to be sure of their personal recognition within that body, they need to feel clearly identified by their teacher. For pupils unaccustomed to achieving recognition as significant individuals by approved methods, corporal punishment provides an alternative route to this end. The pupil then behaves disruptively so that the teacher will, by punishing, signify that he/she has been noticed. It may also help the pupil acquire significance in the eye of fellow pupils in the situation where the teacher's reliance on corporal punishment has prejudiced a class against him/her.

6. It is logically incompatible with the ideas of a community based on mutual respect and care for the welfare and dignity of the individual. Attention has been drawn to the way in which it disturbs those timid children who are least likely to be its targets directly. Many of those misdeeds held to warrant corporal punishment, such as bullying, destructiveness, dishonesty, truancy, rudeness and persistent laziness, are indicators of problems needing help if the pupil is to lead a satisfying life in the community. Corporal punishment does not contribute to the kinds of relationships and atmosphere most likely to promote such help.

7. To sanction corporal punishment in schools may be to deny teachers the guidance and support which they might otherwise seek in relation to other modes of operation.

Research has shown that appropriate planned punishment can improve behaviour and has thrown light on some of the ways in which it can be most effective. It should be devised so that it is:

1. applied consistently: the same kind of misbehaviour should be predictably punished by the same consequence, rather than according to the mood of the teacher. Most often, consistency will require that a misdemeanour is punished in the same way every time it occurs. It would be difficult to justify corporal punishment with such frequency;

2. applied as a natural consequence of particular misbehaviour rather than as condemnation of the individual as a worthwhile person. The latter approach can lead to a lowering of self-

esteem, and there is evidence that such a decrement leads to a lowering of moral controls;

3.   applied by somebody who is warm and caring rather than hostile or punitive in attitude;

4.   not so severe that the pupil is strongly motivated to avoid detection as a possible alternative to improving his/her behaviour;

5.   not an example of aggressive behaviour which we would not wish to see in the pupils themselves, i.e. not a bad example;

6.   fair and reasonable, so that it does not provoke retaliation and can be seen as constructive by the pupil;

7.   accompanied by guidance in, and reward for, the alternative behaviour desired;

8.   accompanied, where necessary, by explanation of the reasons for it;

9.   applied soon after the misbehaviour rather than some time later;

10.   applied, where possible, to the intention rather than to the misdemeanour itself, as this has been shown to be more effective. Plainly, it would be hard to justify the use of corporal punishment in this way.

1.4   Common Sense

To many people, the theories they come across in a number of the social sciences – psychology, management, sociology, criminology – are common sense. That is, the theories or findings are already commonplace, and hence the research is thought to be a trivial, expensive and pointless exercise describing or providing what we already know. Being sensitive to this criticism, which is naturally seen as misplaced, social scientists have often confronted this point at the beginning of their textbooks, warning readers of the dangers of common sense which lulls people into the false belief that they understand other people. Some have even provocatively mentioned the term 'uncommon sense' in their papers and titles.

For instance, McKeachie and Doyle (1966) begin their general psychology textbook by asking 'How is a scientific explanation different from common sense?' and present the following figure and explanation (Figure 1.1).

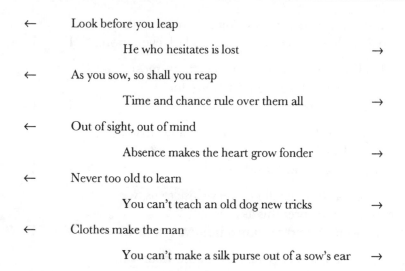

← Look before you leap	
	He who hesitates is lost →
← As you sow, so shall you reap	
	Time and chance rule over them all →
← Out of sight, out of mind	
	Absence makes the heart grow fonder →
← Never too old to learn	
	You can't teach an old dog new tricks →
← Clothes make the man	
	You can't make a silk purse out of a sow's ear →

Figure 1.1: The trouble with folk wisdom is that it gives no guide for determining which of the two contradictory sayings is appropriate in a particular situation, thus the usefulness of such sayings is quite limited.

Source: Reprinted with permission from McKeachie and Doyle (1966).

Why not test yourself? Below are 39 statements derived from various sources that you must decide are either True or False. See how much common sense helps you to give the correct answer. These are from Furnham and Oakley (1995).

Test 2: Common Sense

		True	False
1.	In general, women conform more than men.	T	F
2.	In bargaining with others, it is best to start with a moderate offer – one close to the final agreement desired.	T	F
3.	In making decisions, committees tend to be more conservative than individuals.	T	F
4.	Dangerous riots are most likely to occur when temperatures reach extremely high levels (e.g. around 95–100°F).	T	F
5.	The more persons present at the scene of an emergency, the more likely are the victims to receive help.	T	F

6. If you pay someone for doing something they enjoy, they will come to like this task even more. T   F

7. In choosing their romantic partners, most people show a strong preference for extremely attractive persons. T   F

8. If you want to get someone to change his or her views, is it best to offer this person a very large reward for doing so. T   F

9. When a stranger stands very close to us, we usually interpret this as a sign of friendliness and react in a positive manner. T   F

10. Most people feel sympathy for the victims of serious accidents or natural disasters and do not hold such persons responsible for the harm they have suffered. T   F

11. Unpleasant environmental conditions (e.g. crowding, loud noise, high temperatures) produce immediate reductions in performance on many tasks. T   F

12. Directive, authoritative leaders are generally best in attaining high levels of productivity from their subordinates. T   F

13. In most cases, individuals act in ways that are consistent with their attitudes about various issues. T   F

14. Top executives are usually extremely competitive, hard-driving types. T   F

15. Most persons are much more concerned with the size of their own salary than with the salary of others. T   F

16. Direct, face-to-face communication usually enhances cooperation between individuals. T   F

17. Most persons prefer challenging jobs with a great deal of freedom and autonomy. T   F

18. The behaviour of most lower animals – insects, reptiles and amphibians, most rodents and birds – is instinctive, i.e. unaffected by learning. T   F

19. For the first week of life, a baby sees nothing but a grey blue regardless of what he or she 'looks at'.   T   F

20. A child learns to talk more quickly if the adults around him/her habitually repeat the word he/she is trying to say, using proper pronunciation.   T   F

21. The best way to get a chronically noisy schoolchild to settle down and pay attention is to punish him/her.   T   F

22. Slow learners remember more of what they learn than fast learners.   T   F

23. Highly intelligent people – 'geniuses' – tend to be physically frail and socially isolated.   T   F

24. On average, you cannot predict from a person's grades at school and college whether he or she will do well in a career.   T   F

25. Most national and ethnic stereotypes are completely false.   T   F

26. In small amounts alcohol is a stimulant.   T   F

27. LSD causes chromosome damage.   T   F

28. The largest drug problem in Britain, in terms of the number of people affected, is marijuana.   T   F

29. Psychiatry is a subdivision of psychology.   T   F

30. Most mentally retarded people are also mentally ill.   T   F

31. Electroshock therapy is an outmoded technique rarely used in today's mental hospitals.   T   F

32. The more severe the disorder, the more intensive the therapy required to cure it, for example: schizophrenics usually respond best to psychoanalysis.   T   F

33. Quite a few psychological characteristics of men and women appear to be inborn in all cultures, for example, women are more emotional and sexually less aggressive than men.   T   F

34. No reputable psychologist 'believes in'
     such irrational phenomena as ESP,
     hypnosis, or the bizarre mental and
     physical achievements of Eastern yogis.   T   F

35. To change people's behaviour toward
     members of ethnic minority groups, we
     must first change their attitudes.   T   F

36. The basis of the baby's love for its mother
     is the fact that the mother fills his/her
     physiological needs for food etc.   T   F

37. The more highly motivated you are, the
     better you will be at solving complex
     problems.   T   F

38. The best way to ensure that a desired
     behaviour will persist after training is
     completed is to reward the behaviour
     every single time it occurs throughout
     training (rather than intermittently).   T   F

39. A schizophrenic is someone with a split
     personality.   T   F

Total up the Fs because they are all false for different reasons which
have been discovered by psychological experiments or observations.
If you scored 30 or more 'falses' well done! If you scored below 10
'falses' you will definitely benefit from reading on.

People believe psychology, along with other social sciences, is
simple common sense for various reasons. First, many findings are
well known, intuitive, unsurprising, uninformative. Second, psychological explanations which are the 'stuff of personal experience' are
amenable to common sense and should have explanations in terms
of common sense, not jargon or trivia. A third, related reason is that
many experimental findings or social science writings appear not to
contradict widely held views of human nature. Nearly all psychological research which has demonstrated that people are cruel, unin-
sightful, self-centred, compliant, or anti-social has been criticised
more than those findings that have painted the opposite picture. So
unless the results paint a picture of humans rather different from
how we like to view them, most people say the research results are
simply common sense.

Some people believe that all of science is common sense. Paradoxically, it is the 'hard' scientists who are most convinced that all science is just common sense. Huxley (1902), a famous British scientist, noted in an essay:

> Science is nothing but trained and organized Common Sense, differing from the latter only as a veteran may differ from a raw recruit: and its methods differ from those of Common Sense only as far as the guardsman's cut and thrust differ from the manner in which a savage wields his club.... (p. 42)

Whitehead, another well-known scientist, is reputed to have said that 'Science is rooted in the whole apparatus of Common Sense thought'. Other scientists have dismissed common sense as a source of ideas, let alone testable theories; some psychologists have been particularly dismissive of the importance of common sense. Skinner (1972) wrote: 'What, after all, have we to show for non-scientific or prescientific good judgement, or common sense, or the insights gained through personal experience? It is science of nothing' (p.160). Eysenck (1957), in his celebrated book *Sense and Non-Sense in Psychology*, states:

> This is only one example of what appears to be an almost universal belief to the effect that anyone is competent to discuss psychological problems, whether he has taken the trouble to study the subject or not and that while everybody's opinion is of equal value, that of the professional psychologist must be excluded at all costs because he might spoil the fun by producing some facts which would completely upset the speculation and the wonderful dream castles so laboriously constructed by the layman. (p.13)

Thus for these eminent psychologists common sense is a dangerous area from which to draw ideas as these are often misguided or untestable. Even worse, various 'common-sense' ideas may be based not on simple surmise but prejudice and political ideology. Moreover, one can cite extensive literature that illustrates lay persons' 'faulty' reasoning, e.g. the readily observed failure of lay people to make appropriate use of disconfirmatory information in problem solving and the overwhelming preference for confirmatory strategies in logical reasoning tasks. For example, if you want to find out whether somebody is an extrovert you can ask whether he or she has many friends, likes going out, and really enjoys parties (confirmatory) or, alternatively, whether they are rather shy in company (disconfirmatory). Lay people prefer to use the first of these two approaches and to ignore any disconfirmatory information which might be available.

There are many other well-established findings showing human irrationality in everyday settings. For example, people overestimate the frequency of well-publicised events (deaths due to being murdered or having cancer) while underestimating less publicised events such as dying from asthma or diabetes. Similarly, when considering, say, the relative job performance of two people, the absolute number of successes is given greater weight than the relative number of successes to failures – people ignore the denominator. There are many, many examples of this type of faulty reasoning.

So the argument ebbs and flows. Is psychology a science? Is science a good thing? Is science common sense? Consider the quotes from Furnham and Oakley (1995) set out in Table 1.3.

TABLE 1.3: A battery of quotes for and against science and common sense

Pro-science
- A scientist is a man who would rather count than guess. *M. Gluckman*
- Science is organized common sense where many a beautiful theory is filled by an ugly fact. *T. H. Huxley*
- Science may be described as the art of systematic oversimplification. *K. Popper*
- The man of science does not discover in order to know: He wants to know in order to discover. *A.N. Whitehead*
- Science increases our power in proportion as it lowers our pride. *C. Bernard*
- Science is what you know, philosophy is what you don't know. *B. Russell*
- You know very well that unless you are a scientist, it's much more important for a theory to be shapely, than for it to be true. *C. Hampton*

Anti-science
- Science is always wrong: it never solves a problem without creating ten more. *G.B. Shaw*
- I am tired of all this thing called science....We have spent millions on that sort of thing for the last few years, and it is time it should be stopped. *S. Cameron*
- One of the most pernicious falsehoods ever to be universally accepted is that scientific method is the only reliable way to truth. *R. Bube*
- Traditional scientific method has always been, at the very least, 20–20 hindsight. It's good for seeing where you've been. *R. Pirsig*
- Though many have tried, no one has ever yet explained away the decisive fact that science, which can do so much, cannot decide what it ought to do. *J.W. Krutch*
- Look at those cows and remember that the greatest scientists in the world have not discovered how to make grass into milk. *M. Pulin*

Pro-common sense
- It is a thousand times better to have common sense without education than to have education without common sense. *R. Ingersol*
- Common sense in an uncommon degree is what the world calls wisdom. *S.T. Coleridge*
- The philosophy of one century is the common sense of the next. *H.W. Beecher*
- The best prophet is common sense. *Euripides*

TABLE 1.3: Contd.

- If a man has common sense he has all the sense there is. *S. Rayburn*
- Common sense is instinct and enough of it is genius. *H.W. Shaw*
- Common sense is the wick of the candle. *R.W. Emerson*
- Fine sense and exalted sense are not half so useful as common sense. *B. Gracian*
- The crown of all faculties is common sense. It is not enough to do the right thing: it must be done at the right time, and place. *W. Matthews*

Anti common sense

- Common sense is the collection of prejudices people have accrued by the age of 18. *A. Einstein*
- Logic is one thing and common sense another. *E. Hubbard.*
- Common sense is in spite of, not the result of, education. *V. Hugo*
- Common sense is, of all kinds, the most uncommon. *T. Edwards*
- Common sense, however logical and sound, is after all only one human attitude among many others, and like everything human, it may have its limitations – or negative side. *W. Barrett*
- Common sense is the most fairly distributed thing in the world, for each thinks he is so well endowed with it that even those who are hardest to satisfy in all other matters are not in the habit of desiring more of it than they already have. *R. Descartes*
- If common sense were as unerring as calculus, as some suggest, I don't understand why so many mistakes are made so often by so many people. *C. Winkel*

It should be clear that there is no agreement on this issue! It could be argued that psychology is, in part, the scientific study of common sense.

1.5   Knowledge about Psychology

We have looked at superstition and common sense. Finally, we shall look at your psychological knowledge. This is a multiple-choice test devised by McClutcheon (1986) that asks you to guess the correct answer – out of four. It has been used by Furnham in a number of studies (Furnham, 1993) and is published in Furnham and Oakley (1995).

Test 3: Knowledge about Psychology

The following quiz allows you to demonstrate what you know about psychology. The items have been selected to represent a wide variety of topics and to reflect public interest in psychological issues. For each item one choice is clearly better than the others as determined by examining the relevant scientific evidence. The test is not timed, but try not to linger very long on any item.

1.   Over the last 20 years the total number of deaths or severe
      injuries in the USA caused by 'maniacs' who put razor blades
      or poison in Hallowe'en pumpkins is:
      (a)   Zero to 25
      (b)   26 to 50
      (c)   51 to 500
      (d)   more than 500

2.   Most of the research supports the conclusion that ... are more
      likely to occur when the moon is full:
      (a)   traffic accidents
      (b)   homicides
      (c)   both of the above
      (d)   neither of the above

3.   Regular marijuana usage eventually causes people to use:
      (a)   cocaine
      (b)   heroin
      (c)   both of the above
      (d)   neither of the above

4.   Some of the learning principles which apply to birds and fish
      also apply to:
      (a)   cockroaches
      (b)   humans
      (c)   both of the above
      (d)   neither of the above

5.   Consider the old saying 'Beauty is only skin deep'. Generally
      speaking, research shows that physically attractive people are
      ... than physically unattractive persons:
      (a)   likely to be more psychologically stable than
      (b)   equal in psychological stability to
      (c)   likely to be less psychologically stable than
      (d)   likely to be far less psychologically stable than

6.   Generally speaking, the saying 'Opposites attract' is ...
      description of how people come to like one another:
      (a)   an almost true
      (b)   a very accurate
      (c)   a somewhat accurate
      (d)   usually an inaccurate

7.   Eyewitnesses to crime often give testimony in court that is:
      (a)   very inaccurate
      (b)   very accurate
      (c)   irrelevant
      (d)   deliberately false

8.   The polygraph lie detector test, as a measure of whether someone is lying or telling the truth, is accurate:
    (a)   91 to 100% of the time
    (b)   75 to 90% of the time
    (c)   55 to 74% of the time
    (d)   54% of the time or worse

9.   The earliest human beings are capable of learning is:
    (a)   when they are still in the womb. At that time learning ability is already highly developed. For example, playing the piano a lot during pregnancy will eventually cause the child to learn more easily to play the piano.
    (b)   when they are still in the womb. At that time learning ability is very limited. Foetuses are capable of learning only very simple tasks.
    (c)   at birth. At that time learning ability is already highly developed. For example, playing the piano a lot for several months immediately following the birth of a child will eventually cause the child to learn more easily to play the piano.
    (d)   at birth. At that time learning ability is very limited. Newborns are capable of learning only very simple tasks.

10.   Which of these statements about the value of teenage employment is/are true?
    (a)   jobs help teenagers learn the value of money
    (b)   having a job teaches teenagers to respect work
    (c)   neither of the above
    (d)   both of the above

11.   Sigmund Freud's psychoanalytic theory is an excellent example of:
    (a)   what a well-constructed scientific theory should be like
    (b)   a theory that is accepted today by almost all American/British psychologists
    (c)   both of the above
    (d)   neither of the above

12.   Several bartenders and policemen had a chance to observe (one at a time) several target persons walk and talk for a few minutes. These target persons were either legally drunk or sober, and they were pretending to be either drunk or sober. Which group was accurate in determining whether the target persons were actually drunk?
    (a)   most of the bartenders
    (b)   most of the policeman

(c)   both of the above
(d)   neither of the above
13.   Research on the effects of pornography depicting consenting
      adults shows that it causes:
      (a)   an increase in aggression
      (b)   an increase in sex crimes
      (c)   neither
      (d)   both
14.   Research suggests that if you know someone's attitude about X
      you can predict behaviour relevant to X with:
      (a)   100% accuracy
      (b)   80% accuracy
      (c)   a small amount of accuracy
      (d)   no accuracy whatsoever
15.   Which of these statements is/are true?
      (a)   education can be improved by opening more private
      schools
      (b)   student achievement in private schools exceeds that in
      public schools
      (c)   both of the above
      (d)   neither of the above
16.   In normal human beings the:
      (a)   two hemispheres of the brain work independently
      (b)   'right-brained' are more creative than the 'left-brained'
      (c)   neither of the above
      (d)   both of the above
17.   The percentage of child-abusing parents who are neither
      psychotic, mentally retarded, nor brain-damaged is approxi-
      mately:
      (a)   90%
      (b)   65%
      (c)   40%
      (d)   15%
18.   From a psychological standpoint the most accurate statement
      about feeding infants is:
      (a)   breast is best
      (b)   bottle-fed infants develop the most pleasant personalities
      (c)   cup-fed infants become unusually well-adjusted adults
      (d)   that the three methods are about equal
19.   On a four-choice multiple-choice test, such as this one, if you
      decided to change an answer the most likely consequence is:
      (a)   a change from the right answer to a wrong one

(b)   a change from one wrong answer to another wrong one

(c)   a change from a wrong answer to the right one

(d)   that all three possibilities are about equally likely

20.   Alcohol consumption in small doses causes people to become:

(a)   more aggressive

(b)   sexually aroused

(c)   both of the above

(d)   neither of the above

21.   Testosterone is a hormone that is important for human male sexual behaviour. If you were greatly to increase the amount of it in the bloodstream of a normal, healthy young man the most likely result would be:

(a)   a large increase in sexual behaviour

(b)   a moderate increase in sexual behaviour

(c)   little or no increase in sexual behaviour

(d)   a decrease in sexual behaviour

22.   Under hypnosis a person will, if asked by the hypnotist:

(a)   recall childhood events with very high accuracy

(b)   be able to perform physical feats of strength that would otherwise be impossible

(c)   both of the above

(d)   neither of the above

23.   Psychologists have been accused of torturing laboratory animals. Objective studies designed to investigate these claims have found that animals are:

(a)   never subjected to any pain or harm

(b)   killed or badly injured in about 40% of all experiments

(c)   rarely killed or caused much suffering during an experiment

(d)   given electric shocks in about 35% of all experiments

24.   Approximately ... per cent of all American psychologists are primarily 'psychotherapists'; they try to help patients who have psychological problems:

(a)   95

(b)   75

(c)   55

(d)   40

25.   IQ tests given to 10-year-old children usually provide moderately accurate predictions about how:

(a)   well adjusted you will be as an adult

(b)   well you will do academically in high school

(c)   many and which people should be hired for an easy job

(d) none of the above

26. Which of these groups is likely to be more violent as deter-
     mined by several measures of violence?
     (a) those with less than a high school education
     (b) high school graduates
     (c) college graduates
     (d) there is very little difference among the three

27. Having a dry mouth is ... why people drink fluids.
     (a) the single most important reason
     (b) one of the most important reasons
     (c) a moderately important reason
     (d) a relatively unimportant reason

28. Schizophrenic patients are:
     (a) usually not dangerous to others
     (b) moderately dangerous to others
     (c) very dangerous to others
     (d) dangerous only when their personalities 'split'

29. Research generally supports the idea that criminals are more
     likely than non-criminals to:
     (a) be ugly
     (b) be obese
     (c) both of the above
     (d) neither of the above

30. The Rorschach Method, in which subjects tell what they 'see'
     in several inkblots, is one of the most famous of all psychologi-
     cal tests. Which of these statements is accurate?
     (a) many testing experts feel that it is virtually worthless
     (b) the instructions for giving the Rorschach are always given
          the same way to each subject
     (c) both of the above
     (d) neither of the above

31. A persuasive message is flashed on a screen so quickly that you
     can't see it, or whispered on an audio tape so softly that you
     can't hear it (subliminal perception). Which of the following
     statements about subliminal perception is most accurate?
     (a) studies show that subliminal perception is impossible
     (b) the effect is powerful enough to make people buy
          expensive items they don't want
     (c) it has produced weak effects in the laboratory
     (d) it is so influential that it can cause honest people to
          commit crimes

32. In making judgements about the amount of control they have

in a situation, or judgements about their own social skills, the most accurate estimates are likely to be made by:

(a) depressed patients
(b) psychotic patients
(c) normal people
(d) people suffering from asthma

33. Biorhythm theory holds that there are three monthly cycles: emotional, intellectual and physical. This theory has been found to be ... in predicting injuries and the quality of human performance:

(a) very successful except for the intellectual cycle
(b) very successful
(c) moderately successful
(d) mostly unsuccessful

34. Many hospitals encourage immediate contact between parents and newborns for several minutes right after birth because this is thought to be necessary for 'bonding' to occur. Evidence that this procedure causes close relationships to develop ('bonding') between parents and child is:

(a) very strong
(b) moderately strong
(c) strong only in Mormon and Catholic families
(d) weak

35. The 'only' child usually turns out to be:

(a) 'spoiled'
(b) about average in psychological adjustment
(c) less intelligent than children who have three or more siblings
(d) lonely

36. People who typically spend nine or more hours sleeping at night tend to be ... as compared with those who sleep six hours or less:

(a) more concerned about personal achievement
(b) a little more lazy
(c) a lot more lazy
(d) less anxious

37. After training has been completed the best way to make sure that a desired behaviour will continue at a high rate is to:

(a) reward it every time it occurs
(b) reward it occasionally and irregularly
(c) reward it regularly once out of every 50 times it occurs
(d) use mild punishment when the behaviour does not occur

38.   When natural disasters such a hurricanes and floods strike,
      which of these is a common response?
      (a)   a large percentage of the people flee an approaching
            disaster
      (b)   most people panic and lose their capacity to make good
            decisions
      (c)   neither of the above
      (d)   both of the above
39.   Generally speaking, young geniuses (those with very high IQ
      scores) are found to:
      (a)   be somewhat weaker physically than normal children
      (b)   'burn out' quickly. As adults they lead average lives
      (c)   both of the above
      (d)   neither of the above
40.   One electric shock of low intensity, delivered directly to the
      cortex of the human brain, is most likely to result in:
      (a)   pain, but no tissue destruction
      (b)   pain, and much tissue destruction
      (c)   much tissue destruction, but little pain
      (d)   none of the above
41.   As a predictor of personality, handwriting analysis is generally:
      (a)   worthless
      (b)   slightly better than worthless
      (c)   fairly accurate
      (d)   very accurate
42.   People who participate in dangerous sports like auto racing or
      sky diving are:
      (a)   better adjusted psychologically than the average person
      (b)   about average in adjustment
      (c)   about average except for a strong death wish
      (d)   severely disturbed
43.   Astrology ... as a predictor of human personality:
      (a)   has no accuracy
      (b)   has a small degree of accuracy
      (c)   is moderately accurate
      (d)   is very accurate
44.   Which statement best describes the relationship between sleep
      and learning?
      (a)   it is possible to learn efficiently while you are in deep sleep
      (b)   learning is efficient when it is followed by sleep
      (c)   it is a great idea to sleep, then study immediately upon
            awakening

    (d)   sleep is totally unrelated to learning efficiency

45.   Does research on sleep show that (1) sleepwalkers are acting out their dreams and (2) sleeptalkers often give away their secrets during sleep?
    (a)   number one is true but number two is not
    (b)   number two is true but number one is not
    (c)   both are false
    (d)   both are true.

46.   Which of these statements about suicide are true?
    (a)   those who threaten to commit suicide are serious
    (b)   questioning a person about his/her suicidal ideas may 'put the idea in their head', making an attempt likely
    (c)   both of the above
    (d)   neither of the above

47.   Many experts believe that adult humans with no brain damage use ... of their brain cells:
    (a)   most
    (b)   about 25%
    (c)   about 10%
    (d)   less than 5%

48.   Most reading difficulties in children are caused by:
    (a)   dyslexia
    (b)   the brain's reversal of words (i.e. 'saw' instead of 'was')
    (c)   neither of the above
    (d)   both of the above

49.   A psychic is one who can predict the future without the use of past events. When tested under controlled laboratory conditions psychics usually show success rates that are about ... percentage points above chance levels.
    (a)   5
    (b)   25
    (c)   45
    (d)   65

50.   Every year during the Christmas season the:
    (a)   number of admissions to mental hospitals rises rapidly
    (b)   frequency of suicide increases
    (c)   both of the above
    (d)   neither of the above

51.   In 1973 it was proposed that hyperactivity in children could be successfully treated by reducing the intake of food additives (Feingold diet). Most of the evidence gathered to test this hypothesis has found that:

    (a)   hyperactive children actually become more hyperactive
    (b)   the diet has little or no effect on hyperactivity
    (c)   hyperactive children show moderate improvement
    (d)   the diet results in a large reduction in hyperactivity

52.   Blind people are able to avoid obstacles because they:
    (a)   have a special sense which compensates for their absence of vision
    (b)   have a greater ability to hear than sighted persons
    (c)   both of the above
    (d)   neither of the above

53.   The term 'blue Monday' means that people are more likely to feel 'blue' (sad, in a bad mood, depressed) on Monday than any other day of the week. Evidence suggests that Monday is about:
    (a)   30% 'bluer' than the other days
    (b)   20% 'bluer' than the other weekdays
    (c)   as 'blue' as other weekdays
    (d)   as happy as Saturday and Sunday

54.   It has been claimed that some rock and roll songs, when played backwards, contain messages that promote illegal drug use and immoral behaviour (backmasking). It is further claimed that these messages cause people to behave illegally and immorally. Research on backmasking suggests that it has ... effect on behaviour:
    (a)   a strong negative
    (b)   a weak negative
    (c)   no negative
    (d)   a weak positive

55.   When rioters are compared with non-rioters from the same community, which of these kinds of people are likely to be over-represented in groups of rioters?
    (a)   poorly educated
    (b)   those who suffer from a variety of psychological disorders
    (c)   neither of the above
    (d)   both of the above

56.   Generally speaking, the most accurate description of the relationship between neatness and work productivity is:
    (a)   productivity is much higher in neat settings
    (b)   productivity is a little bit higher in neat settings
    (c)   productivity is the same in neat and messy settings
    (d)   productivity is a little bit higher in messy settings

57.   The statement 'In order to permanently change someone's

behaviour you must first change that person's attitude', has been found to be:

(a) false, if the person can be persuaded to change behaviour for a large sum of money

(b) false, if the person can be persuaded to change behaviour for a small sum of money

(c) false, if the person is forced to change his/her behaviour

(d) true

58. It has been documented that some mentally retarded persons have remarkable achievements in one area. For example, some otherwise retarded persons can add huge sum of numbers quickly and accurately, while others are very musically talented. How common is this?

(a) nearly all retarded persons have one remarkable skill

(b) about half do

(c) about one-fourth do

(d) very few do

59. There are many different programmes designed to help people who want to give up cigarette smoking. In the long run (6 to 12 months after the programme is over) the average amount of smoking reduction is:

(a) about 35-50%

(b) less than it is for those who try to quit on their own

(c) both of the above

(d) neither of the above

60. When persons who are found not guilty by reason of insanity are eventually released they usually:

(a) commit crimes of greater severity then the original one

(b) commit crimes of about the same severity as the original one

(c) commit no new crimes

(d) are usually found not guilty by reason of insanity for a new offence

61. 'Scared Straight' (Juvenile Awareness Project) is a programme which attempts to reduce juvenile delinquency by exposing young offenders to the harsh realities of prison life. Inmates try to scare young offenders with their description of the horrors of prison life, so that they will go 'straight'. This programme has been shown to be ... in reducing juvenile delinquency:

(a) 100% effective

(b) very effective

(c) moderately effective

(d) ineffective

62.   When black and white defendants are tried on similar
      offences, blacks are ... more likely to be found guilty and be
      given longer sentences than whites.
      (a) no
      (b) 1–10%
      (c) 15–22%
      (d) 25 to 35%

63.   It is evening and growing dark, but there is just enough light to
      see some colour. A person approaches you wearing a shirt of a
      solid colour. The colour will be most easy to identify correctly
      if it is:
      (a) red
      (b) orange
      (c) yellow
      (d) blue

64.   Brainstorming is a group problem-solving situation in which
      members are encouraged to present as many solutions as
      possible, no matter how unusual they might seem. Members
      are not permitted to criticise any ideas, but they are encour-
      aged to elaborate on them. When compared with an appropri-
      ate control group of people working alone brainstorming has
      been shown to be:
      (a) much better
      (b) somewhat better
      (c) about as good
      (d) worse

Here are the correct answers:

No.	Ans	No.	Ans	No.	Ans
1.	A	15.	B	29.	A
2.	D	16.	C	30.	A
3.	C	17.	A	31.	C
4.	C	18.	D	32.	A
5.	A	19.	C	33.	D
6	D	20.	D	34.	D
7.	A	21.	C	35.	B
8.	C	22.	D	36.	A
9.	B	23.	C	37.	B
10.	C	24.	D	38.	C
11.	D	25.	B	39.	D
12.	D	26.	D	40.	D
13.	C	27.	D	41.	B
14.	C	28.	A	42.	A

43.	A	51.	B	59.	D
44.	B	52.	D	60.	C
45.	C	53.	C	61.	D
46.	A	54.	C	62.	B
47.	A	55.	C	63.	D
48.	C	56.	C	64.	D
49.	A	57.	B		
50.	D	58.	D		

Total your answers. How did you do? We would expect a psychology student to get about 50, and an intelligent lay person somewhere between 20 and 35. Certainly all of these issues and topics are examined in a psychology course. Do you still think psychology is just common sense? Which of the answers you got wrong were you most surprised about? Those topics might be an excellent starting point for your further reading.

1.6   Beware the Fortune Cookie

Is psychology as (non)scientific as astrology or graphology? As many people in fact seem to believe in astrology as in psychology: they are victim to some of the oldest tricks in the trade.

Why do so many people from all backgrounds believe in, consult and act upon astrological and graphological predictions? The same is true of tarot cards, crystal ball readings and other hocus-pocus. Some businesses in Britain use the services of a graphologist while the French frequently consult astrologers. Patient research by impartial researchers has by and large failed to find any replicable theoretically based or explicable significant findings. This is perhaps far more true of graphology than of astrology for which there is equivocal evidence. Both are falsifiable and both have been falsified, yet people still believe. In short graphology and astrology are bunkum. Yet many people are hoodwinked. Why?

There are two sorts of answers to this question. One concerns the reliability and validity of alternative, more scientifically acceptable, ways of assessing, describing or measuring people. Like ability tests, high unemployment has meant unprecedented numbers of people applying for jobs and bewildered selectors are turning to any means of assessment that they trust in, understand or can afford. Some trust school grades or the predictiveness of leisure pursuits (always the source of greatest lies in an application form) despite the evidence that they are weak predictors of occupational success. However, distrust of psychology, the emergence of numerous fairly bogus consultancies and the excessive use of poorly psychometrised tests means that both because of the costs and the poor performance of some of these tests, distraught and over-burdened selectors are turning elsewhere for easy answers.

Some have turned to graphology. Yet there are literally dozens of scientific studies that exist again and again challenge the validity of graphology in accurately describing personality or predicting behaviour (Beyerstein and Beyerstein, 1992).

Furnham (1988) reviewed these studies noting the following typical conclusions from studies examining the validity of graphological analysis.

1.   'It was concluded that the analyst could not accurately predict personality from handwriting.' This was based on a study of Vestewig, Santee and Moss (1976) from Wright State University, who got six handwriting experts to rate 48 specimens of handwriting on 15 personality variables.

2.   'No evidence was found for the validity of the graphological signs.' This is from Lester, McLaughlin and Nosal (1977), who used 16 graphological signs of extroversion to try to predict from handwriting samples the extroversion of 109 subjects whose personality test scores were known.

3.   'Thus the results did not support the claim that the three handwriting measures were valid indices of extraversion.' This is based on the study by Rosenthal and Lines (1978), who attempted to correlated three graphological indices with the extroversion scores of 58 students.

4.   'There is thus little support here for the validity of graphological analysis.' This was based on a recent study by Eysenck and Gudjonsson (1986), who employed a professional graphologist to analyse handwriting from 99 subjects and then fill out personality questionnaires as she thought would have been done by the respondents.

5.   'The graphologists did not perform significantly better than a chance mode.' This was the conclusion of Ben-Shaktar and colleagues (1986) at the Hebrew University, who asked graphologists to judge the profession, out of eight possibilities, of 40 successful professionals.

6. 'Although the literature on the topic suffers from significant methodological negligence, the general trend of findings is to suggest that graphology is not a viable assessment method.' This conclusion comes from Klimoski and Rafael (1983), at Ohio State University, after a careful review of the literature' (p. 65).

After excellent empirical studies in the area Ben-Shaktar and his Israeli colleagues (1986, p.652) have thoughtfully concluded thus:

1. Although it would not be surprising if it were found that sloppy handwriting characterised sloppy writers, stylised calligraphy indicated some artistic flair, and bold, energetic people had bold, energetic handwriting, there is no reason to believe that traits such as honesty, insight, leadership, responsibility, warmth and promiscuity find any kind of expression in graphological features. Some may have no somatic expression at all. Indeed, if a correspondence were to be empirically found between graphological features and such traits, it would be a major theoretical challenge to account for it.

2. There are not enough constraints in graphological analysis, and the very richness of handwriting can be its downfall. Unless the graphologist makes firm commitments to the nature of the correspondence between handwriting and personality, one can find *ad hoc* corroboration for any claim.

3. The *a priori* intuitions supporting graphology listed above operate on a much wider range of texts than those graphologists find acceptable. As graphologists practise their craft, it appears that from a graphological viewpoint, handwriting – rather than being a robust and stable form of expressive behaviour – is actually extremely sensitive to extraneous influences that have nothing to do with personality (e.g., whether the script is copied or not, or the paper lined or not).

4. It is noteworthy that most graphologists decline to predict the sex of the writer from handwriting, although even lay people can diagnose a writer's sex from handwriting correctly about 70% of the time. They explain this by insisting that handwriting only reveals psychological, rather than biological, gender. Although common sense would agree that some women are masculine and some men effeminate, it would be somewhat perverse to argue against the presumption that most women must be feminine and most men masculine. Could the graphologists simply be reluctant to predict so readily verifi-

able – or falsifiable – a variable?

However, the more plausible reason why people believe in graphology and astrology is paradoxical. Graphological and astrological 'interpretations' or 'readings' are indeed true, but (and it is an important but) they are true because they consist of vague positive generalisations with high base-rate validity (i.e. they are true of most people) yet are supposedly derived specifically for a named person.

For nearly 40 years psychologists have been investigating the Barnum Effect. It was the famous circus-act producer Phineas T. Barnum who said 'There's a sucker born every minute' and had as his formula for success 'A little something for everybody'. The Barnum Effect refers to the phenomenon whereby people accept personality feedback about themselves, whether it is universally valid or trivial, because it is supposedly derived from personality assessment procedures. In other words, people believe in astrology and graphology because they fall victim to the fallacy of personal validation, which means that people accept the generalisations, the trite bogus descriptions which are true of nearly everybody, to be specifically true of themselves.

Consider a psychological study to illustrate this point. An American psychologist called Stagner (1948) gave a group of personnel managers a well-established personality test. But instead of scoring it and giving them the actual results, he gave each of them bogus feedback in the form of 13 statements derived from horoscopes, graphological analyses and so on. Each manager was then asked to read over the feedback (supposedly derived for him/herself from the 'scientific' test) and decide how accurate the assessment was by marking each sentence on a scale (a) amazingly accurate; (b) rather good; (c) about half and half; (d) more wrong than right; (e) almost entirely wrong. Table 1.5 shows the results – over half felt their profile was an amazingly accurate description of them, while 40% thought it was rather good. Almost none believed it to be very wrong.

If you add together the first two columns and look at those two considered most accurate, 'You prefer a certain amount of change and variety and become dissatisfied when hemmed in by restrictions and limitations' and 'While you have personality weaknesses you are generally able to compensate for them', and least accurate, 'Your sexual adjustment has presented problems for you' and 'Some of your aspirations tend to pretty unrealistic', you see the importance of positive general feedback. People definitely and not unnaturally have a penchant for the positive. Many researchers have replicated this

TABLE 1.5: Evaluations of items by 68 personnel managers when presented as a 'personality' analysis

	Judgement as to accuracy of item: percentage[1] choosing				
	a[2]	b	c	d	e
A. You have a great need for other people to like and admire you	39	46	13	1	1
B. You have a tendency to be critical of yourself	46	36	15	3	0
C. You have a great deal of unused capacity which you have not turned to your advantage	37	36	18	1	4
D. Whilst you have some personality weakness, you are generally able to compensate for them	34	55	9	0	0
E. Your sexual adjustment has presented problems for you	15	16	16	33	19
F. Disciplined and self-controlled outside, you tend to be worrisome and insecure inside	40	21	22	10	4
G. At times you have serious doubts as to whether you have made the right decision or done the right thing	37	31	19	18	4
H. You prefer a certain amount of change and variety and become dissatisfied when hemmed in by restriction and limitations	63	28	7	1	1
I. You pride yourself as an independent thinker and do not accept others' statements without satisfactory proof	49	32	12	4	4
J. You have found it unwise to be frank in revealing yourself to others	31	37	22	6	4
K. At time you are extroverted, affable, sociable, whilst at other times you are introverted, wary, reserved	43	25	18	9	5
L. Some of your aspirations tend to be pretty unrealistic	12	16	22	43	7
M. Security is one of your major goals in life	40	31	15	9	5

Notes: [1] Not all percentages add to 100% because of omissions by an occasional subject.
[2] Definitions of scale steps as follows: (a) amazingly accurate, (b) rather good, (c) about half and half, (d) more wrong than right, (e) almost entirely

result. A French psychologist advertised his services as an astrologer in various newspapers and received hundreds of requests for his services. He replied to each letter by sending out mimeographed identical copies of a single, ambiguous, 'horoscope'. More than 200 clearly gullible clients actually wrote back praising his accuracy and perceptiveness. An Australian professor regularly asks his first-year students to write down in frank detail their dreams, or he might ask them to describe in detail what they see in an inkblot – the more mystical the task the better. A week later he gives them the 13 statements shown in the table for rating as before. Only after they have publicly declared their belief in the test are they encouraged to swap feedback. The humilation of being so easily fooled is a powerful learning experience.

Furnham (1994) a recently 'tricked' his students with a 'medical Barnum'. They were told the following:

> Trichology Diagnosis. There are many ways of determining a person's state of health. For instance, by examining heart beats, urine specimens, blood pressure etc., modern medicine attempts to measure body functioning. But there are other methods which have been used for thousands of years. For instance, by examining the state of a person's pupils it has been possible to diagnose certain illnesses.
>
> There has also been a longstanding interest in the extent to which a careful physical and chemical analysis of hair can give very interesting clues to body health. For instance, the evidence that Napoleon was poisoned was provided by a close analysis of his hair. More recently, DNA analysis can be done by the examination of a person's hair.
>
> This study is an attempt to examine if **hair analysis** or **trichosis diagnosis** can be used to diagnose the health of otherwise normal healthy individuals. We want you to provide 2–5 hairs (preferably from the back of the head) and put them in an envelope with your name on it. It takes some time to do this analysis so it will not be until next week that we give you the feedback which will be put in the same envelope.

All students agreed to do this but the request did cause anxiety. Three wanted to know if the test could detect drug-taking and one whether it would detect cancer. Students were reassured that it could not but that this form of analysis was a good indicator of general health.

The following week 52 of the 60 arrived at the time-tabled lab and were shown the advertising from an organisation that purports to do such an analysis. They were given the envelope which contained their hair samples which now included, along with their own samples, two pages typed in different script. The one page consisted of a paragraph of the medical Barnum items which they were asked to rate. A second page set out the items one by one (24 in all) and subjects were asked to rate them on a seven-point scale for accuracy (7 being extremely accurate; 1 being not accurate at all). In order to encourage beliefs in this feedback, results were printed in various typefaces and in different orders. Thus if one subject happened to glance at his/her neighbour's printout it would not appear the same. They were told not to confer, warned about social desirability and encouraged to give their honest answers. The overall results are in Table 1.6.

One third of the feedback items got a score of 60% or above. Some of the highest ratings were about normality (18, 20), which is to be expected given this sample. Other items rated as accurate referred to *variability* in behaviour (6, sleeplessness; 10, tiredness; 15, appetite; 17, anxiety; 22, food craving). The item which yielded the lowest score (i.e. rated by the majority as inaccurate) referred to quite specific physical behaviours (13, nosebleeding; 21, urine colour). Interestingly, nearly two-thirds believed the health-industry themes about their diet benefiting from more fresh fruit and vegetables (item 1).

Research on the Barnum Effect has, however, shown that belief in this bogus feedback is influenced by a number of important factors, some to do with the client and the consultant (their personality, naïvety, etc.) and some to do with the nature of the test and the feedback situation itself. Women are not more susceptible than men, though of course generally naïve or gullible people are (tautologically!) more susceptible to this effect. However, the status or prestige of the consultant is only marginally important which is of course good news for the more bogus people in this field.

However, some variables are crucial. One of the most important is perceived specificity of the information required. The more detailed the questions, the better – so you have to specify exact time, date and place of birth to astrologers. In one study an American researcher gave all his subjects the same horoscope and found that those who were told that the interpretation was based on the year, month and day of birth judged it to be more accurate than those who were led to believe that it was based only on the year and

TABLE 1.6: Ratings of the feedback from the 'medical Barnum' (%)

	Accuracy (0–100)	Those giving maximum (100%) accurate scores
1. Your diet, while adequate, would benefit from an increase in fresh fruit and vegetables	65.6	19.1
2. You are probably hairier than most other people of your sex and age	44.9	4.3
3. Not all your measurements are symmetrical (e.g. your hands, feet, breasts are not exactly the same size/cup)	55.6	2.1
4. Your sex drive is very variable	56.3	4.3
5. There is evidence of a tendency to arthritis in your family	47.7	12.8
6. You are prone to feel the cold more than other people	58.0	19.1
7. Your skin texture changes under stress	54.4	10.6
8. You are prone to occasional patterns of sleeplessness	62.6	25.5
9. Your metabolic rate is at the 40 percentile (just below average for your age and sex)	50.1	4.2
10. You sometimes feel very tired for no reason	64.7	23.4
11. You can get depressed for no apparent reason	58.7	14.9
12. You are occasionally aware that your breath smells for no reason	44.9	2.1
13. Your nose bleeds occasionally	34.9	8.5
14. You are more prone to tooth decay than others	42.8	10.6
15. Your appetite varies extensively	63.5	23.4
16. You have a tendency to put on weight easily	44.6	8.5
17. You sometimes experience symptoms of anxiety (e.g. tension headaches, indigestion)	65.9	23.4
18. There are no major hereditary defects in your family	75.6	34.0
19. Your bowel movements are not always regular	51.3	8.5
20. Your cardiovascular efficiency is average for your age and sex	67.7	14.9
21. You experience frequent changes in your urine colour	41.3	4.3
22. You occasionally get a craving for certain food	66.5	25.5
23. Your body fat distribution is not perfectly normal	56.8	12.8
24. You frequently get indigestion	43.7	4.3

Reprinted with permission

month. Again and again studies show that after people receive general statements they think pertain just to them their faith in the procedure and in the diagnostician increases. A client's satisfaction is no measure of how well the diagnostician has differentiated him or her from others, but it is utterly dependent on the extent to which they believe it is specific to them.

The second factor belies the truth that we are all hungry for compliments but sceptical of criticism. That is, the feedback must be favourable. It need not be entirely, utterly positive but if it is by-and-large positive with the occasional mildly negative comment (that itself may be a compliment) people will believe it. This can easily be demonstrated by giving the well-used 13 statements Table 1.5 with the opposite primarily negative meaning (i.e. 'You do not pride yourself as an independent thinker and accept others' statements without satisfactory proof'). People do not readily accept the negative version even if it is seemingly specifically tailored to them. This confirms another principle in personality measurement – the 'Pollyanna Principle', which suggests that there is a universal human tendency to use or accept positive words or feedback more frequently, diversely and facilely than negative words and feedback. It has been shown that according to the evaluation of two judges there were five times as many favourable as unfavourable statements in highly acceptable interpretations and twice as many unfavourable statements in rarely accepted interpretations.

Hence the popularity of astrology and graphology; feedback is based on specific information (time and place of birth for astrology; slant and size of writing, correctness of letters, dotting of i's and crossing of t's, use of loops etc. in graphology). It is nearly always favourable. It is often the anxious (worried, depressed, insecure) who visit astrologers, graphologists, fortune tellers. They are particularly sensitive to objective positive information about themselves and the future. Therefore, the very type of feedback and the predisposition of clients make acceptance highly probable. Thus if the general description seems true (and it probably is) people frequently conclude that it must be even more true when even more information is given. Furthermore, this process is enhanced over time for two reasons. Since Freud it has been known that people selectively remember more positive events about themselves than negative and are thus likely to remember more feedback that coincides with their own views of themselves than information that is less relevant or contradictory. Second, of course, people have to pay for the consultation. Perhaps one needs a wealth warning in every astrological statement!

There are other attractions of astrological and graphological reading. They not only give useful, 'fascinating' information about oneself, but they are also claimed to predict the future, thus reducing anxieties and uncertainties about what will happen. Also, unlike other forms of therapy which require psychological work and/or behaviour change to obtain any benefit, in graphology one merely has to supply a writing specimen, or in astrology the exact time and place of birth. There is much to gain and little to lose at the astrologist's/graphologist's. Not surprisingly, then, a comfortable collaborative illusion of scientific validity emerges, formed between the buyer and seller of astrological readings and handwriting analyses.

There is one other reason why people validate graphology and astrology: the self-fulfilling prophecy. It is quite possible that if one is told 'As a Virgo, you are particularly honest', this may lead one to notice and subsequently selectively recall all or any, albeit trivial instances, of behavioural confirmation (pointing out that a person had dropped a bus ticket; giving back excess change). The self-fulfilling prophecy may work on both a conceptual and a behavioural basis. Thus Virgos come to include the trait of honesty in their self-concept but also they may actually become slightly or occasionally more honest. In this way graphology and astrology predictions may come true because accepting the predictions partly dictates that our behaviour will change appropriately!

Beware the fortune cookie, the graphologist, the astrologer! The moral of the story, of course, is that you can impress anyone with the perspicacity of your psychological insights as long as they are vague, relevant for most people, generally favourable, but personalised just for you. Fortune tellers have exploited this fact for hundreds of years. Crystal balls have been replaced by tarot cards or simple pen and ink, but the principle remains the same. 'The fault of false belief, dear Reader, is not in our stars, it is in ourselves.'

1.7   Maxims for Distinguishing Science from Non-science

At various points in time, people have 'demonstrated' various psychic powers from spoon bending to remote viewing. Where these have been investigated, nearly all have proved to be unreplicable or explicable in terms of 'trickery' or conventional scientific explanations. Marks and Kammann (1980) have sceptically analysed and appraised claims about ESP, precognition, clairvoyance, telepathy, psychokinesis and other related phenomena. They conclude their book with an appendix called 'Modes for rationales or the art of doubt'. These maxims are attempts to prevent lay people being fooled by bogus 'psychic phenomena'. The 10 rules are:

1. *If-what-then-what* – make the theorist be specific by asking what the theory predicts.
2. *Disprovability* – ask the theorist what piece of evidence would be required to disprove his/her theory.
3. *Burden of proof* – it is for the theorist to prove or substantiate his/her belief in the theory, rather than your disbelief.
4. *Alternative thinking* – it is possible that other phenomena (i.e. mediating variables) explain the theorist's evidence, just as well as the phenomena he/she cites.
5. *Missing negative cases* – very often, negative cases (those which 'disprove' a theory) are omitted, so making the data look stronger. These need to be sought out.
6. *Personal observation* – subjective validations are not sufficient unless accompanied by detailed recorded observations.
7. *Testimonials* – personal experience is poor evidence because often people are not fully aware of forces acting upon them or their real needs and motives.
8. *Sources* – it is worth examining the credibility of the source of a theory, i.e. where it is published, debated, etc., as these sources are frequently dubious.
9. *Emotional commitment* – the more a person is ego-involved in a theory, the less rationally and sceptically it may be assessed.
10. *Ad hominen technique* – 'First a believer may hold certain authorities to be infallible, and quote their opinions as evidence. Second, he may try to place contrary believers into a category of bad people and thus reject their arguments out of hand. Third, he may turn against you, accusing you of bad motives or stupidity. All of these arguments are fallacious, and it is not only important to recognise them, but also not to use them. The object is to learn, not to win' (Marks and Kamman, 1980, p.226).

In a wonderful paper called 'Cold reading: how to convince strangers that you know all about them' Hyman (1977) lets people into the secrets of how to become a palmist, graphologist, fortune-cookie reader etc. All 13 of his rules are repeated here lest the inquiring layman is hoodwinked by the trickster.

Whether you prefer to use the formula reading or to employ the more flexible technique of the cold reader, the following bits of advice will help to contribute to your success as a character reader.

1.   *Remember that the key ingredient of a successful character reader is confidence.* If you *look* and *act* as if you believe in what you are doing, you will be able to sell even a bad reading to most of your subjects.

The laboratory studies support this rule. Many readings are accepted as accurate because the statements do fit most people. But even readings that would ordinarily be rejected as inaccurate will be accepted if the reader is viewed as a person with prestige or as someone who knows what he is doing.

One danger of playing the role of reader is that you will persuade yourself that you really are divining true character. This happened to me. I started reading palms when I was in my teens as a way to supplement my income from doing magic and mental shows. When I started I did not believe in palmistry. But I knew that to 'sell' it I had to act as if I did. After a few years I became a firm believer in palmistry. One day the late Dr Stanley Jaks, who was a professional mentalist and a man I respected, tactfully suggested that it would make an interesting experiment if I deliberately gave readings opposite to what the lines indicated. I tried this out with a few clients. To my surprise and horror my readings were just as successful as ever. Ever since then I have been interested in the powerful forces that convince us, reader and client alike, that something is so when it really isn't.

2.   Make creative use of the latest statistical abstracts, polls, and surveys. This can provide you with a wealth of material about what various subclasses of our society believe, do, want, worry about, and so on. For example if you can ascertain about a client such things as the part of the country he comes from, the size of the city he was brought up in, his parents' religion and vocations, his educational level and age, you already are in possession of information that should enable you to predict with high probability his voting preferences, his beliefs on many issues, and other traits.

3.   Set the stage for your reading. Profess a modesty about your talents. Make no excessive claims. This catches your subject

off guard. You are not challenging him to a battle of wits. You
can read his character; whether he cares to believe you or not
is his concern.

4.   Gain his cooperation in advance. Emphasize that the success
        of the reading depends as much upon his sincere cooperation
        as upon your efforts. (After all, you imply, you already have a
        successful career at reading characters. You are not on trial –
        he is.) State that due to difficulties of language and communi-
        cation, you may not always convey the exact meaning which
        you intend. In these cases he is to strive to reinterpret the
        message in terms of his own vocabulary and life.

    You accomplish two invaluable ends with this dodge. You have
an alibi in case the reading doesn't click; it's his fault, not yours!
And your subject will strive to fit your generalities to his specific life
occurrences. Later, when he recalls the reading he will recall it in
terms of specifics; thus you gain credit for much more than you
actually said.

    Of all the pieces of advice this is the most crucial. To the extent
that the client is made an active participant in the reading the reading will succeed. The good reader, deliberately or unwittingly, is the
one who forces the client to actively search his memory to make
sense of the reader's statements.

5.   Use a gimmick such as a crystal ball, tarot cards, or palm
        reading. The use of palmistry, say, serves two useful purposes.
        It lends an air of novelty to the reading; but, more impor-
        tantly, it serves as a cover for you to stall and to formulate
        your next statement. While you are trying to think of some-
        thing to say next, you are apparently carefully studying a new
        wrinkle or line in the hand. Holding hands, in addition to
        any emotional thrills you may give or receive thereby, is
        another good way of detecting the reactions of the subject to
        what you are saying (the principle is the same as 'muscle
        reading').

    It helps, in the case of palmistry or other gimmicks, to study
some manuals so that you know roughly what the various diagnos-
tic signs are supposed to mean. A clever way of using such
gimmicks to pin down a client's problem is to use a variant of
'Twenty Questions,' somewhat like this: Tell the client you have
only a limited amount of time for the reading. You could focus on

the heart line, which deals with emotional entanglements; or the fate line, which deals with vocational pursuits and money matters; the head line, which deals with personal problems; the health line, and so on. Ask him or her which one to focus on first. This quickly pins down the major category of problem on the client's mind.

6.   Have a list of stock phrases at the tip of your tongue. Even if you are doing a cold reading, the liberal sprinkling of stock phrases amidst your regular reading will add body to the reading and will fill in time as you try to formulate more precise characterizations. You can use the statements in the preceding stock spiels as a start. Memorize a few of them before undertaking your initial ventures into character reading. Palmistry, tarot, and other fortune-telling manuals also are rich sources of good phrases.

7.   Keep your eyes open. Also use your other senses. We have seen how to size up a client on the basis of clothing, jewellery, mannerisms, and speech. Even a crude classification on such a basis can provide sufficient information for a good reading. Watch the impact of your statements upon the subject. Very quickly you will learn when you are 'hitting home' and when you are 'missing the boat.'

8.   Use the technique of 'fishing.' This is simply a device for getting the subject to tell you about himself. Then you rephrase what he has told you into a coherent sketch and feed it back to him. One version of fishing is to phrase each statement in the form of a question. Then wait for the subject to reply (or react). If the reaction is positive, then the reader turns the statement into a positive assertion. Often the subject will respond by answering the implied question and then some. Later he will tend to forget that he was the source of your information. By making your statements into questions you also force the subject to search through his memory to retrieve specific instances to fit your general statement.

9.   Learn to be a good listener. During the course of a reading your client will be bursting to talk about incidents that are brought up. The good reader allows the client to talk at will. On one occasion I observed a tea-leaf reader. The client actually spent 75 percent of the total time talking. Afterwards when I questioned the client about the reading she vehemently insisted that she had not uttered a single word during

during the course of the reading. The client praised the reader for having so astutely told her what in fact she herself had spoken.

Another value of listening is that most clients who seek the services of a reader actually want someone to listen to their problems. In addition many clients have already made up their minds about what choices they are going to make. They merely want support to carry out their decisions.

10. Dramatize your reading. Give back what little information you do have or pick up a little bit at a time. Make it seem more than it is. Build word pictures around each divulgence. Don't be afraid of hamming it up.

11. Always give the impression that you know more than you are saying. The successful reader, like the family doctor, always acts as if he knows much more. Once you persuade the client that you know one item of information about him that you could not possibly have obtained through normal channels, the client will automatically assume you know all. At this point he will typically open up and confide in you.

12. Don't be afraid to flatter your subject every chance you get. An occasional subject will protest such flattery, but will still cherish it. In such cases you can further flatter him by saying, 'You are always suspicious of people who flatter you. You just can't believe that someone will say good of you unless he is trying to achieve some ulterior goal.'

13. Finally, remember the golden rule: Tell the client what he wants to hear. (pp.26–29)

Conclusion

In this chapter we have introduced psychology as the systematic study of behaviour and the basic mechanisms which influence ideas, feelings and thoughts. We have examined whether psychological insight is really just 'organised common sense' and whether commonly held superstitions are really true. We have looked at some myths surrounding three specific areas – happiness, alcoholism and crime – and shown how psychological research can help our understanding. The reader's current knowledge of psychology and degree of interest in various topics have been tested in a quiz. Finally, we have examined the validity of graphology and astrology, sometimes incorrectly described as branches of psychology or sciences in their own right, and looked at the psychological basis for people's belief in them.

We hope you believe the following: that psychology encompasses the study of (among other things) common sense, and many of its theories and findings are clearly not simply common sense; that it attempts a scientific approach to understanding behaviour; and that it may give useful insights into other 'ologies' (such as astrology) which purport, erroneously, to describe human behaviour.

Chapter 2:
The Background to
Modern Psychology

2.1   Introduction

Essay writers like to start with definitions. Although they are not
difficult to find, rather different definitions of psychology exist and it
is not certain how useful they are. Most are too general and vague to
be useful. Others are too specific and do not capture the range of
things studied by psychologists. Definitions that have been proposed
include the science of the mind, the scientific study of behaviour, the
study of mental experience. The problem is really that, because
psychology is such a diverse discipline with many different branches,
it is rather difficult to come up with just one, simple but comprehensive, definition.

There is a story, possibly a myth, concerning the folly of searching
for or relying too heavily on definitions. A young man had been
appointed to a lectureship at a famous university and he was fortunate
in having six months before assuming the job to prepare all his
lectures. He was given the 'Introduction to Psychology' class as his
major teaching task and he thought it might be good idea to begin
with defining what psychology is (and is not). It soon became apparent
to him that this was a difficult task – at least to get it right – but he
determined to carry on until he got a comprehensive and correct definition that accurately described all the varied types, methods and
theories in psychology. But it took so long that by the time term had
begun he still had not finished the first part of the first lecture – the
definition. However, as Colman (1988) has suggested, it is important to
say what psychology is not; that is to describe related disciplines that
are essentially different from, but occasionally confused with, psychology:

- *Psychiatry*: A branch of medicine that specialises in the prevention, diagnosis and treatment of mental illness. Psychologists are not usually medically trained; psychiatrists always are. Clinical psychologists are often interested in the same phenomena as psychiatrists but tend to develop different theories of their cause or methods for treatment.
- *Psychoanalysis*: This is a theory of mental life (both structure and function) and a method of psychotherapy devised by Sigmund Freud. It places heavy emphasis on unconscious processes. It also involves a lengthy training process. Some psychologists and psychiatrists go on to become psychoanalysts but they make up a small percentage of the total.
- *Psychometrics*: This is the study of mental testing and involves the development and validation of aptitude, ability and attitude, IQ and personality tests. It is a small but important branch of psychology.
- *Parapsychology*: This is the study of paranormal behaviour, particularly extra-sensory perception (ESP) and psychokinesis. It has a long history and is dedicated to the difficult and painstaking research, sometimes conducted by psychologists, that looks particularly for the evidence for ESP. However, many psychologists are dismissive of this branch of psychology, pointing to very few replicable findings from all the research done.

Psychology has influenced and is influenced by many disciplines:

PSYCHOLOGY

NATURAL SCIENCES	SOCIAL SCIENCES	HUMANITIES
Zoology	Political Science	Biography
Physics	Economics	Linguistics
Chemistry	Sociology	History
Medicine	Anthropology	Philosophy
Biology	Education	
Computer science		
Mathematics		

Although it is a hybrid science it is not derivative of others (like management science), having its own specific unit of analysis, methods and theories.

2.2   Different Approaches to Psychology

For many different reasons – what they are studying, how they have been trained, what their theories are – psychologists tend to be attracted to different approaches or traditions in psychology. While most psychologists tend to have a basic leaning toward one or another of these approaches, they generally borrow from all. There are five broad approaches to explaining behaviour: the behavioural, the psychoanalytic, the phenomenological/humanistic, the cognitive and the neurobiological.

The Behavioural Approach

Behaviourists believe that humans or animals are the result of whatever has happened to them in their life experience: a product of the learning from the various stimuli (and responses) they have been exposed to. Thus, the criminal is the end product of learning bad habits and the altruist the opposite. Factors in the environment and reactions to them are the most important predictors of behaviour. If you have a moral environment, you have a good person; an immoral environment equals a bad person; a good mother and father to imitate results in a good child, and later in a good parent and so forth. We are what we have learned to be. Change the environment and you also change the end product. Reward certain behaviour and you get more of it; punish it and you should get less. Most behaviourists pay little attention to the inner workings or thoughts/feelings/motives of individuals, preferring to focus on observable behaviour. Behaviourists believe that observable phenomena (that is, behaviours that you can see and measure) are the stuff of psychological science, rather than, say, unconscious wishes or beliefs which one cannot directly observe. It is sometimes called black box psychology because it is not interested in what goes on inside the person but more what goes in (stimuli) and what comes out (responses). It was particularly popular from the 1930s to the 1960s although is somewhat in decline now.

The Psychoanalytic Approach

The psychoanalysts by and large emphasise the primitive animal nature within us (the id). Psychoanalysts emphasise an inner self preoccupied with sex, aggression and basic bodily needs, all of which operate at the unconscious level. This particular philosophy started with Sigmund Freud who maintained that we seek primarily self-gratification. It should be noted, however, that today's followers of psychoanalysis have modified Freud's basic beliefs because they seemed too extreme. In any case, psychoanalysts stand in stark contrast with the humanistic group (see below). The Freudian view is that often unconscious motives, needs and drives determine our behaviour and often symbolic fears and even physical illness are the direct result of unconscious conflict. (See Chapter 4 for a full discussion of the ideas of Freud.) Psychoanalysts, now largely independent of academic psychology, remain a small but distinct group working on traditional problems in a traditional way.

The Phenomenological/Humanistic Approach

In direct contrast with the behaviourists are psychologists who emphasise processes occurring inside the person as a basic force for explaining human behaviour. The word 'phenomenon' here refers to personal understandings or ways of seeing and making sense of the world that are forever changing. The phenomenologists argue that, no matter what is actually happening in the environment, each person is unique — that what is really seen or understood from that environment is changed or altered by the person to fit his or her own beliefs or needs. The term humanistic comes from humane, or a belief in the basic goodness of people, and suggests that by our very nature we are capable of reaching 'higher states' of existence.

The criminal or the mental patient, according to this approach, develops poor behaviour patterns because the environment doesn't provide the proper atmosphere for growth and development. The distinction between the phenomenologists and the behaviourists is that, for the former group, growth is internal and this growth will go on unless the environment is very difficult and stifling. Humanists believe individuals can become whatever they wish. The important feature of this approach is the emotional interpretation that each of us gives to what happens in the environment. The death of a parent has a different meaning for individual A than it does for individual B. This is because each of us has different internal experiences we bring to bear on the outside event. Compared with the behaviourists' view, the outside event is of secondary importance; humanists focus almost exclusively on the inner working of the unique person. This approach, sometimes called the third force in psychology, has never been influential although its heyday was in the 1960s.

The Cognitive Approach

The cognitive psychologists emphasise thought processes, reasoning and problem solving. For cognitive psychology, the most important human ability is our capacity to take information from the environment, analyse this information in a systematic (though often biased and erroneous) way, and come up with a solution to a problem. Cognitive psychologists stress that we are thinking creatures who often make mistakes, able to compare things we have seen in the past with what we are presently seeing and thus make judgements about them. Humanism is too vague for them because it leaves everything to a process that is not clear. The cognitivists attempt to develop a working model of human thought and this model is an elaborate, organised theory of how we process information. Cognitive psychological approaches to all aspects of behaviour swept into fashion in the late 1960s and remain popular today. Humans are seen as rationalising not rational and cognitive psychologists have taken delight in showing how people use psycho-logic rather than pure logic in thinking about themselves, others and the world around them.

The Neurobiological Approach

There are two different ways of understanding the response a person might have to some kind of event in the physical environment. One way is to view the situation as primarily psychological (literally related to the mind) and the other is to see the response as neuro- (nerve cells) biological (physical; including chemical, muscular). Consider a person fleeing from a bird (ornithophobia). Some psychologists focus on the background and learning experiences of this individual in order to explain the behaviour. Neurobiologists take a different approach. They describe the behaviour in terms of the neurobiological changes that are taking place in the person as the result of previous experiences. For example, the person has learned to become terrified of pigeons in the past, and seeing a pigeon in the present triggers the same set of physical alterations (chemicals in the blood, heart-rate changes, sweating etc.) that occurred in the earlier experiences. Neurobiologists are interested in the biological foundations of behaviour and tend to focus on physiological processes. Many search for the explanation for problems and illness in the physics and chemistry of the brain. Some argue they are reductionists and attempt to reduce psychology (a social science) to the physical sciences.

There are also other approaches such as the *ethological* or *evolutionary* approach which looks at the development and change of behaviour over time. It relies on the Darwinian idea of natural selection and attempts to explain why certain ideas and behaviour patterns have endured whilst others have been lost. Both neuro- and evolutionary psychology have made huge strides over the past two decades. This approach is currently among the most popular.

How do the various approaches understand or explain the same problem? In the following case, that of a failure of memory. Furnham and Oakley (1995) suggest one can illustrate the different approaches best by considering the everyday problem of John Smith. John is 40 years old and lives as he has always done, with his mother. He has never been married, but has many friends and a good job as an accountant. He seemed happy, prosperous and healthy. During the past six months he has become depressed and is forgetting things. He had always remembered his mother's birthday, but this year he forgot about it completely, which hurt her. He met a woman he really liked, set up a date with her a week later, only to discover that he had to cancel it because he had forgotten an out-of-town meeting that he had to attend. Usually logical and methodical he is clearly not himself and has become very quiet, introspective and scatty.

Behavioural analysis

According to the behaviourists, when John was a child he was consoled by his mother rather than scolded when he did things wrong. Not only was he rewarded by her attention, but she encouraged him to stay home because he was ill (so rewarding a hypochondriac). The behaviourists might then argue that John has learned very bad habits. He is currently unhappy with his life – for whatever reason – and is using the same behaviour to get attention that worked in the past, only instead of forgetting little things, he is forgetting significant dates. He has, in short, learned the benefits of forgetting, and is trying to attract sympathy and help.

Psychoanalytic analysis

For the psychoanalysts, who emphasise basic needs such as sex and aggression and unconscious motives, John may be suffering from a classic conflict of wanting a relationship with this new woman friend as well as with his mother. Thus, John is trying to keep the two 'love affairs' going at the same time. This may not be working because he is becoming frustrated in his desires and hence becoming more aggressive, as when his unconscious causes him to forget his mother's birthday. The longer this goes on, the more John feels guilty; the more guilty he becomes, the more aggressive he becomes. The more aggressive he becomes the more he strikes out at others by 'forgetting' that which is important to others. His forgetting is a 'solution' to the conflict.

Phenomenological/Humanistic analysis

In the view of phenomenologists John's inner world has suffered a number of blows because things have not been going right, and he is more and more distracted. While some might guess John is experiencing considerable conflict, we don't know this because such a general statement could apply to many people. We have to find out what it is specifically that bothers John. It will probably be something in his environment causing him to lose steam in his personal development. Every effort will be made to understand him and to realign his environment (work and home situation) into a more fitting setting for his goals. We have to know how he currently sees his life situation and get to understanding his way of interpreting his situation.

Cognitive analysis

Cognitive psychologists focus on current thinking skills rather than on previous learning or on unconscious impulses. Thus, the cognitivists would get John to analyse explicitly and rationally exactly what his life is like, and what kinds of things he is saying to himself that are not reasonable. They would probably focus on what, when and how he forgets particular things and how he tries to remember. He may have inappropriate strategies or poor methods of remembering and these can easily be taught to him (say, through using visioning or mnemonics). John will have to make a formal, logical plan of action to improve his life at home and at work, and his relationship with the 'other woman' and his mother. Then, they claim, his memory will improve all by itself.

Neurobiological analysis

One of the keys to an active memory is a reasonably high level of activating chemicals in the brain. Thus, if we are excited, we firmly lock into our memory the event that brought about the excitement. But John is showing symptoms that are just the opposite: he has been depressed much of the time lately. This depression is lowering the level of activating chemicals necessary for useful day-to-day remembering. So, John's problem may be explained by the neurobiologists by focusing on chemical events and physiological changes. This could be corrected by chemicals (drugs), exercise or adopting a new 'mind set'.

Of course, it is possible that a psychologist may favour a combination of approaches. But the above everyday example shows how psychologists from the different branches of psychology focus on quite different factors and offer different explanations.

Psychologists with different interests and different approaches tend to specialise in different areas, of which there are now many. Kalat (1993) has outlined 14 different specialities in psychology (see Table 2.1).

Further different specialities tend to adopt different approaches. Thus many counselling psychologists are phenomenologists, experimental psychologists are cognitivists and biopsychologists are influenced by neurobiological approaches.

2.3   Fundamental Differences

Because of their different interests and backgrounds, there are fundamental and significant differences between beliefs and approaches of psychologists. It should be pointed out that these fundamental philosophical differences are relevant to all the social sciences, indeed all science not only psychology. Kimble (1984) has listed 12 different areas of contention. Each has an opposite, A vs B.

1. Most Important Values

A. The most important values that govern research and scholarship are *scientific values*. Although humanistic values play a role, that role is a subordinate one. The immediate goal of scholarship is the advancement of scientific knowledge. In cases where human values and scientific values appear to be in conflict, raising questions as to whether research is worth doing, scientific costs and benefits contribute more to the decision than human costs and benefits. Scholarship, it is argued, places no responsibility on the scholar personally to apply the products of scholarship for the good of society. The strongest criticisms one can make of a research project are methodological not moral criticisms. A study that is unsound in these terms cannot be justified by any apparent degree of relevance to the human condition and is therefore pointless.

B. The most important values that govern research and scholarship are *humanistic values*. Although scientific values play a role, that role is a subordinate one because the immediate goal of scholarship is the improvement of the human condition. In cases where scientific

TABLE 2.1: Some major specialisations in psychology

Specialisation	General interest	Example of specific interest or research topic
Clinical Psychologist	Emotional difficulties	How can people be helped to overcome severe anxiety?
Community Psychologist	Organisations and social structures	Would improved job opportunities decrease certain types of psychological distress?
Counselling Psychologist	Helping people to make important decisions and to achieve their potential	Should this person consider changing careers?
Developmental Psychologist	Changes in behaviour as people grow older	At what age can a child first distinguish between appearance and reality?
Educational Psychologist	Improvement of learning in school	What is the best way to test a student's knowledge?
Environmental Psychologist	The influences of noise, heat, crowding and other environmental conditions on human behaviour	How can a building be designed to maximise the comfort of the people who use it?
Ergonomist	Communication between person and machine	How can an aeroplane cockpit be redesigned to increase safety?
Experimental Psychologist	Sensation, perception, learning, thinking, memory	Do people have several kinds of memory?
Industrial and Organisational Psychologist	People at work, production efficiency	Should jobs be made simple and foolproof or interesting and challenging?
Personality Researcher	Personality differences among individuals	Why are certain people shy and others gregarious?
Biopsychologist	Relationship between brain and behaviour	What body signals indicate hunger and satiety?
Psychometrician	Measurement of intelligence, personality and interest	How fair or unfair are current IQ tests? Can we devise better tests?
School Psychologist	Problems that affect schoolchildren	How should the school handle a child who regularly disrupts the classroom?
Social Psychologist	Group behaviour, social influences	What methods of persuasion are most effective in changing attitudes?

values and human values appear to be in conflict, raising questions
as to whether a bit of research is worth doing, human costs and benefits must contribute more to the decision than scientific costs and
benefits. Scholarship puts the scholar in a position of personal
responsibility to apply the products of scholarship for the good of
society. The strongest criticism one can make of a study is in terms of
relevance to the human good. A study that lacks such relevance
cannot be justified by any appeal to scientific values and is pointless.

Scientific values		*Human values*
Increasing scientific knowledge		Improving the human condition
Methodological strength	VS	Relevance to social good
No obligation to apply		Personal obligation

2. Degree of Lawfulness of Behaviour

A. *All behaviour is caused* by physical, physiological or experimental
variables. In principle it is possible to discover exact laws relating
even individual behaviour to these variables. Behaviour is understandable, predictable, controllable.
B. The concept of *causality probably does not apply to behaviour*, certainly
not to individual behaviour. There is nothing lawful about behaviour
except perhaps at the level of statistical averages. Even in principle,
behaviour must be regarded as incomprehensible, unpredictable and
beyond control.

Determinism		*Indeterminism*
Lawful		Not lawful
Understandable	VS	Incomprehensible
Predictable		Unpredictable
Controllable		Uncontrollable

3. Sources of Basic Knowledge

A. The final source of psychological knowledge is to be found in *sense
data* obtained by observation (through the five senses). Such observations must be ones that can be carried out by any properly trained
and equipped observer. Our concepts must be defined operationally
in terms that can be tested by public observation. The primary object
of observation is the behaviour of other organisms and the circumstances under which behaviour occurs. Psychology is the science of
'the other' and introspective. Self-report can contribute little.
B. The final source of psychological knowledge is to be found in the
intuitions we all have. Empathy produces better understanding than

observation. The concept of public testability must be rejected. Operational definitions (objective definitions of what behaviour means) hamper progress in psychology more than they promote it. Observations can never substitute for the knowledge contained in common sense. An analysis of language as we use it will yield more useful concepts than operational definitions. Self-report is more valid than observations made on others.

Objectivism		Intuitionism
Sense data		Empathy
Public observation	VS	Self-report
Operational definition		Linguistic analysis
Information from investigation		Common sense

4. Methodological Strategy

A. Psychology's most important enterprise is the *collection of data*. With data available, theory construction will be a relatively straightforward matter. Induction (collecting and inferring from evidence) contributes more to scientific progress than deduction. Investigation is more important than theory construction. Evidence counts for more than argument, reasoning and interpretation in producing scientific progress.

B. Psychology's most important enterprise is the *interpretation of data*. With theories available, data have a relatively straightforward theoretical meaning. Deduction (logical analysis) contributes more to scientific progress than induction. Theory construction is more important than investigation. Argument, reasoning and interpretation count for more than evidence in producing scientific progress.

Data		Theory
Investigation		Interpretation
Induction	VS	Deduction
Evidence		Argument

5. Setting for Discovery

A. The most important setting for psychological investigations is the *laboratory*; the most important method is experimentation. Whatever we lose as a result of artificiality is more than made up for by what we gain in control. Precision is more important than ecological validity (a natural, real environment). Manipulating variables produces more useful information than anything that can be accomplished by naturalistic observation. Hypothesis testing is a more powerful tool than correlation.

B. The most important setting for psychological investigations is the *real world* in which people and animals live. Whatever we lose by way of control is more than made up for by what we gain by working in a natural rather than artificial situation. Ecological validity is more important than precision (of measurement). Naturalistic observation produces more useful information than anything that can be accomplished by manipulating variables. Correlation (looking at the relationship between variables) is a more powerful tool than hypothesis testing.

Laboratory observation		*Field study*
Experimentation		Survey/case study
Manipulation of variables		Naturalistic observation
Hypothesis testing	VS	Correlation
Control of variables		Reality
Precision		Ecological validity

6. Temporal Aspects of Lawfulness

A. The behaviour of an organism is the *product of its history*; behaviour cannot be understood except by reference to the past. Although observations that can be made in the here and now can contribute, the preferred approach is a developmental approach; the most powerful studies are longitudinal studies over time which show clear causal links.

B. Although the behaviour of an organism may be a product of its history, it is possible and preferable to attempt to understand it in terms of observations that can be made in the *here and now*. The preferred approach is a descriptive approach. The most powerful studies are cross-sectional studies.

Historical		*Ahistorical*
Developmental approach	VS	Descriptive approach
Longitudinal study		Cross-sectional study

7. Position of Nature/Nurture Issue

A. The most important influences on behaviour are *physiological*. Although an interactionist model is the only sound one (taking account of both nature and nurture), hereditary factors carry a heavier weight than environmental ones in the interactionist equation. Physiology is more important than personal experiences when it comes to understanding behaviour. Psychology is more a biological science than a social one because biological variations contribute more to psychological processes than variations in environment.

B. The most important influences on behaviour are in the *environ-*

ment. Although an interactionist model is obvious, environmental factors carry a heavier weight than hereditary ones in the interactionism equation. The particular natures of the social and physical environment are more important than physiology when it comes to understanding behaviour. Psychology is more a social science than a biological one because environmental variations contribute more to psychological processes than variations in biology.

Heredity		*Environment*
Physiology	VS	Situation
Biological science		Social science

8. Generality of Laws

A. The laws of behaviour are, or someday will be, very general (*nomothetic*) laws, applying to all members of a given species, and they apply in some measure to a range of species. The concept of 'standard behaviour' is a sound one; there is no such thing as a unique individual except in the sense that unique functioning of the general laws may apply in individual cases. The laws of behaviour also generalise to a wide range of situations. Universalism is a better concept than contextualism.

B. Laws of behaviour that apply to all members of a species can never be discovered. Although regularities can be discovered, they apply only to the behaviour of specific individuals. These (*idiographic*) laws of individual human behaviour are not relevant to all members of species. Every individual is unique. The laws of behaviour are specific to situations as well as to individuals. Contextualism is a better concept than universalism.

Nomothetic		*Idiographic*
Species general		Species specific
'Standard man'	VS	Individual uniqueness
Universalism		Contextualism

9. Concreteness of Concepts

A. Useful concepts in psychology (mind, emotion) refer to actually existing physiological entities or relationships. They are '*hypothetical constructs*'. In our research, our main aim should be the discovery of the physical bases for terms such as habit, attitude, drive and temperament.

B. Useful concepts in psychology are unlikely to correspond to actually existing physiological entities or relationships. They are '*intervening variables*'. In the Stimulus–Organism–Response model 'O' stands for organism, but more at a conceptual than a biological level. In our research, it is a waste of time to search for physical bases for terms such as habit, attitudes, drive and temperament.

Hypothetical construct		*Intervening variables*
Biological reality	VS	Abstract conception

10. Level of Analysis

A. Progress in psychology requires the analysis of behaviour, experience and stimulus situations into their *elements* (most feasible basic units of analysis). Only then can we proceed to the task of determining the rules of synthesis by which these elements combine to produce complex behaviour and experience. The construction of the nervous system is designed to deal with elements. Elements must, therefore, be basic; the wholes of behaviour and experience must be made up of these parts. The idea that the whole is greater than the sum of its parts is nonsense.
B. Progress in psychology requires the recognition of the unanalysability of behaviour, experience and the environment. We live in an organised perceptual world, not a fragmented physical one. The whole has priority; attempts to extract mental or behavioural elements from it are bad science. Parts have meaning only in the context of *wholes*. If the nervous system processes only elements, this casts doubt on physiological interpretation because it fails to recognise that wholes are in fact greater than the sums of their parts. To deny that is nonsense.

Elementism		*Holism*
Molecular		Molar
Wholes constructed from parts	VS	Wholes give meaning to parts

11. Factors Leading to Action

A. Explicitly or implicitly, a common idea in theories of psychology is that behaviour is a joint product of cognitive (intellectual) and affective (emotional) factors. In the control of behaviour *cognitive factors are more important* than affective factors. Reason is more important than emotion. Thinking is more important than motivation; intellect is more important than impulse; the human organism is more rational than irrational.
B. Explicitly or implicitly a common idea in theories of psychology is that behaviour is a joint product of cognitive and affective factors. In the control of behaviour *affective factors are more important* than cognitive

factors. Emotion is more important than reason. Motivation is more important than thinking; impulse is more important than intellect; the human organism is more irrational than rational.

Cognition		*Affect*
Reason		Emotion
Thinking	VS	Motivation
Intellect		Impulse
Rational		Irrational

12. Conception of Organism

A. The mode of action of organisms is *reaction* to stimulation. Behaviour is an automatic expression of the laws of behaviour. Situational and physiological variables have effects on behaviour over which the organism has little or no control. The chief rules of mental life are reactive rules of associationism. Perception, learning and memory are more associative processes than they are constructive processes.
B. The mode of action of organisms is active *creativity*. Behaviour is much more than an automatic expression of the laws of behaviour. The effects on behaviour of situational and physiological variables are something over which the organism has considerable voluntary control. The chief rules of mental life are creative rules of constructionism. Perception, learning and memory are more constructive processes than they are associative processes.

Reactivity		*Creativity*
Automaticity	VS	Voluntary control
Associationism		Constructivism

Kimble (1984) argued that current academic psychology has two distinct cultures, labelled scientific and humanistic, which differ on specific explicit values. *Scientific*: 'All behaviour is caused by physical, physiological or experimental variables. In principle it is possible to discover exact laws relating every individual's behaviour to these variables. Behaviour is understandable, predictable, controllable.' *Humanistic*: 'The concept of causality probably does not apply to behaviour, certainly not to individual behaviour. There is nothing lawful about behaviour except perhaps at the level of statistical averages. Even in principle, behaviour must be regarded as incomprehensible, unpredictable and beyond control' (p. 835). This is most clearly seen in his 12-point table which emphasises some of the major differences in the discipline (see Table 2.2). It should be

emphasised that these are not lay theoretical approaches but the
positions of polarised academic psychologists who are frequently
explicit about their assumptions. Psychologists of a tough-minded
natural science approach tend to favour the 'scientific' approach,
whereas psychologists in the tender-minded, social science school
tend to value the more 'humanistic' approach.

TABLE 2.2: Scales and subscales of the epistemic differential	
Scale	Relating opposing ideas
1. Most important values: scientific vs human	Increasing knowledge vs improving human condition; methodological strength vs relevance; obligation to apply vs no such obligation
2. Degree of lawfulness of behaviour: determinism vs indeterminism	Lawful vs unlawful; understandable vs incomprehensible; predictable vs unpredictable; controllable vs uncontrollable
3. Source of basic knowledge: objectivism vs intuitionism	Sense data vs empathy; observation vs self-report; operational definition vs linguistic analysis; investigation vs common sense
4. Methodological strategy: data vs theory	Investigation vs interpretation; induction vs deduction; evidence vs argument
5. Setting for discovery: laboratory vs field	Experimentation vs survey/case study; manipulation vs naturalistic observation; hypothesis testing vs correlation; control vs realism; precision vs ecological validity
6. Temporal aspects of lawfulness: historical vs ahistorical	Development vs descriptive approach; longitudinal historical vs cross-sectional study
7. Position on nature/nurture issue: heredity vs environment	Physiology vs situation; biological vs social science
8. Generality of laws: nomothetic vs idiographic	Species general vs species specific; 'standard man' vs individual uniqueness; universalism vs contextualism
9. Concreteness of concepts: hypothetical constructs vs intervening variables	Biological reality vs abstract conception
10. Level of analysis: elementism vs holism	Molecular vs molar; part vs whole
11. Factor leading to action: cognition vs affect	Reason vs emotion; thinking vs motivation; intellect vs impulse
12. Conception of organisms: reactivity vs creativity	Automaticity vs voluntary control; associationism vs constructivism

The idea that psychology is not value free but value laden has also been taken up by Krasner and Houts (1984) who also demonstrated the existence of two groups, which they called *behavioural* and *non-behavioural*. They showed that people who endorsed freedom of enquiry as opposed to ethical constraints on research, and who favoured social Darwinism as opposed to social altruism, favoured the behavioural over the experimental approach to psychology. Essentially the same point is being made: psychologists as a group tend to polarise on various discipline-specific epistemological assumptions and values.

Indeed some researchers have suggested that certain psychology textbooks have strong epistemological (theory of knowledge) biases. For instance, Hogan and Schroeder (1981) claim that authors of textbooks introduce the following behaviouristic biases: (a) they ignore traditional topics such as thoughts, feelings, sensations, states of mind; (b) they equate 'scientific study' with a search for causal relationships, relationships inferred from the covariation of events; (c) they equate 'scientific study' with laboratory experimentation and statistical analysis, implying thereby that non-experimental methodologies are unscientific or worthless.

This finding or claim is disputed by Brown and Brown (1982) whose analysis of texts showed little evidence of glaring behaviourist, environmentalist or liberal biases in treating the topics of emotion, personality assessment and instincts. But it is difficult to be even-handed when very fundamental beliefs are involved.

2.4   What goes on in Psychology

By this stage we hope we have given you some idea of what in general psychology is, how it developed as a science and some of the major points of disagreement between psychologists. But what do psychologists actually do? In particular what do psychology students do, what do researchers in psychology do and what do the increasing band of people who have chosen to make their career in psychology do?

Psychology in Schools, Colleges and Universities

One way of discovering what a student in psychology might be taught in school, a college or at university is to take a look at a general textbook in psychology, such as one of the those listed in Chapter 6. A typical list of textbook contents is as follows (Furnham

and Oakley, 1995). Each of the areas receives about equal consideration.

- *The Nature of Psychology*. This section would be expected to
  include an exploration of psychology as a science, its history
  and the major issues it addresses.
- *Methods of Psychological Research*. A review of the major
  approaches to research and varieties of research methods,
  including how to design experiments and an introduction to
  the use of statistics in psychology.
- *Biological Processes*. Without a brain, a nervous system and the
  body they serve there would be no psychology! So psychologists learn about nerve cells and the way they work, about
  hormones and how the brain is constructed. This section
  might also consider how nervous systems change through
  maturation or through experience and the importance of
  heredity and our evolutionary history in making us what we
  are today
- *Sensation and Perception*. A consideration of how our bodies detect
  light, sound, odour and touch and how our brains convert these
  raw sensations into perceptions; that is, our experience of things
  we can see, hear, smell, feel and interact with, of size and shape,
  of depth and colour. Sometimes this conversion process goes
  awry and what we perceive is an illusion.
- *Consciousness and Altered Mental States*. An exploration of how and
  why our mental experience varies during sleep and dreaming,
  in hypnosis or when we meditate or take drugs of various sorts.
- *Learning and Conditioning*. An account of the varieties of learning
  in humans and animals and the principles which underlie it.
- *Memory*. A consideration of different types of memory, such as
  working memory, short-term and long-term memory and the
  effects of brain injuries on memory. An increasingly important
  topic is memory, and its shortcomings, in everyday situations.
- *Language and Thought*. Explores the mechanisms of thinking,
  reasoning, decision making and problem solving. The development, use and understanding of language and the relationship between thought and language are other central issues
- *Psychological Development*. Describes stages of development in
  physical abilities and mental processes from birth (or even
  before), through childhood, adolescence and into adulthood.
  Particularly important topics are the development of
  language, of a sense of self and of moral reasoning as well as

the contribution of experience versus inbuilt factors to these developments.

- *Motivation.* Why do we do things? What moves us to action? Among the answers on offer are hunger, thirst, sex, curiosity and the need to achieve. Again the question arises – are we born with these motives, or do we acquire them?

- *Emotion.* How is an emotional experience produced – in our bodies or in our minds? Other concerns are the ways in which emotion is expressed through facial expressions and body language, the effects of emotion on memory, judgement and so on. Aggression is often the emotion most heavily featured.

- *Mental Abilities and Their Measurement.* Describes the design and use of tests and measures in psychology. Key problems discussed include the nature of intelligence and possibly the role of heredity.

- *Personality and Individual Differences.* Our unique personality is what distinguishes us from others. The question of how personality is formed and developed is often presented in textbooks by contrasting major theories, such as the psychoanalytic or social-learning approaches.

- *Abnormal Psychology.* Looks at the various ways in which our psychological adjustment and mental health can break down. It ranges from the commonplace problems of anxiety and stress, and how we cope with them, to less common conditions such as phobias (abnormal fears), eating disorders (anorexia and bulimia), depression and schizophrenia.

- *Psychological Therapies.* A wide variety of approaches to treating psychological disorders are described, contrasted and evaluated from psychodynamic therapy, based on Freud's theories, to the more recent behavioural and cognitive therapies.

- *Social Psychology and Interpersonal Relations.* Much to the annoyance of social psychologists this topic is commonly treated last in psychology textbooks. It covers a wide range of issues such as the way we understand our own behaviour and that of others, how our attitudes are formed and change, why we are attracted to some people and not others, why we conform to social pressures, why we sometimes help our fellow humans and why we sometimes ignore or even harm them. Gender issues would have been raised in many of the earlier sections but have become a particular focus for some social psychologists in recent years.

Cognitive Science

One development in psychology which it is important for the potential student to know about is the emergence of cognitive science as an
identifiable field of study. Cognitive science is the science of the
mind. It is concerned with those parts of psychology which focus on
'cognitive processes' (literally mental processes related to 'knowing')
such as perceiving, remembering, reasoning, decision making and
problem solving. It is concerned with the way information is
processed and represented in human brains and human minds in
order to bring about these cognitive capabilities and the intelligent
behaviour which depends on them. It seeks to understand and to
model the fundamental properties of the brain and mind that make
it possible for humans to see, think and feel, and to communicate.
The possibility that the same, or similar, mental processes can be
simulated by inanimate information processing systems such as
computers has generated a powerful new subject closely associated
with cognitive science, that of 'artificial intelligence'. Most importantly, though, cognitive science extends beyond the boundaries of
psychology to include other disciplines such as anthropology, philosophy, neuroscience, linguistics and computer science. Cognitive
science is not usually treated separately in schools or colleges but one
possibility at university level is to study cognitive science alongside
psychology or one of the other related disciplines.

Conclusion

There are different schools of psychological research each with its
own theories, concepts and methods. They define and research
different problems but approach the same problem quite differently.
It is possible to list some of the fundamental points of disagreement
between psychologists that are shared by most other social sciences.
Crudely they divide into the scientific vs the humanistic approach.
Most academic psychology is dominated by the scientific approach.
Despite a certain amount of disillusionment with how successful this
approach has been, new areas of research, particularly in neurobiology, have meant increasing rather than decreasing interest in the
scientific approach. But increasing specialisms means that the discipline of psychology is fragmenting. Once an island in the sea of
knowledge, psychology now looks like a far-flung archipelago with
islands drifting ever further apart.

Chapter 3:
Is Psychology a
Science?

Psychologists study everything from shopping obsessions and klepto-
mania to hearing in the bat and remembering in the dolphin. They
study issues as diverse as learning, perception and social behaviour.
As such they need a wide range of methods to investigate the issues
that fascinate them. Self-evidently, animals cannot give self-reports;
and certain behaviours such as altruism (selfless behaviour) need to
be studied in a natural setting.

Consider the following problem: imagine that the innocence or
guilt of an accused person is utterly and exclusively dependent on
whether they can read or not. It is your job as a psychologist to determine this relatively simple fact. How would you do it? Remember
that if they are guilty (and can read) they may be pretty clever in out-
smarting you. Think about it. Probably the best way is to use the
Stroop technique used by psychologists for more than 60 years. If
you write the word red in green, yellow in blue, purple in orange and
then get the person – who supposedly cannot read – to say what
colours (not words) they see, those who can read get interference and
hence take longer to say the colour but those who cannot read have
no problem. Imagine reading out the colour of words in Icelandic or
Afrikaans – because (most) people cannot understand these
languages they have no problem identifying the colours. Only those
who can read the language suffer interference.

The Stroop technique in fact has many other applications as well.
How psychologists go about their research is in itself interesting.
They have to be imaginative and flexible because of the diversity of
things they study, and because people are aware they are being studied, their behaviour may not be typical.

3.1   The Assumptions of Science

Although it is open to much debate, most psychologists accept certain assumptions about science and knowledge. Nachmias and Nachmias (1986) list six:

1.   Behaviour is orderly and regular: there is a pattern to behaviour which can be understood (predicted and measured).
2.   We can understand behaviour/know nature: we can, through observation and experimentation, come to understand the causes of behaviour.
3.   Relative knowledge to superior ignorance: scientific knowledge is incomplete, tentative and changing, not absolute.
4.   Natural phenomena have natural causes: no supernatural explanation for behaviour need be posited.
5.   Nothing is self-evident: all claims for scientific truth need to be demonstrated objectively.
6.   Scientific knowledge is acquired from empirical observation and experiments.

Scientific empiricism involves making observations that meet the following criteria:

1.   They are *objective*. That is, they are not influenced by any preconceived ideas about how the results 'should' turn out. Patterns may be observed by anybody.
2.   They are *systematic*. Observations or experiments should be carried out in an orderly way; for example, when observing behaviour, experimenters should know exactly what behaviours they are looking for and how to record them accurately. Disciplined observation is crucial.
3.   They are *replicable*. All observations can be repeated by others, with the same results. Even if an observation is done objectively and systematically, the results are suspect if they cannot be obtained by others. If results are not replicable they are not reliable, and not universally true.

What makes a good researcher in psychology or any other science? Hall (1984) has listed nine factors.

1.   *Enthusiasm*. One main criterion is to have fun while doing research. The activity of research should be as absorbing as

any game requiring skill and concentration that fills the researcher with enthusiasm.

2.   *Open-mindedness.* The practice of good research requires that the scientist observe with a keen, attentive, inquisitive and open mind, because some discoveries are made serendipitously. Open-mindedness also allows us to learn from our mistakes and from the advice and criticisms offered by others. It also means being able to let go of pet theories that are demonstrably wrong.

3.   *Common sense.* The *principle of the drunkard's search* is this: A drunkard lost his house key and began searching for it under a street lamp even though he had dropped the key some distance away. Asked why he didn't look where he had dropped it, he replied, 'There is more light here!' Considerable effort is lost when the researcher fails to use common sense and looks in a convenient place, but not in the most likely place, for the answers to his or her research questions. But, as noted before, this seemingly well-distributed quality is in fact quite rare.

4.   *Role-taking ability.* Good researchers must think of themselves as the users of the research, not just as the persons who have generated it. In order to anticipate criticisms, researchers must be able to cast themselves in the role of the critic or objective observer. The people being studied constitute yet another group inextricably connected with the research, and their unique role is part and parcel of the findings. It is important to be able to empathise with them and to examine the research procedures and results from this subjective viewpoint.

5.   *Inventiveness.* Aspects of creativity are required in the good researcher. The most crucial is the ability to develop good, clear hypotheses and know how to test them. It also requires: finding solutions to problems of financial resources, laboratory space, equipment, recruitment and scheduling of research participants; responding to emergencies during the conduct of research; finding new ways to analyse data, if called for; and coming up with convincing interpretations of results.

6.   *Confidence in one's own judgements.* 'Since all the sciences, and especially psychology, are still immersed in such tremendous realms of the uncertain and the unknown, the best that any individual scientist, especially any psychologist, can do seems to be to follow his or her judgement, however inadequate that may be' (Tolman, 1959, pp.93, 152).

7.   *Consistency and care about details.* Taking pride in one's work will

80

All in the Mind

provide a constructive attitude with which to approach what might seem like the relentless detail-work involved in doing research. There is no substitute for accurate and complete records, properly organised and analysed data, and facts stated precisely.

8. *Ability to communicate.* It has been stated, 'The literature of science, a permanent record of the communication between scientists, is also the history of science: a record of truth, of observations and opinions, of hypotheses that have been ignored or have been found wanting or have withstood the test of further observation and experiment. Scientists must write clearly, unambiguously and simply, so that their discoveries may be known to others' (Barrass, 1978, p.25).

9. *Honesty.* Scientists should demand integrity and scholarship, and abhor dishonesty and sloppiness. However, there is evidence that fraud in science is not uncommon and that it exists in many parts of the scientific community. As a consequence, various institutions, including leading scientific organisations, are currently seeking ways of policing the scientific community for fraud and misconduct. Fraud is devastating to science, because it undermines the basic respect for the literature on which the advancement of science depends.

Skinner, one of the most famous psychologists of this century, suggested four quite simple maxims for young psychological scientists:

1. Cultivate intellectual honesty.
2. Avoid premature conclusions.
3. Search for orderly, lawful relationships among events.
4. Ask questions that are potentially answerable using currently available measuring techniques.

Recommendations for the Researcher

In a wily but perspicacious article on research in the social sciences Aiken (1994) gives some guidelines to researchers in the behavioural sciences under five headings:

A. Planning
1. Some people are simply not cut out to do research: research is difficult and time-consuming and potential researchers may lack the stamina, motivation or ability.

2.   Most good (and bad) research ideas have been thought of before: as Aiken notes so graphically 'One's head should hurt before rather than after the research is conducted' (p. 851) to make sure the research is worth doing.

3.   All worthwhile research has not been done during the past decade: do not assume that recent research is necessarily best or exclusive.

4.   A research investigation should begin with a question: indeed, the more involved and interested one is in the question, the more likely one is to pursue an answer.

5.   If there is more than one way to do or say something, always choose the simplest way: seek for parsimony not over-simplification.

6.   Garbage in, garbage out: 'One should not expect a high-speed computer to compensate for fuzzy ideas and inadequate methodology' (p. 850).

7.   Much scientific research is trivial: a lot of research gathers dust on library shelves and rehashes what is already known.

8.   Researchers should not wait until the data are collected to consult a statistician: analysis should be thought of in the planning, rather than the implementation, stage.

9.   The best-laid plans of researchers often go wrong: many things can go wrong despite best intentions and great care.

B. Implementation

1.   A shotgun approach is usually messy: measuring too much with no clear hypotheses leads to poor results.

2.   Be aware of, and beware of confounding variables: because there may be factors that determine the cause of both variables A and B, which then appear naturally correlated, but are not.

3.   In making measurements, stay off the ceiling and the floor: be careful of measurements that are either too easy or too difficult; or where most people either agree or disagree.

4.   The sample of subjects with which one chooses to work is probably atypical: getting a truly random or representative sample is very difficult and expensive.

5.   Laboratory research is not necessary more controlled, and field is not necessarily more real: location alone does not determine either control or reality.

6.   Not all social science research consists of surveys: many psychological studies measure behaviour rather than self-report.

7. Most research in the behavioural sciences is basically correla-
    tional: in fact most laboratory research attempts to investigate
    causal not only correlational relationships.
8. Watch out for the jingle and jangle fallacy in selecting instru-
    ments: jingle assumes measures with (much) the same name
    measure the same thing; whereas jangle is the opposite –
    those with different names measure different things.
9. Some people cannot seem to tell the difference between an
    independent and a dependent groups design: the former
    assigns people at random to conditions; the latter may involve
    repeated measures.

C. Analysing
1. There is more to research than collecting and analysing data:
    interpretation and inference are equally important.
2. Do not rely on a fancy statistical procedure to correct design
    errors: it is better to get the design right in the first place.
3. Do not use cannons to shoot flies: relying on sophisticated
    statistics may lead to interpretation errors when the variables
    are correlated.
4. Pay attention to statistical power and sample size: results are
    likely to be more robust when more powerful tests are used
    and when the sample is both big and representative.
5. Minds may be changed, but not statistical significance levels:
    one must state before the analysis what the acceptable level is
    and this should be honoured.
6. Correlations (and chi-square tests) are chronically abused and
    misused: cause is inferred from correlation and it is ignored
    that significance is quite different from the variance accounted
    for.

D. Interpreting
1. Absence of evidence is not evidence of absence: not proving
    your hypothesis does not mean that it is necessarily untrue.
2. Do not argue with the facts if they are actually factual: if a
    well-conducted study proves one wrong, pet theories are
    clearly no longer defensible.
3. All kinds of effects may get in the way of a clear interpretation
    of results: all sorts of well-known effects (Hawthorne, Halo)
    can bias the data and can (in part) be controlled if anticipated.
4. Research results are seldom conclusive: few experiments are
    crucial in deciding facts – research findings often lead to other

Newman University
Library
Tel: 0121 476 1181 ext 1208

Borrowed Items 03/01/2015 21:48
XXXX3817

em Title	Due Date
Why psychology?	26/01/2015 23:59
All in the mind : the ssence of psychology	26/01/2015 23:59
Children, rights and hildhood	07/01/2015 23:59
Children in society : ontemporary theory, olicy and practice	09/01/2015 23:59
Sociology	09/01/2015 23:59
buse of care and ustody orders and nderstanding school hobia	23/01/2015 23:59
Equality and social olicy	23/01/2015 23:59
Childhood experiences f domestic violence	23/01/2015 23:59
Well-being of children n the UK	23/01/2015 23:59
iscourse on inequality	23/01/2015 23:59
Child care today	23/01/2015 23:59
Crime and inequality	23/01/2015 23:59
How children develop	23/01/2015 23:59
Children and ommunities	23/01/2015 23:59
ssata : an utobiography	23/01/2015 23:59

Amount Outstanding: £6.00

Indicates items borrowed today
hankyou for using Newman Library
www.newman.ac.uk/library
brary@newman.ac.uk

questions and issues becoming more complicated.

5.   Causation implies correlation, but correlation does not imply causation: this well-known truism is true!

6.   Interactions are usually more interesting than main effects: this tells us to what extent factors are related in a cooperative, competitive or compensating matter such as the trade-off between speed and accuracy.

7.   Statistical significance is not equivalent to practical significance: the former only alerts to the possibility of the latter.

E. Reporting

1.   Always keep the 'dear reader' in mind: writing should be economical without being telegraphese and not full of jargon.

2.   Strive for well-integrated paragraphs and papers: all papers should flow.

3.   It is easy to overlook one's mistakes: others need to help check one's work.

4.   Good computer software does not guarantee good writing.

5.   Don't be in a hurry to stop working on a paper: put a paper aside for a while and resume work on it later when refreshed.

3.2   Horse Sense

The story of the mathematical horse is well known in psychology and very illustrative of the scientific method (Kalat, 1993). Because of his long-lasting fame at the turn of the century many people know about 'Clever Hans' the mind-reading horse.

People flocked to see the horse Hans perform his amazing feats. Hans was owned by a Mr van Osten, who was so impressed by the horse's abilities that he built a large 'answer board' for Hans to use. If people gave the owner a question for Hans, he would look directly at the horse and repeat the question in what seemed a normal tone of voice. Hans would then lift his hoof and tap out the answer. Thus if asked, 'What is 2 + 2?' Hans would tap the ground four times. But if the question was 'Who is King of England?' Hans would point to the letters on the answer board that spelled out the correct response. After Hans had given the correct answer the owner would reward the animal by patting it or give it food as a reward. Was the horse unusually gifted or were the audience being hoodwinked?

There were a number of intriguing aspects of Hans's performance. If people tried to trick him, he could detect it. For instance, if someone said, '2 + 2 is 5, isn't it?' Hans would usually signal 'No',

using the answer board. Many people believed this response proved
Hans was an 'independent thinker' and was not just responding to
subtle cues given him by his owner. Also, Hans would respond to
questions given to him even by strangers. Thus, the horse obviously
was not just picking up on unintentional cues from his owner.

Interestingly, if the answer to your question was a long one, Hans
would tap much more rapidly than if the answer were short. Many
took this as evidence that Hans was so bright, he knew the length of
the answer *before he started responding*. Of course if the horse merely
started and stopped responding when given some cue by his owner
the animal obviously would not know in advance which answers
were going to be long and which would be short.

Given these facts, it is not surprising that most people who
observed the performing horse concluded Hans was an equine
telepath. Yet some sceptics remained convinced that the animal was
merely reacting to cues of some kind from the people who asked
Hans questions. The controversy became so heated that, in 1904,
several of the best-known scientists in Germany formed a 'commission' to study the animal. The commission included a zoologist, a
physiologist, a veterinarian, a psychologist, the director of the Berlin
Zoo and the manager of a circus. After months of study, the commission issued its report. These distinguished scientists stated boldly that
they could find no evidence Hans was responding to external cues
from his questioners and Hans was therefore a special case, and
perhaps really could read minds ... or at least do arithmetic.

However, the psychologist on the commission, clearly not satisfied, told one of his graduate students to look into the matter. This
student simply did not believe that Hans could 'read minds'. So, for
many months, he observed very carefully as the owner talked to his
horse. Then, in a *controlled and systematic* way, the student began to
change the conditions under which Hans worked. The student was
clearly using experimental not just observation methods.

The student put blinkers on Hans so the animal could not watch
the people who were asking him the questions. The horse's ability to
respond correctly decreased significantly. This result strongly suggested
that Hans was responding to some unintentional visual cue given him
by the person asking the questions. And when this bright student found
ways to keep Hans from hearing the tiny noises that people made when
asking him questions, Hans did even worse. And, when both visual and
auditory cues were cut out after someone asked the horse a question,
Hans either refused to respond or gave the wrong answer.

To test the animal's ability to 'think independently', the enterprising student then asked Hans to add two numbers, such as 23 + 49. Hans immediately responded by tapping out 72. Then he asked a friend of his to select a number at random and whisper it in the horse's ear. The student then did the same, and asked Hans to add the two numbers. If *either* the intrepid student or his friend knew *both* numbers, Hans invariably got the correct answer, but if neither was aware of what number the other had chosen, the horse usually failed the test.

These results indicated that Clever Hans was indeed a 'genius of a horse', but was not a mind-reader. The animal was superb at reading 'body-language' cues that questioners almost always gave to the animal. But these were so slight and so subtle that most people were completely unaware they were giving Hans signals. In this sense the sceptics were right all along.

Indeed it was established that the moment most people finished asking Hans a question, they inclined their heads slightly forward. This was a signal to Hans to start tapping and when Hans had tapped out the correct response, the people leaned back (just slightly). This cue told Hans to stop tapping. Some other questioners inhaled sharply when Hans had reached the right number of taps (perhaps out of shock). Similar cues helped the animal point his hoof to letters on the 'answer board' that the horse owner had constructed.

People tended to lean further toward when they asked questions requiring longer answers than when they asked questions with short answers. This response gave Hans his cue as to how fast to tap. Indeed, the horse was so sensitive to slight head movements that if anyone present raised an eyebrow or twitched a nostril while Hans was responding, he would stop instantly.

Once the student became aware that Clever Hans was reacting to the body-language cues he was giving the horse, he deliberately tried to stop making these tell-tale movements when he asked Hans questions. But no matter how hard he struggled to control his body language, Hans could almost always detect some sort of signal that told the animal when and how to respond. As all liars know it is difficult to hide non-verbal cues completely.

The Clever Hans story is important for several reasons. First, it showed that most of us continually give cues in our body language that suggest how we feel and what we are thinking about. Usually, we are unaware we are giving off these signals, but they are detectable to anyone who is trained to notice. Sixty years later psychologists began to take a serious interest in non-verbal behaviour!

Second, the student's research demonstrates how critical *scientific experiments* are to understanding human behaviour. The commission of distinguished scientists who studied Clever Hans observed the horse carefully, asked questions, and gave the matter a lot of thought and concluded that Hans could 'read minds'. But they did not do scientific experiments to test out their conclusions. The student observed the animal first, because the scientific method always begins with careful observations. But he took the next crucial step. He guessed at the environmental stimuli (or cues) that could be affecting the horse's behaviour, and thentific experiments led the student to quite a different set of conclusions about Clever Hans than the commission had reached. Exactly the same issue arose with those who observed spoon-benders and the like today.

One of the main purposes of any science is that of solving 'mysteries'. The cause of much human behaviour is indeed a puzzle for the psychologist. We could just use our 'hunches', of course, and make wild guesses about the answer. B he altered these stimulus cues in a very systematic way. This creative use of scienut scientists prefer to adopt a logical process of some kind when trying to find the solution to the puzzle.

The approach most scientists use is called the *scientific method*, which is based on the belief that most observable patterns of behaviour have *measurable causes*. To use the scientific method properly, you must follow several steps:

1.   One has to recognise that a problem or phenomenon of some kind exists which needs an explanation, and that it probably has a natural cause. Perceiving and defining the problem carefully and clearly is the first step.
2.   One makes as many initial observations about the circumstance of the phenomena as possible. These observations are made as exact and complete as possible. (This leads to forming a hypothesis.)
3.   One uses the results of initial observations to come up with a tentative solution or 'first guess' as to what the answer is. This may be stated as an experimental hypothesis, although more than one can be tested at a time.
4.   One then draws up a plan for testing objectively whether or not the first hunch about the solution was correct. This test may merely involve making further observations about the puzzling affair. Or it may more usually involve performing an experiment in which one 'does something' to the phenomenon in order to get a reaction of some kind.

5.   Whether one merely observes things or whether one under-
      takes an experiment of some kind, one then looks over the data
      gathered and tries to decide whether the tentative solution to
      the problem was right or wrong. If the initial hypothesis was
      wrong, it must be revised and one needs to make some more
      observations to derive and test other hypotheses. But if the first
      hunch was correct, one probably will refine the solution to the
      phenomenon by testing it again and again. And to do so, one
      needs to make further predictions about future events.

6.   If these further predictions turn out to be accurate, then most
      likely the solution to the puzzle was correct. But if the predic-
      tions were incorrect, one should realise that one 'erred' some-
      where along the way. And thus one will have to start the
      problem-solving process all over again (Kalat, 1993).

All scientists strive for, but rarely achieve, disinterested objectivity.
For example, the student (above) was objective in his study of Clever
Hans. His initial hypothesis was that the horse was responding to
unconscious cues from the owner and other questioners. Interestingly, the owner never charged anyone for talking to Hans, and
made not a penny out of the animal's fame. But the student
researcher did not allow his affection for either the man or the horse
to get in the way of his pursuit of objectivity. According to Kalat
(1993) the owner, on the other hand, let his emotions blind him to
what was really going on. He loved Hans and went into a deep
depression after the student's report was accepted. A few months
later he died, a bitter and very disappointed man. It is not easy to be
dispassionate, unbiased and objective when doing psychological
research. Indeed many would argue that it is impossible, even undesirable. But most empirical psychologists strive for that end believing
that the only way we will understand ourselves is through careful
observation and experimentation.

3.3   The Research Process

Scientific knowledge is knowledge obtained by both reason and
experience (observation). Logical validity and experimental verifica-
tion are the criteria employed by scientists to evaluate claims for
knowledge. These two criteria are translated into the research activities of scientists through the research process (see Figure 3.1). The
research process can be viewed as the overall scheme of scientific

activities in which scientists engage in order to produce knowledge; it is the paradigm of scientific inquiry.

Problem $\rightarrow$ Hypothesis $\rightarrow$ Research design $\rightarrow$ Measurement

Generalisation $\leftarrow$ Data analysis $\leftarrow$ Data collection $\leftarrow$

Figure 3.1: The principal stages of the research process

As illustrated in Figure 3.1, the research process consists of seven principal stages: problem, hypothesis, research design, measurement, data collection, data analysis and generalisation. Each of these stages is interrelated with theory in the sense that each is affected by it as well as affects it. The most characteristic feature of the research process is its *cyclic nature*. It often starts with a problem and ends in a tentative generalisation based on the experimental evidence. The generalisation ending one cycle is the beginning of the next cycle. This cyclic process continues indefinitely, reflecting the progress of a scientific discipline.

The research process is also *self-correcting*. Tentative generalisations to research problems are tested logically and empirically. If these generalisations are rejected, new ones are formulated and tested. In the process of formulation all research operations are re-evaluated because the rejection of a tentative generalisation might be due not to its being invalid, but to deficiencies in performing the research operations. To minimise the risk of rejecting true generalisation, one re-examines each of the stages in the research process prior to the formulation of new generalisations.

Psychology, and all science, is united by its methodology. What sets the scientific approach apart from other modes of acquiring knowledge is the assumptions upon which it is grounded and its methodology.

The methodology of the scientific approach serves two major purposes: rules for communication (to other researchers and the wider world) and rules for logical and valid reasoning. These systems of rules allow us to understand, explain and predict our environments and ourselves in a manner that other systems for generating knowledge cannot allow us to do.

Scientific knowledge is knowledge provable by both reason and observation. The scientific methodology requires strict adherence to the rules of logic and observation. Such adherence should not be seen as encouraging conformity but rather helping to know the correct use of the rules. Naturally psychologists, like other scientific communities, are involved in power struggles that are not always conducive to the progress of science. These struggles and fashions are inevitable. But claims for knowledge are accepted only in so far as they are congruent with the assumptions of science and its methodology.

3.4   Pure vs Applied Research

Psychologists do practise in the 'real world', and also conduct research in the laboratory. Some do 'blue-sky' research which attempts to understand important processes and mechanisms for their own sake – why people dream; why some people are colour-blind; why visual illusions occur. Others, however, start with practical problems they have been asked to solve. They are applied psychologists.

Robson (1994) has noted 16 characteristics which distinguish 'real-world' applied research from pure research.

In applied enquiry the emphasis tends to be on:

1.	*solving problems*	rather than	*just gaining knowledge*
2.	*predicting effects*	rather than	*finding causes*
3.	*getting large effects* (looking for robust results)	rather than	*relationships between variables* (and assessing statistical significance)

and

	concern for actionable factors (where changes are feasible)		
4.	*developing and testing programmes, interventions, services, etc.*	rather than	*developing and testing, theories*
5.	*field*	rather than	*laboratory*
6.	*outside organisation* (industry, business, school, etc.)	rather than	*research institution*
7.	*strict time constraints*	rather than	*as long as the problem needs*
8.	*strict cost constraints*	rather than	*as much finance as the problem needs* (or the work is not attempted)
9.	*little consistency of topic from one study to the next*	rather than	*high consistency from one study to the next*

10.	*topic initiated by sponsor*	rather than	*topic initiated by researcher*
11.	*often generalist researchers* (need for familiarity with range of methods)	rather than	*typically highly specialist researchers* (need to be at forefront of their discipline)
12.	*little use of 'true' experiments*	rather than	*much use of 'true' experiments*
13.	*multiple methods*	rather than	*single methods*
14.	*orientated to the client* (generally, and particularly in reporting)	rather than	*orientated to academic peers*
15.	*currently viewed as dubious by many academics*	rather than	*high academic prestige*
16.	*need for well-developed social skills*	rather than	*some need for social skills*

(Robson, 1994, pp.11–12. Reprinted with permission.)

He furthers the distinction between laboratory, pure studies and applied research by citing actual published studies.

	Laboratory	Real world
Giving bad news	Subject has to inform partner in the lab	Coroner announcing death of next of kin
Interpersonal attraction	Anticipating interaction with a stranger: traits are listed as more or less similar to one's own	'Fear and loathing' at a college social function
Behaviour on a train	Response to an 'implanted' crisis	Defence of common territory
Reactions to fear	Anticipating an electric shock	Learning first hand how to work on high steel in a 21-storey building
Superstition	Predicting sequence in which bulbs will light up	'Poker parlours' in California
Loosening of internal controls in response to anonymity	Students delivering shock when clothed in lab gowns and hoods	Tenants in high-rise housing exposed to danger
Impression formation	Students reading lists of adjectives	Folk-singers trying to 'psyche out' an audience

(Robson, 1994, pp. 11–12. Reprinted with permission.)

He very helpfully shows diagrammatically how they differ (see Figure 3.2).

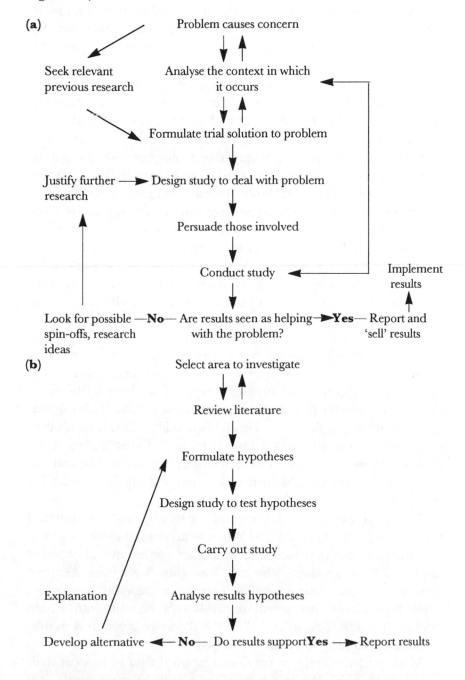

Figure 3.2: A model for the real-world enquiry process involved and, as a contrast, the traditional type of model given in most research methodological texts. Reprinted with permission.

Cursory comparison of the models indicates several differences. As already stressed, the focus in real-world enquiry shifts from the usual scientific task to the solution of a problem or resolution of an issue. The model is also substantially more complex, with a greater number of processes involved and more, and more complex, interactions between the various stages (p. 452).

But how do academic research psychologists interested in pure research differ in their approach from management consultants in the applied world? Furnham and Pendleton (1991) consider 11 differences.

For the academic, research may have a 'blue-skies' air about it. Its aim is to achieve insight, understanding or knowledge that may not be useful, applicable or saleable. The aim is to know the cause of things and to have a comprehensive understanding of the issue under investigation. While, for many academics 'pure' research is the major aim, for the business executive research is nearly always 'applied'. Research is action orientated, problem solving, operation intended. In this sense, the aim is much clearer and probably short term. Academics start with a puzzle, consultants with a problem, and the former are satisfied to know and understand, whereas the latter want to use the knowledge and sell it.

Consultants are time-conscious, high-urgency people, driven by deadlines. They want the answer now and are perplexed by the apparently sluggish, procrastinatory ways of academics who resist the immediate fix-it nature of consultancy jobs. Consultants certainly adhere to Benjamin Franklin's maxims: 'Lost time is never found again; remember that time is money'. Expectations about time and its use are remarkably different in the two worlds, and this is a source of considerable frustration, particularly for consultants dealing with academics.

To a large extent, academics and consultants look for different things in solutions to problems. Whereas academics value elegance, parsimony, scope, precision and testability, consultants often value applicability, comprehensibility and feasibility. Academics like theories and solutions that are reliable, testable, logically consistent, explicit, verifiable and systematic. Although the consultant might admire these characteristics, unless the theory or solution is usable, or at least insightful, it is near worthless.

Most academics rely on original, empirical data to support their advice or theories. While the database can be of many kinds, it is important that it is representative, comprehensive, correctly sampled and measured, and free of 'noise' and errors. Some consultants are happy with a secondhand empirical base, non-original sources and particularly illustrative case-histories to make a point. Whereas the source of the data may be all-important for academics, it is not as crucial for people in business who do not have to persuade others on the basis of their data. In this sense, the two are probably epistemologically divided as well, the former being empiricists, the latter rationalists.

The levels of complexity of theory, or model, often differ in the two worlds. Academics' level of analysis is frequently complex and they expect the audience, whoever that is, to deal with the complexity. Consultants strive to simplify and clarify, in order to help the audience or the client to comprehend. Academics are often scathing about the simple-minded solutions of consultants, while the consultant sees the academic as needlessly obfuscating an issue that can be presented much more clearly.

The way in which uncertainty, or the unknown, is dealt with is very different in the two worlds. Among academics, the issue is usually dealt with statistically by offering probabilities on the likelihood of various outcomes. Academics, then, expect people to be able to interpret the application of results themselves. Consultants often find they have to deal with the uncertainty issue personally, by reassurance or interpretation. In some senses, consultants feel they need to 'own the problem', while academics take a more distant, uninvolved approach.

Consultants like to sell ideas, solutions and 'theories', and they usually prefer to do so face to face. As polished presenters, consultants might have slick slides, memorable mnemonics and helpful hand-outs, but their preference is for the live medium. Academics prefer documents, tables and charts, and seem happiest giving and receiving information in this form. Not even skilled at chalk-and-talk, most academics feel most secure communicating in writing; hence, their love of word processors but not car phones or, worse, video phones.

For academics, self-presentation, in terms of dress and equipment, is irrelevant because they value what is being said, and the quality of ideas, over packaging. Often shabby, nearly always unfashionable and frequently something of an eyesore, the academic is easy to spot, even in a crowd. For consultants, the opposite is true. They know that their clients will be acutely aware of the messages that are sent by such small things as the type of watch, size of briefcase and elegance of technology used. Consultants never underestimate the packaging of services because they have come to learn the extent to which impression-management can influence customer satisfaction. In this sense, academics are rugged individualists and consultants smart mimics.

Academics rely on their ability to persuade, often by the quality of their data. The numbers do the talking. Consultants, on the other hand, often use rhetoric – and with some success. This is not to suggest that there are not some extremely skilled rhetoricians among academics, or that consultants are empirically naïve, but that, when looking at their reports and presentations, academics prefer the disinterested nature of empirical data and consultants the power of persuasive words.

Whereas, for consultants and their clients, value for money has always been important, academics are only recently having to argue the potential benefits of their work in relation to its costs. For most academics, cost–benefit analyses are impossible to calculate: they will cite many examples of chance discoveries which have followed from blue-skies research. Consultants have to demonstrate value in the short term.

Finally, it seems that academics and consultants not only have different personalities but that they value certain characteristics differently. Academics tend to be phlegmatic, stable introverts – respecting others, thoughtful, controlled, reliable, reserved, calm, even-tempered types. Consultants, on the other hand, tend to be sanguine, stable extroverts – active, impulsive, optimistic, responsive, easygoing and sociable. These differences occur partly out of necessity – consultants have to get on with people, to socialise and to persuade. Academics, meanwhile, have to spend long periods alone in libraries and laboratories collecting data very carefully.

There are, no doubt, hundreds of exceptions to the rules listed here – instances where the differences either do not occur or occur in the opposite way to that described. Certainly, there are academics who can deal well with the commercial world, and consultants whose training and methods are rigorous. The problem remains, however, that academics and business people still do not fully understand one another. They come from different cultures, hold different values and expectations, and have different aims and strategies of communication (see Figure 3.3)

3.5   Major Methods of Research

Psychological researchers have to be eclectic in their research methodology: different problems require different methods to

	Academics	Consultants
Major aims	Insight and knowledge	Action and operation
Speed of solution	Low urgency	High urgency
Type of solution valued	Elegant and critical	Applicable and comprehensible
Source of data	Direct empirical base	Secondhand empirical base
Level of complexity	Frequently complex	Frequently simple
Dealing with uncertainty	Dealt with statistically	Dealt with personally
Preferred medium of presentation	Written documents/tables	Face to face
Self-presentation	Irrelevant, often shabby	Important, fashionably smart
Means of persuasion	Empirical data	Rhetoric
Cost–benefit analysis	Irrelevant	Crucial
Type of personality valued	Introvert	Extrovert

Figure 3.3: Characteristics which separate the two worlds of academics and consultants

analyse them. A number of very different methods are available to the researcher to investigate psychological issues, test theories or explore ideas. Practical and ethical issues as well as personal preferences dictate which method is used, although often it is determined by the philosophic training of the researcher. Ideally, the research question should dictate which method is used and often this is the case. The following are the major methods (Furnham and Oakley, 1995).

Psychology in the Laboratory

Some people argue it is impossible to study real behaviour in the cold, clinical laboratory. The research psychologist's aim is to test the effects of one or more independent variables on one or more dependent variables, i.e. does heat affect aggression; does eye contact affect liking; does the order of information received affect the way it is remembered? *Independent variables* in an experiment are those factors that are controlled or arranged by the experimenter and may often be considered the cause of behaviour. *Dependent variables* refer to those behaviours of the subject that are observed or recorded by the experimenter. Thus, if one is interested in whether television viewing encourages violence the independent variable may be the amount and type of TV programmes watched and the dependent variable some measure of violent behaviour in the viewers.

Most characteristic of the laboratory experiment is the psychologist's ability to control and vary the independent variables (those which are changed). Indeed, this aspect of control is one of the most important features of the laboratory experiment. Numerous extraneous variables can be eliminated or manipulated, such as light, noise, distraction, other people present. One could also control how far people sit from one another, or the size or temperature of the place where they meet, or through what medium they interact with each other in everyday situations.

The laboratory experiment also offers another important advantage: the ability to assign subjects randomly to conditions. In order for a psychologist to draw conclusions regarding cause and effect, he or she must be sure that the pattern of results was not due to some systematic difference in the groups being compared (i.e. volunteers vs non-volunteers; who comes first and so on). On average, *randomisation* ensures an equality of subject characteristics across the various experimental conditions.

Another characteristic of the laboratory experiment is the *manipulation* check. It is still important for psychologists to be sure that the subjects in the experiment perceive the manipulation as it is intended. That is, if you want to induce anxiety in subjects (perhaps by threatening them with a painful shock), you might measure their heart rate or ask them afterwards how scared they were. In other words, did they believe the experimenter; did they see the situation in the way he/she wanted them to?

Advantages

Principal among the advantages is the ability of the experimenter to control the independent variables and to assign subjects randomly to conditions. These two capabilities provide some basis for conclusions regarding cause and effect. Furthermore, the laboratory allows the investigator to 'sort out' factors – to simplify the more complex events of the natural world by breaking them down into their component parts. Psychologists can, in short, control what their subjects see and experience and note how they subsequently react.

Disadvantages

Although the laboratory experiment has considerable advantages in terms of its ability to isolate and control variables, it has substantial disadvantages as well. In recent years, these disadvantages have become the topic of considerable debate. Four of the major issues of concern have been the possible irrelevance of the laboratory setting; the reactions of subjects to the laboratory setting; the possible influence of experimenters on their results, and deception and ethics.

Many of the situations created in the laboratory bear little direct relationship to the situations a person encounters in real organisational life. They are too sterile, artificial and staged. One can distinguish between *experimental realism* and mundane realism: in the laboratory, one can devise situations that have impact and that evoke valid psychological processes (experimental realism), even if the situation itself does not look like the real world (mundane realism) (see Chapter 7). Yet, it remains true that many laboratory tasks seem suspiciously artificial and their *external validity* has not been demonstrated. External validity refers to the 'generalisability' of research findings to the 'outside world', to other populations, treatment variables and measurement variables. For some, if the situation is artificial so are the experimental subjects' reactions to it.

A second criticism of the laboratory experiment focuses on the reactions of subjects to the laboratory setting. These reactions may involve *demand characteristics* and *evaluation apprehension*. The first term refers to the fact that the experimental setting may evoke certain perceived demands. That is, expectations on the part of subjects to act in the way that they think the experimenter would wish. Some try to charm and ingratiate themselves to the experimenter (sycophants) or to do the opposite. In short, subjects believe they should (and do) behave in a particular, not necessarily natural, way. Evaluation apprehension refers to the concerns (anxieties) that a subject has about being observed and judged while in the laboratory setting.

A third criticism of the laboratory experiment concerns *experimenter expectancies*. It has been shown in a variety of situations that an experimenter who knows the hypothesis of the study can unknowingly influence the results of the study. The influence of these experimenter expectancies can be controlled to a large extent. For example, many experiments involve instructions that have been tape recorded in advance, thus assuring consistency in experimenter approach to all subjects. Other techniques include the use of a 'blind' experimenter, wherein the individual conducting the experiments is not informed of the experimental hypotheses and thus is less likely to exert a systematic bias on the results. In medicine, drug trials are usually double blind – neither the doctor administering the drug nor the patient receiving it knows whether it is the real thing or a placebo.

A fourth problem concerns the *ethics* of laboratory research, particularly when deception is involved. In order to ensure subjects are naïve or unaware about the point of the study (and to reduce demand characteristics and evaluation apprehension) they are often deceived or indeed lied to about the study. Although they are fully debriefed afterwards, the ethical problems must be faced (see Chapter 7).

Despite these well-understood problems, the majority of psychological studies are conducted in laboratories, because the advantages are seen to outweigh the disadvantages. This is probably less true of studies of social behaviour but very common in studies of cognitive behaviour.

Field Experiments

In contrast with the laboratory experiment, the setting of the field experiment is a natural one and the subjects are not generally aware that they are in an experiment. Rather than contriving an artificial situation in a laboratory, the investigator who uses a field experiment to test a hypothesis is looking at behaviour in its *natural setting*. For example, in order to study altruism (unselfish helping or pro-social behaviour) a psychologist may get an actor to collapse in the street, or lie bottle-in-hand in the gutter while the experimenter observes the behaviour of passers-by. What circumstances (blood, alcohol present) determine whether passers-by do or do not help (see Chapter 7)?

Advantages

The advantages of the field experiment are that by focusing on behaviour in a natural setting, the experimenter can be much more certain of the *external validity* of his or her findings: that people are behaving naturally. Furthermore, the problems of reactivity and the subjects' desire to be seen in a positive light are eliminated. In addition, because control over the independent variable and principles of randomisation are maintained, the field experiment allows the same possibilities for conclusions about cause and effect as does the laboratory experiment.

Disadvantages

Although the field experiment may seem to combine ideally the application of the strict rules of experimentation with the realism of natural behaviour settings, it too has some disadvantages, which relate to the nature of the independent variable, the nature of the dependent variable, the ethics of the experiment and the practical difficulties involved.

Because the experimenter is working in a complex natural setting where many events may be occurring simultaneously, the independent variable (i.e. the drunk in the gutter) in the study must be obvious to the potential subject. Subtle manipulations of a variable (is the person bleeding or not?) may simply go unnoticed. The experimental independent variable is, in effect, competing with all the other stimuli present in the setting

The dependent variable (the behaviour one measures) in a field experiment needs to be selected carefully. The experimenters must be able to readily observe and reliably judge the dependent-variable behaviour. But this is not always possible because things get in the way. Remember in the 'real world' one does not have the control of the laboratory. An additional problem in field experimentation concerns ethics. Is it reasonable for the investigator to involve individuals in an experiment without their knowledge or permission? Is it ethical to observe and film people without their knowledge? Is it acceptable to stage events that cause distress and anxiety to passers-by? Finally, the field experiment often poses practical problems. In contrast with the investigator in the laboratory, the investigator in the field has no control over the majority of events in the environment; unexpected events may reduce or destroy the effectiveness of the manipulation.

Quasi-experimental Research

The defining characteristics of quasi-experimental research are that the investigator does not have full experimental control over the independent variables but does have extensive control over how, when and for whom the dependent variable is measured (Rosnow and Rosenthal, 1992). Generally these experiments involve behaviour in a natural setting and focus on the effect of intervention in a system of ongoing behaviour. For instance, imagine the television stations in a particular part of the country go on strike. This allows one the perfect and rare opportunity to see what people do when deprived of the all-pervasive television compared with those who are not.

In other cases, the intervention may be a natural disaster, such as flood, earthquake or tornado. Power blackouts could serve as the independent variable in a study of reactions to stressful events. The introduction of new laws in one state/county but not in adjacent others provides excellent quasi-experimental opportunities to investigate their effects. Psychologists have no control over the independent variable (strikes, law changes), but they could carefully select a set of dependent variables to measure the effect of the phenomenon. Consider whether TV advertisements trying to stop drink-driving work: if one region runs ads of this sort and another doesn't (perhaps because of cost) one can see what effect they have by measuring actual drink-related behaviour after the series of advertisements and comparing the two regions.

Advantages

One unique advantage of quasi-experimental research conducted in a natural setting is that it allows for the study of very powerful variables that cannot be manipulated or controlled by any psychologists. Quasi-experimental research deals with policy decisions that have consequences for very large numbers of people. The broad impact of such decisions gives considerable weight to the external validity of the study, in a manner that can rarely be matched in the more limited laboratory or field experiment.

Disadvantages

Because the investigator has no control over (or ability to predict) the primary independent variable in quasi-experimental research, it is always possible that other uncontrolled variables are affecting the dependent-variable behaviour. Also, random assignment of subjects to conditions can rarely be assumed in the quasi-experimental design. Often such research must literally be done 'on the run'. Furthermore, the arbitrariness of events in the quasi-experimental world precludes the experimenter's ability to vary factors according to any theoretical model. To a large extent quasi-experimental psychologists have to be opportunists trying to find situations that allow them to test their theories.

Field Study

Most field studies preferred by anthropologists are characterised by their in-depth study of a limited group of people. Rather than manipulate some aspect of the environment and observe the changes that occur, the investigator in the field study records as much information as possible about the characteristics of that situation without altering the situation in any substantial way. This is the method of journalists, historians and sociologists as well as psychologists. Most often, people in the environment are aware of the investigator's presence and the general purpose of the investigation. Many times the investigator is a *participant observer* – that is, someone actively engaged in the activities of the group while at the same time maintaining records of the group members' behaviours.

Observation and accurate, reliable recording are the key elements of the field-study method. Considerable time must be devoted in advance to understand the environment and become aware of the kinds of behaviours that are most likely to occur, and which types of behaviour are to be recorded.

Once categories of behaviour are selected for observation, the investigator must devise specific methods of recording the desired information. The observer must conduct a series of preliminary investigations to *determine the reliability* of the measures. In other

words, it must be demonstrated that a series of different observers
watching the same event and using the methods chosen to record
observations will code the behaviour in the same way.

Advantages

The major advantage lies in realism: the focus of the study is on
events as they normally occur in a *real-life setting*. Furthermore,
because most field studies take place over an extended period of
time, they provide information about the sequence and development
of behaviours that cannot be gained in the one-shot observation typical of field and laboratory experiments. Additionally, the duration of
the field study generally allows for the collection of several different
types of dependent measures. The data from field studies are rich,
varied and nearly always fascinating.

Disadvantages

Although well-conducted field studies provide a wealth of unique
data, the lack of control in such settings can be a problem. A second
potential problem in the field study is the subjects' awareness of the
investigator's observations. When subjects are aware of being
observed, their behaviour may be reactive – that is, influenced by the
process of observation. Most experienced observers believe,
however, that in a long-term field study the subjects become indifferent to the observer's presence, though the problem remains a serious
one in briefer studies. There are often serious problems of reliability
if, as often happens, we only have one observer. What if our observer
is biased or hoodwinked by the people he or she is studying? In short,
few field-study findings are demonstrably reliable.

Archival Research

Archival research refers to the analysis of any existing records that
have been produced or maintained by persons or organisations other
than the experimenter. The original reason for collecting the records
was not a psychological experiment but rather to track, monitor or
control specific types of behaviour. Newspaper reports and government records of aeroplane fatalities are two examples of archival
data. Psychologists may be interested in meteorological records;
admissions of people of different ethnic groups to mental hospitals
and a company's absenteeism records. Other sources of material
include books and magazines, folk stories of preliterate societies,

personal letters and speeches by public figures. Many organisations keep records in archives which they may be prepared to share with serious researchers.

Advantages

First, it allows the investigator to test hypotheses over a wider range of time and societies than would otherwise be possible. Trends can be examined and related to other known variables. Demonstrating the validity of a hypothesis in a number of different cultures and historical periods, instead of being restricted to a specific group in the present time and place, gives considerable confidence in the validity of that hypothesis as a test of human behaviour in general.

A second advantage of the archival method is that it uses unobtrusive measures which did not cause reactivity in the participants at the time they were collected. Because the information used in archival research was originally collected for some other purpose, there is little or no chance that demand characteristics or evaluation apprehension will be problems.

Disadvantages

Although psychologists doing archival research did not collect the data personally, they may encounter some difficulties in terms of data availability. Frequently a researcher will not be able to locate the kind of data needed to test a hypothesis. Not being able to design the dependent measures, the investigator is left at the mercy of those who collected the data (what they were interested in, how they recorded it and so on). Creativity and ingenuity may be needed to locate the kinds of data needed; in other cases, however, missing or inaccurate records will prevent an adequate experimental test. Even if the material is available, it is sometimes difficult to categorise it in the way necessary to answer the research question. Such procedures are time consuming, although the development of computer programs has provided welcome assistance in some instances.

Simulation and Role Playing

The aim of simulations or role plays is to imitate some aspect of a real-world situation in order to gain more understanding of people's psychological processes. Subjects in these studies are typically asked to *role play*: to adopt a part and act as if they were in the real situation. In advance of their participation, the subjects are fully informed about the situation and are asked to develop their part to the best of their ability. They may be given a part script and the setting may be totally real, but all concerned know that it is a simulation.

Advantages

The success of simulation or role-play study depends heavily on the degree of involvement that the setting can engender. If the subjects become deeply involved in the simulation it may well approximate the real-life conditions that it intends to match. Furthermore, because participants are fully informed of the purposes of the study in advance, they take on the role of co-investigators, a role that is both ethically and humanistically more satisfying in many respects than the more typical experimental subject role in which the subject is unaware of many of the experimenter's intentions. An additional advantage of the simulation is that it may allow the investigator to study in the laboratory phenomena and situations that are difficult to study in the real world.

Disadvantages

In spite of their advantages, simulation and role playing are two of the most controversial methods in the social psychological reper-toire. Critics of the method claim that when one asks subjects to act as if they are in a certain role, the subjects will do only what they think they *might* do and not necessarily what they *would* do in the real situation (Nachmias and Nachmias, 1986). That is, the actions and reactions of actors may be interesting, clever and insightful but they are not typical.

In addition, the problems of experimental demands and evalua-tion apprehension, discussed earlier in relation to laboratory experi-ments, are even more serious when the subject is fully informed of the purposes of the study. On the other hand, proponents of role playing argue that, to some degree, the participant in an experiment is always playing a role, whether it is the general role of subject or a more specific role defined by the investigator.

Questionnaires and Interviews

Although many other methods in psychology make use of question-naires as part of their procedures, survey and interview methods rely solely on this type of information. In both cases, the investigator defines an area for research and designs a set of questions that will elicit the beliefs, attitudes and self-reported experiences of the respondent in relation to the research topic.

Designing a good questionnaire is not as simple as it may appear. Problems include the wording of questions, the provision of sufficient responses, and the format of the questionnaire itself. Considerable pretesting is necessary to ensure that the questions are objective, unbiased, understandable to the average respondent, and specific enough to elicit the desired information.

When the questionnaire is being presented by an interviewer, precautions against biasing the responses are necessary. The issue of experimenter bias, discussed earlier in relation to laboratory experiments, can be a problem in the interview method if the interviewer consciously or unconsciously encourages some responses and discourages or seems uninterested in others. Thus, interviewers must be carefully trained to standardise the delivery of questions to respondents. In addition, the interview method requires some skills on the part of the interviewer in developing rapport, so that the respondent will be willing to answer questions in a straightforward and honest manner. Interviews are notoriously unreliable if not conducted by highly trained personnel.

In questionnaires, surveys and interviews, the investigator must be concerned with *sampling procedures*, i.e. who should be asked to complete the questionnaire so that one can get a representative picture. Unless the sample is representative of the population from which it is drawn the results will not give accurate readings.

Advantages

A major advantage of both survey questionnaires and interviews is that they allow the investigator to formulate questions very specifically. Rather than devising a situation to elicit desired behaviour or finding a natural situation in which to observe that behaviour, constructors of questionnaires question people directly about the behaviour or area under investigation. They can also provide a range of answers (pretested for comprehensiveness as well as comprehensibility) to make it easy for the respondent. Survey questionnaires are easier and more economical to use than interview procedures. In addition, they provide a greater anonymity for the respondent, which is important in the case of sensitive or personal issues. Face-to-face interviews, on the other hand, allow the interviewer to gather additional information from observation. Furthermore, the interviewer can clarify questions that may be confusing to the respondent and ensure that the person intended to answer the questions is indeed the person responding.

Disadvantages

Perhaps the major difficulty with self-report data, whether from interviews or surveys, is the issue of accuracy. Some questions may lead to embellishments by the respondent, who attempts to appear in a favourable light. As suggested earlier, survey questionnaires and interviews also have opposite sets of weaknesses. The survey questionnaire gives the investigator less control over the situation and cannot ensure the conditions under which the questionnaire is being administered, who is answering it and whether the respondent fully understands the questions. The interview is more costly, more time consuming and is more susceptible to bias. Most people have experienced both questionnaires and interviews and know some of their obvious shortcomings.

Tests

Over the years psychologists have constructed a huge number of tests to measure such things as ability, skill, vocational preferences or even art appreciation. Some of the best-known tests are those measuring intelligence and those measuring personality. Test scores can be used as either an independent or a dependent variable. As an independent variable one can see whether test scores predict different types of behaviour, i.e. do IQ scores predict school results – or one may be interested in how training courses affect test results. Tests are widely used and equally widely criticised.

Advantages

The advantages of testing include the fact that tests provide numeric information, which means that individuals can more easily be compared on the same criteria. They can be particularly useful in an occupational setting, for example, in selection of candidates for a particular job. In interviews, different questions are asked of different candidates, and the answers often forgotten. Tests provide comparable profiles. Also, with data-based records, one can trace a person's development over time. In fact, by going back to test results kept in a person's file one can actually see if, and by how much, the tests were predictive of occupational success. Tests give explicit and specific scores on temperament and ability rather than vague, ambiguous, coded platitudes that are so often found in references. A percentage or a test score (provided of course that it is valid) makes for much clearer thinking about personal characteristics than terms such as 'satisfactory', 'sufficient' or 'high-flyer'. Good norms demonstrate a candidate's scores relative to the population so that people know how they match up.

Tests, it is argued, are fairer because they eliminate corruption and favouritism. That is, if a person does not have the ability or has a 'dangerous' profile, they will not be chosen irrespective of their other 'assets'. Moreover, tests are comprehensive in that they cover all of the basic dimensions of personality and ability from which other occupational behaviour patterns derive. A good test battery can give a complete picture of individual functioning.

Psychological tests are scientific in that they are soundly empirically based on proven theoretical foundations– that is, they are reliable, valid and able to discriminate the good from the mediocre, and the average from the bad. Tests also increase the psychological concepts and language of those who use them. This gives those who are not trained in personality theory a very useful set of concepts that they can use to identify and distinguish human characteristics in the workplace.

Data resulting from the tests can be used to settle practical arguments. That is, objective numbers provide the sort of clear evidence to justify decisions. Finally, tests give testers and testees alike interesting and powerful insights into their own beliefs and behaviours. They might also be used to explain to candidates why they have been rejected.

Disadvantages

An obvious and common complaint is that these tests are fakeable – that is, people like to describe themselves in a positive light and receive a 'desirable' score so that they may be accepted. Yet this faking in a way reflects their 'real' personality. Some tests have lie scores to attempt to overcome this (see Chapter 5).

Also, some respondents do not have sufficient self-insight to report on their own feelings and behaviour – that is, it is not that people lie but they cannot, rather than will not, give accurate answers about themselves. Tests are sometimes dismissed as unreliable in that all sorts of temporary factors – test anxiety, boredom, weariness, a headache, period pains – lead people to give different answers on different occasions. Although this is partly true, this factor makes only a small difference. Most importantly, tests may be invalid – they do not measure what they say they are measuring and the scores do not predict behaviour over time. For many tests, this is indeed the Achilles' heel and they are lamentably short of robust proof of their validity. It is supremely important that tests have predictive validity, i.e. that scores predict behaviour accurately. Intelligence tests are frequently but incorrectly accused of not being valid; that is, not really measuring intelligence.

It is also true that people have to be sufficiently literate or articulate to do these tests, not to mention sufficiently familiar with jargon. Many believe that their personnel could not answer them properly, they would take up too much time, or they would cause needless embarrassment. Another relevant criticism is that there are no good norms, at least for the populations they want to test. Hence it is frequently argued that many psychological tests are unfair, and biased in favour of White Anglo-Saxon Protestants (WASPs); hence white males tend to do better or get a more attractive profile, and therefore get selected more often than, say, black females. They therefore fly in the face of antidiscriminatory legislation.

Also, freedom of information legislation may mean that candidates would be able to see and hence challenge the scores themselves, their interpretation and the decision made on them. The less objective the recorded data, the better for those unprepared to give negative feedback. As (ability and personality) tests become well known, people could buy copies and practise so that they know the correct or most desirable answers. This happens extensively with General Measure Aptitude Tests (GMATs), and results could be seen to have more to do with preparation and practice than actual ability.

Unobtrusive Measures

Many of the methods of collecting data outlined above are reactive – the self-consciousness of the subjects may affect the nature of the results. People may be guilty, embarrassed, clumsy or simply nervous when being questioned or watched, hence psychologists have tried what are called unobtrusive measures. One of the most famous is the lost letter technique where psychologists 'lose' a letter, perhaps addressed to a local or a foreign person, and count whether prejudice is manifest by the finders 'helpfully' posting it or ripping it up. Some psychologists have even advocated 'garbology'. That is, going through people's rubbish to find out what they have thrown away such as empty alcohol bottles and so on. Responses to advertisements of different kinds have also been examined.

Critics point out that these measures are rarely very reliable. They also note some of the ethical problems in fooling people. There are also no control factors so one cannot be certain what chance events are affecting the behaviour examined.

Advantages

The major advantage of using unobtrusive measures is that they are usually free of the self-conscious manipulation of obtrusive measures. Take the drinking of alcohol: most people underestimate how much they drink and very heavy drinkers may strenuously deny the extent of their drinking. But actually counting their discarded bottles gives one a very real indication of the extent of their habit.

Disadvantages

The primary disadvantage of the use of unobtrusive measures such as measuring the wear on the tyres of a disabled person's wheelchair to measure their mobility is that one cannot be absolutely sure what caused the behaviour to occur. In other words all sorts of other factors which you may not know about may have affected the thing that you are measuring.

The range of research methods used by psychologists gives one a good idea of the variety of problems they investigate and the way they do it. Experimental psychologists often use laboratory-based studies and social psychologists frequently use questionnaires. Developmental and animal psychologists frequently use detailed observation techniques. No one method is correct, though given the balance of advantages and disadvantages it does seem the case that certain psychological processes are best measured by some approaches rather than others.

Psychology, like all sciences, is changing and hence new methods are being developed or old methods rediscovered. There is for instance a renewed interest among social psychologists in qualitative methods such as group discussions, focus groups and in-depth interviews. The material that emerges (recorded and then transcribed on to paper) is subjected to various forms of analysis, such as discourse analysis which attempts to discover the theories, ideas and motives behind the speakers involved.

Some methodologies move in and out of fashion, but others

TABLE 3.4: Comparison of five methods of research

Definition	Case Study	Observational study		Experiment	
		Naturalistic observation	Survey	Correlation	Experiment
	Detailed description of a single individual	Detailed description of what people or animals do under natural conditions	Description of selected aspects of a population of individuals	Description of the relationship between two variables	Description of the relationships between an independent variable and a dependent variable
Number of individuals studied	Usually one	Usually many	Many	Many	At least a few in each group
Manipulated by investigator	Nothing	Nothing	Questions	Nothing	Independent variable
Advantages	Suitable for studying rare conditions	Unintrusive, natural, source of new information	Determines characteristics of a population	Suitable for studying variables that are impossible or impractical to control	Useful for determining cause-and-effect relationships
Example	Intensive report of the childhood of someone who became a murderer	Report on changes in society's television watching habits	Survey of how many hours per week most people watch TV programmes	Correlation between hours of watching TV programmes and some measure of violent behaviour	Two groups randomly assigned; one group watches violent TV; the other watches non-violent TV; compare probability of violent behaviour by members of the two groups

From *Introduction to Psychology*, by J. Kalat. Copyright © 1993, 1990, 1986 Wadsworth Publishing Company. By permission of Brooks/Cole Publishing company, a division of International Thomson Publishing Inc., Pacific Grove, CA 93950.

remain quite constant in terms of their use and popularity. It remains true that often the nature of the problem dictates the research method used, although the beliefs of the experimenter are also pretty important in determining which of the different methods is chosen.

Kalat (1993) has provided a nice comparison of five of the above methods, although described in slightly different terminology (see Table 3.4).

Another excellent example is the table provided by Cook (1988) who was interested in comparing the results of different 'tests' in selection (see Table 3.5).

TABLE 3.5: Summary assessment of 10 selection tests by five criteria

| Test | Criteria | | | | |
	Validity	Cost	Practicality	Generality	Legality
Interview	Low	Medium /high	High	High	Untested
References	Moderate	Very low	High	High	A few doubts
Peer ratings	High	Very low	Very limited	Military only	Untested
Biodata	High	Medium	High	High	Some doubts
Ability	High	Low	High	High	Major doubts
Personality	Low	Low	Fair	?White-collar only	Untested
Assessment centre	High	Very high	Fair	Fairly high	No problems
Work sample	High	High	High	Blue-collar only	No problems
Job knowledge	High	Low	High	Blue-collar only	Some doubts
Education	Low	Low	High	High	Major doubts

Source: Cook (1988). *Personnel Selection and Productivity*. Chichester: Wiley.

Not everyone would agree with Cook's criteria. Supervisor/peer assessments, assessment centres, biodata and general mental ability are usually regarded as the best of the remaining methods. References, interviews, personality, and assessment and interest inventories provide low but positive methods. As noted above, however, other facets of selection methods are important. It is worth noting, nevertheless, that for several methods (e.g. references) only very limited information is available. The idea of selection is very simple: select in the good candidates and select out the bad ones. Also, poor or weak candidates are sometimes chosen which selectors learn about to their cost, while sometimes good candidates are rejected yet selectors never know about this group.

Predictably, recent evidence from meta-analytic studies, on the validity of interviews, suggests that different types of interview may have different validities. Self-assessments and handwriting do not provide much support for their use as a predictor of work performance (see Chapter 1).

What should dictate the choice of method for the researcher is the nature of the problem. What all researchers look for is the most sensitive, cost-effective and valid measure of psychological process. It is quite clear that they certainly have enough to choose from.

Chapter 4:
That Man Called
Freud

Without doubt the most famous psychiatrist ever to have lived was Freud. Along with Marx and Darwin it was the ideas of this German-speaking psychiatrist which did most to shape how people in the twentieth century see themselves. He remains, to this day, the most quoted of all psychologists or psychiatrists.

Ask the lay person to name just one psychologist they have ever heard of and they offer Freud. His work is still considered by many some of the best ever done and his books are still extensively read. However, despite all his fame he remains widely misunderstood and misquoted. So much so that a book entitled *What Freud Really Said* has been written (Stafford-Clark, 1970).

Yet many of the concepts and methods of Freud have influenced lay people who have never read his work or even have a slight understanding of what he was trying to say or achieve.

Before we continue, test your knowledge of Freud. Kalat (1993) designed the following short quiz:

Match the Freudian defence mechanisms or ways of protecting oneself in the top list with the situations in the list that follows.

1. Repression	5. Regression
2. Denial	6. Projection
3. Rationalisation	7. Reaction formation
4. Displacement	8. Sublimation

a. _____ A man who is angry with his neighbour goes hunting and kills a deer.

b. _____ Someone with a smoking habit insists that there is no convincing evidence that smoking impairs health.
c. _____ A woman with doubts about her religious faith tries to convert others to her religion.
d. _____ A man who beats his wife writes a book arguing that people have an instinctive need for aggressive behaviour.
e. _____ A woman forgets a doctor's appointment for a test for cancer.
f. _____ Someone who has difficulty dealing with certain people resorts to pouting, crying, and throwing tantrums.
g. _____ A boss takes credit for a good idea suggested by an employee because, 'It's better for me to take the credit so that our department will look good and all the employees will benefit'.
h. _____ Someone with an unacceptable impulse to shout obscenities becomes a writer of novels.

Answers
a. 4, displacement
b. 2, denial
c. 7, reaction formation
d. 6, projection
e. 1, repression
f. 5, regression
g. 3, rationalisation
h. 8, sublimation

If you scored less than 4 out of 8 try this shorter quiz devised by Wade and Tavis (1990). This time you are required to supply the Freudian concept.

Which Freudian concepts do these examples suggest?

1. A 4-year old girl wants to snuggle on Daddy's lap but refuses to kiss her mother.
2. A celibate priest writes poetry about sexual passion and love.
3. A man who is angry at his boss shouts at his kids for making noise.
4. A woman who was molested by her brother for many years assures her friends that she adores him and thinks he is simply perfect.
5. A racist justifies segregation by saying that black men are only interested in sex with white women.

6.   A 9-year-old boy who moves to a new city starts having
       tantrums.

Answers
1. Oedipus complex
2. sublimation
3. displacement
4. reaction formation
5. projection
6. regression

Sigmund Freud (1856–1939), the founder of the theory and therapy
called psychoanalysis, cast a long shadow over this century. Today
there are basically three attitudes toward Freud and psychoanalysis,
the theory he formulated:

PRO: Freud was one of the geniuses of history. With minor exceptions, his basic theory is correct, universal and brilliant. His
description of the causes of human behaviour was a major and
unique breakthrough. This view agrees with Freud's own
appraisal of the importance of psychoanalysis: that it was as
profound a revolution in human thought as Galileo, Darwin
and Einstein created in their respective fields.

EQUIVOCAL: Freud was a great thinker of his time. Although many
of his ideas have lasting value, some are dated, limited to
Freud's time and place, and others are simply wrong. This is
probably the most common current view among psychiatrists
and many clinical psychologists, who still use many of Freud's
terms, ideas and therapeutic methods. Like the proverbial
curate's egg, the theory is good in part.

ANTI: Freud was a fraud: psychoanalysis a dinosaur in the history of
ideas, doomed to extinction, and the most stupendous intellectual confidence trick of the twentieth century. Anti-Freudians
criticise Freud and his modern followers for their lack of scientific rigour, for regarding psychoanalysts as 'the chosen' group
that accepts no dissenters or disbelievers, and for promoting a
costly method of therapy that is not demonstrably better than
any other, indeed may imprison rather than liberate. For some
alchemy is to chemistry as psychoanalysis is to psychiatry.

So what did he believe? Medawar (1969), a Nobel Prize-winning
geneticist, noted that psychoanalytic theory claims that any objec-

tions to the truth of psychoanalysis are not to be treated seriously because they are defences against the painful truths which, for the unanalysed, are too painful even to contemplate. Such objections to Freud's ideas are called resistance to the theory. Medawar argues that this point robs psychoanalysis of all claims to be scientific because, by this device, it shuts itself off from scrutiny and, as we have seen, scientific theories must be, by definition, refutable or in other words testable. Medawar thus dismisses the theory. Others have strongly agreed with him.

Psychology as a science began as an effort to study human consciousness, but Freud compared conscious awareness to the tip of a mental iceberg. Beneath the visible tip, he argued, lay the *unconscious* part of the mind, containing unrevealed wishes, guilty secrets, unspeakable yearnings, and conflicts between desire and duty. These forces, he argued, have far more power over human behaviour than consciousness does, so the true study of human psychology must probe beneath the surface.

To probe the unconscious, Freud developed the *psychoanalytic method*. The unconscious reveals itself, said Freud, in dreams, 'free association' – talking about anything that pops into your head, without worrying about what anyone will think of you – and slips of the tongue. Because so many thoughts and memories are hidden in the unconscious and because patients resist uncovering them, Freud maintained, psychoanalytic therapy can be long and difficult. Some patients may be in therapy for 20 years or more, so much so that it may well look like a form of addiction.

Most people know that Freud and his followers were interested in dreams. Kline (1984) has defined precisely what the Freudians believe about dreams.

1.   All dreams represent a wish. This wish is usually concerned, as often in Freudian theory, with repressed conflicts which cannot find expression in waking life. The wish is therefore an unfulfilled wish. According to this view, dreaming is important for mental health.

2.   Dreams are the guardian of sleep. Dreams are the product of id activity. Without them these wishes from the id would become conscious and flood the ego with anxiety and we would wake. This, indeed, is the basis of nightmares. Awakening from a nightmare occurs when the wish is about to break into consciousness. The nightmare is the result of the attempt to convert the anxiety-laden wish into acceptabdream material.

3. Dreams are shaped by the censor. This id activity is moni-
    tored and charged by the censor (equivalent to the superego, a
    concept which was a relatively late development in psychoan-
    alytic theory) which ensures, by disguising the wish, that it can
    evade the ego. Where this fails, as has been seen, the subject
    awakes.
4. These changes and disguises are known as dreamwork. They
    are primary processes, id activity. Hence a study of dream-
    work is a study of unconscious, primary mental processes.
    This indeed accounts for the importance attached to dreams.
    Normally primary processes, being unconscious, are not
    accessible. Dreamwork is an exception. Analysis of dreams,
    therefore, was described as the royal road to the unconscious.

    This dreamwork is, however, although accessible, not obvious. It
has to be deduced or inferred from the dreams themselves. This
was achieved by obtaining free associations to dreams. Dreams
change and distort reality. The changes and disguises take various
forms. Two common ones are symbolism and condensation. Trivi-
alization and changing into the opposite are also typical dreamwork mechanisms.
    These changes mean essentially that what is dreamed, the mani-
fest content, is relatively harmless. The unfulfilled wish is held in
the latent content. Dream analysis by free association aims to pene-
trate the dreamwork and reveal the latent wish. (pp. 30–31)

Freud was interested in the dynamics, structure and development of
personality.

The Dynamics of Personality

Freud's theory, and the approach of many of his followers, is called
psychodynamic because it is based on the movement of psychological
energy within the person, in the form of attachments, conflicts and
motivations. Freud used nineteenth-century physics ideas of the
'conservation of energy': within any system, he thought, energy can
be shifted or transformed, but the total amount of energy remains the
same. Psychological energy – the energy it takes to carry out psychological processes, such as thinking or dreaming – was, to Freud,
another form of physical energy. The imagery relates to nineteenth-
century inventions such as the steam engine which, by converting
water into steam through heat, was able to power great machines.

Freud believed that energy, if blocked from direct expression, must be displaced on to a substitute. When *displacement* serves a higher cultural socially useful purpose, as in the creation of art or inventions, it is called *sublimation*. Freud himself thought that, for the sake of civilisation and survival, sexual and aggressive energies could and should be displaced or sublimated into socially appropriate and constructive forms. Thus religious orders teach children because they cannot have children; or barren couples may keep pets as substitutes for their parenting energy.

The displacement of energy from one object to another is a key feature of Freud's psychodynamics of personality. Personality differences in habits, attitudes and behaviour patterns stem from the way people displace energy from their early instinctual preferences. Freud called children polymorphous perverts because their perversions and obsessions could take any form.

The Structure of Personality

To Freud, the human personality is made up of three major systems: the *id*, the *ego* and the *superego*.

(1) First the *id* is the reservoir of all psychological energies and inherited instincts. For Freud, the id was the 'true psychic reality' because it represents the inner world of subjective experience. It is unconcerned with objective reality and is unaffected by the environment. The id operates according to the *pleasure principle*, seeking to reduce tension, avoid pain and obtain pleasure. The id is the most primitive part of one's personality.

The id contains two basic, competing instincts: the *life* or sexual instincts (fuelled by psychic energy called the *libido*) and the *death* or aggressive instincts. As instinctive energy builds up in the id, the result is an uncomfortable state of tension. The id may discharge this tension in the form of reflex actions, displacement, physical symptoms or 'wishful thinking' – uncensored mental images and unforbidden thoughts. The energy escapes but manifests itself in odd ways. It is the job of the psychoanalysts to recognise and discover the outward manifestation of the id.

(2) Second, the *ego* is a referee between the needs of the instinct and the demands of society. It obeys the *reality principle*, putting a rein on the id's desire for pleasure until a suitable outlet can be found. The ego thus represents 'reason and good sense'. Freud described the relationship between ego and id this way: 'In relation to the id, [the ego] is like a man on horseback who has to hold in check the

superior strength of the horse; .... Often a rider, if he is not to be parted from his horse, is obliged to guide it where it wants to go; so in the same way the ego constantly carries into action the wishes of the id as if they were its own.'

If a person feels anxious or threatened when those 'wishes of the id' conflict with social reality, the ego has certain weapons at its command to relieve the tension. These weapons, called *defence mechanisms*, have two characteristics: they deny or distort reality, and they usually operate unconsciously. According to Freud, they are often unhealthy patterns that cause emotional problems and self-defeating behaviour. Although there is no single agreed list of all the processes that Freud considered to be defences, we will use the main ones described by Freud's daughter Anna Freud, who became an eminent psychoanalyst herself, and by modern personality researchers.

1.   In *repression*, a threatening idea, memory or emotion is blocked from becoming conscious. It refers to the mind's effort to keep a lid on unacceptable feelings and thoughts in the unconscious, so that you are not even aware of them. Of course repression is only partly successful and can cause havoc with memory.

2.   In *projection*, one's own unacceptable feelings are attributed to someone else. A person who has uncomfortable sexual feelings about members of a different ethnic group may project this discomfort on to them, saying, 'those people are dirty-minded and oversexed'. Some cultures institutionalise the whole process of projection.

3.   In *reaction formation*, the feeling that produces unconscious anxiety is transformed into its opposite in consciousness. Usually, a reaction formation gives itself away by being excessive: the person asserts the feeling too much and is too extravagant and compulsive about demonstrating it.

4.   *Regression*. Freud believed that personality develops in a series of stages, from birth to maturity; each new step, however, produces a certain amount of frustration and anxiety. If these become too great, normal development may be briefly or permanently halted and the child may remain fixated at the current stage; for instance, he or she may not outgrow clinging dependence. People may 'regress' to an earlier stage if they suffer a traumatic experience in a later one. Adults occasionally reveal 'partial fixations' that they never outgrew, such as biting nails, sucking the thumb, and often regress to immature behav-

iour when they are stressed. The temper-tantrums of some adults may be very similar to how they behaved as children.

5.   In *denial*, people simply refuse to admit that something unpleasant is happening or that they are experiencing a taboo emotion. It can often be seen initially in people who are told that they are dying.

6.   *Intellectualisation* and *rationalisation* are higher-level defences that depend on complex cognitive processes. Intellectualisation is the unconscious control of emotions and impulses by excessive dependence on 'rational' interpretations of situations. In rationalisation, the person finds excuses to justify actions that were caused by repressed and unacceptable feelings. Some people find that a university education trains them to be highly sophisticated at rationalisation.

7.   In *displacement*, people release their 'pent-up' emotions (usually anger) on things, animals or other people that are not the real object of their feelings. People use displacement when they perceive the real target as being too threatening to confront directly.

These defence mechanisms, Freud maintained, protect the ego and allow the person to cope with reality. Different personalities emerge because people differ in the defences they use, in how rigid their defences are, and in whether their defences lead to healthy or disturbed functioning.

(3) Third, the *superego*, the last system of personality to develop, represents the voice of morality, the rules of parents and society, the power of authority. The superego consists of the *ego ideal*, those moral and social standards you come to believe are right, and the *conscience*, the inner voice that says you did something wrong. The superego sits in judgement on the activities of the id, handing out miserable feelings (guilt, shame) when you break the rules. Naturally some people have better-developed superegos than others.

According to Freud, the healthy personality must keep all three systems in balance. A person who is too controlled by the id is governed by impulse and selfish desire, while someone who is too controlled by the superego is rigid, moralistic and authoritarian. A person who has a weak ego is unable to balance personal needs and wishes with social duties and realistic limitations.

A wit once described the story of psychoanalysis as the story of a sex-crazed monkey (the id) attacking a naïve spinster (the ego) while being supervised by a nervous bank manager (the superego).

The Development of Personality

Freud thought that personality develops over five stages. Freud called these stages 'psychosexual' because he believed that psychological development depends on the changing expression of sexual energy in different parts of the body as the child matures.

1. The *oral stage* marks the first year of life as babies take in everything through their mouths. The mouth is the focus of sensation and stimulation at this stage. People who remain fixated at the oral stage, he maintained, may, as adults, seek constant 'oral gratification' in such activities as smoking, drinking, overeating, debating, nail biting etc. They may choose dentistry, the law, opera singing, wine-tasting or lecturing, all of which are oral occupations.

2. The *anal stage*, at about age two to three, marks the start of ego development, as the child becomes aware of the self and of the demands of reality. The major issue at this stage is control of bodily wastes, a lesson in self-control that the child learns during toilet training. People who remain fixed at this stage, he thought, may become 'anal retentive', holding everything in, obsessive about neatness and cleanliness. Or they can become just the opposite, 'anal expulsive', that is, messy and disorganised. It is said that those jobs concerned with monitoring, checking, controlling or quality assuring are anal. Because, supposedly, attitudes to money are acquired in this phase, money-related jobs such as accountancy are anal.

3. The *phallic (or Oedipal) stage* lasts roughly from age three to five. Here sexual sensations are located in the penis, for boys, and in the clitoris, for girls. The child wishes to possess the parent of the opposite sex and get rid of the parent of the same sex. Children of this age supposedly announce proudly that 'I'm going to marry Daddy [or Mummy] when I grow up' and reject the same sex 'rival'. Freud labelled this phenomenon the *Oedipus complex*, after the Greek legend of King Oedipus, who unwittingly killed his father and married his mother. Later, some psychoanalysts used the term 'Electra complex' (from another Greek legend) to describe the female version of this conflict, but Freud himself and almost all contemporary psychoanalysts speak of the 'Oedipus complex' for both sexes.

Boys and girls, Freud believed, go through the Oedipal stage differently. Boys at this stage are discovering the pleasure and pride of having a penis. When they see a female for the first time, they are horrified. Their unconscious exclaims (in one way or another), 'Her penis has dropped off! How could this happen? The girl must have been castrated. Who could have done such a thing to her? My powerful father.' This realisation, said Freud, causes little boys to accept the authority of the father, who must have the power to castrate them too. They repress their desire for the mother and decide to be as much like the father as possible. *Identification* is the process by which they take in, much as being their own, the father's standards of conscience and morality. The superego has thus emerged.

Freud admitted that he didn't know what to make of females, who, lacking the penis, couldn't go through the same steps. He speculated that a girl, upon discovering male anatomy, would panic that she had only a puny clitoris instead of a stately penis. She would conclude, said Freud, that she had already been castrated. As a result, girls don't have the powerful motivating fear that boys do to give up their Oedipal feelings. They have only a lingering sense of 'penis envy'.

The healthy female supposedly resolves penis envy by having children. The neurotic female resolves penis envy by behaving like men, perhaps by having a career or becoming too 'masculine'. Women do not develop the strong moral superegos that men do. They feel inferior to men, dislike other women and develop the unfortunate personality traits of passivity, vanity, jealousy and 'masochism' (taking pleasure in being treated badly). Needless to say, feminists take issue with Freud.

By about age five, when the Oedipus complex is resolved, the child's basic personality patterns are formed. Unconscious conflicts with parents, unresolved fixations and guilts, and attitudes toward the same and the opposite sex will continue to replay themselves throughout life.

4. The *latency stage* lasts from the end of the phallic stage to puberty. The child settles down, goes to school, makes friends, develops self-confidence and learns the social rules for appropriate male or female behaviour. Sexual feeling subsides and skills are developed. This is a period of learning social mores and is not typified by psychological trauma of any sort.

5. The *genital stage* begins at puberty and marks the beginning of what Freud considered mature adult sexuality. Sexual energy is now located in the genitals, and, eventually, directed toward sexual intercourse. Not everyone, however, reaches this mature stage.

The defence mechanisms of the ego and the displacement of instinctual energy may prevent people from reaching mature genital sexuality, and keep them fixated on 'immature' forms of sexual behaviour.

Early in Freud's career, many of his women patients (and some men) told him they had been sexually molested in childhood, typically by their fathers, uncles or male friends of the family. At first, Freud concluded that these early experiences of sexual abuse were responsible for his patients' later unhappiness and illness. But he later changed his mind. He decided that his patients must be reporting fantasies, not real events, and that children (all children, not just his patients) fantasise about having sexual relations with their opposite-sex parent. These fantasies are so taboo that children feel guilty about having them. It is their unconscious guilt about wanting sex with the parent, not the actual experience of sexual abuse, that causes illness and emotional problems later on. This issue remains very topical today with various reports of patients who, through hypnosis, remember early childhood abuse.

Over the years psychologists have attempted to evaluate Freudian ideas and practices. The following are among the most common attacks:

1. *Untestable hypotheses.* Many of the ideas in psychoanalysis, old or new, original or revised, are impossible to test one way or the other. They are descriptive observations, more poetic than scientific. Because so much of psychoanalytic theory depends on the subjective interpretation of the analyst, there is no way to decide which analyst is right. Freud saw penis envy; Horney saw womb envy. Freud saw castration fears; others analysts did not. Although the hypotheses may be interesting and part-true, they remain unable to be tested.

2. *Incorrect or time-limited ideas.* Many of Freud's ideas that were put to the test have proved faulty. His notion that our instincts fill an internal 'reservoir', for instance, has been disproved by modern research in physiology. The body does not 'store' anger or other emotions. People can certainly collect grievances and keep a mental list of grudges, but this is not the same as saying they have a fixed amount of aggressive energy. Other Freudian ideas have been shown to be specific to his society rather than universal, timeless principles. Freud's belief that sexual conflicts are behind most personality problems, for example, was probably truer in Victorian times than today. Anthropologists have accused him of being a product of his

time and his theories only relevant to middle-aged, neurotic Viennese of his day.

3.   *The 'patients-represent-everyone' fallacy*. Freud and his followers generalised inappropriately from patients in therapy to all human beings. To be accurate, the observer would have to study a random sample of women, children or homosexuals who are not in therapy. In fact the theory was based on a very small number of far-from-normal patients.

4.   *The 'looking-backward' or 'faulty memory' fallacy*. Looking backward over lives means arranging events sequentially. We assume that if A came before B, then A caused B. Psychoanalysts often make this error, and looking backward also depends on a person's memories, which are highly subject to distortion.

5.   *An overemphasis on unconscious processes rather than real experiences*. Freud's emphasis on the unconscious had a powerful effect, then and now, not just for theoretical reasons but also for practical ones. It was a great step forward to discover that people are not always aware of their actual desires or of the motives behind their behaviour. However, some psychologists today believe that the emphasis on the unconscious went too far, overshadowing the importance of real events and conscious thoughts. Since Freud, the problems of conscious thought and behaviour have proved equally intriguing.

Klein (1984) spelled out nine objections which he argued have been effective in persuading most academic psychologists that Freudian theory is unscientific and not worthy of serious study.

1.   The sample which formed the basis of Freud's data was composed in the main of Viennese neurotic, hysterical, Jewish ladies, a *fin de siècle* phenomenon of a dying European tradition. From so limited a sample it is impossible to extrapolate theories about all human beings.

2.   In the psychoanalytic writings of Freud and most of his followers, almost no data are reported. What is presented is an interpretation of unknown data, sometimes mixed with accounts of what a patient said. There is, therefore, no way of checking the interpretations, for consistency for instance.

3.   Freud saw 4 to 5 patients a day, each for an hour. It was his custom, after dinner, to write up these cases. He did not take notes during the session for fear of spoiling the rapport with his patients. It is, therefore, pertinent to question the accuracy

of Freud's recollection of his data. Freud's own conception of repression would suggest that Freud would not remember data that failed to fit his hypotheses.

4.   Freud eschewed quantification. Lack of quantification enforces a vagueness to the theorizing which is, *per se*, not good.

5.   The same lack of quantification means that there is no (and cannot be any) statistical analysis. This, in turn, means that it is impossible to estimate to what extent any observations are likely to have arisen by chance. Without such statistical analyses, even clearly reported data are impossible to interpret.

6.   Furthermore, and this is a serious objection, the theory is not refutable and refutability lies at the heart of scientific theorizing (Popper, 1959). For example, what contrary evidence could be adduced to the late Freudian claim that two drives energize human behaviour, Eros (the life instinct) and Thanatos (the death instinct)?

7.   Freudian theory fails to predict. It is able to explain, *post hoc*, but this is a function of its vagueness rather than its explanatory power.

8.   Finally, psychoanalytic therapy (the *raison d'être*, after all, for the theory) did not work. Indeed exposure to psychoanalysis probably prevented recovery, which in 70 per cent of cases occurred spontaneously.

9.   The conclusion drawn from this battery of objections is that psychoanalysis is an unscientific nonsense, best relegated to the history of ideas, along with phlogiston, the flat earth and the Ptolemaic theory of a geocentric universe. (p. 17)

In a spirit of fairmindedness he does attempt to answer some of these points. Thus he believes:

1.   The objection of sampling, though true, is almost equally applicable to all branches of psychology, except perhaps the psychometry of human abilities.

2.   The claim that failure of the analytic therapy implies failure of the theory contains a logical fallacy. As it cannot be demonstrated that a particular theory is applied either well or badly, then neither success of therapy nor its failure can be attributed to the underlying theory.

3.   It is possible to conceptualise Freudian theory not only as one huge theory but also as a *collection of hypotheses*. Not all these

hypotheses will turn out to be correct. However, the failure of one hypothesis does not imply the failure of all. In other words, it is in order to argue that psychoanalytic theory consists of a collection of hypotheses, some false, others true. It therefore makes no sense to reject psychoanalysis as a whole, as do psychologists in general, or to accept it, as do psychoanalysts. What is really required is to sift through these hypotheses one by one in the light of empirical evidence which is the essence of the scientific method. Thus, at a stroke, psychoanalysis in this conception is transformed from unscientific to scientific.

4. As regards the efficiency of psychoanalytic therapy it is wrong to say that psychoanalysis is an effective therapy. It is equally wrong to say that it is ineffective. There is no definitive evidence either way.

Chapter 5:
Psychology at Work

5.1 Management and Common Sense

Working adults spend about one-third of their day at work (eight hours out of 24). Work is central to our lives and therefore of considerable interest to psychologists.

Organisational and occupational psychologists are crucially interested in work-related behaviour. They have themselves been working most of this century to establish, among other things, what factors predict job productivity, worker satisfaction and the relationship between the two. The sort of questions they ask are many and varied. Baron (1986) gives a typical list:

(1)   Are there actually conditions under which leaders are unnecessary?

(2)   Do female managers differ from male managers in important ways? Or is the existence of such differences basically a myth?

(3)   How do individuals learn about the 'right' way to behave in an organization? (That is, how do they become *socialized* into it?)

(4)   What sources of bias operate in the appraisal of employees' performance?

(5)   Is information carried by the grapevine and other informal channels of communication accurate?

(6)   What are the best techniques for training employees in their jobs?

(7)   What tactics can be used to convert destructive organizational conflict into more constructive encounters?

(8)   How do individuals (or groups) acquire power and influence within an organization?

(9)   What conditions cause people to suffer from 'burnout?' What can be done to prevent such reactions?

(10)   How can resistance to change within an organization be overcome?

(11)   How do new technologies affect the structure and effectiveness of organizations?

(12)   What steps can be taken by American businesses to compete more effectively against their Japanese counterparts?

(13)   What factors lead persons to feel satisfied or dissatisfied with their jobs?

(14)   Are individuals or committees better at making complex decisions? (p. 7)

R. Baron, (1986) *Behaviour in Organizations*, 2nd edn, p.7. Reprinted by permission of Prentice Hall, Upper Saddle River, New Jersey, USA.

What do work psychologists do? Arnold, Robertson and Cooper (1991) suggested there are 12 distinct areas in which they work:

1.   *Selection and assessment*: for all types of job by a variety of methods, including tests and training.

2.   *Training*: identification of training needs; design, delivery and evaluation of training.

3.   *Performance appraisal*: identification of key aspects of job performance, design of systems for accurate performance assessment, training in appraisal techniques.

4.   *Organizational change*: analysis of systems and relationships with a view to possible change; implementation of any such change (e.g. new technology)

5.   *Ergonomics*: analysis and design of work equipment and environments to fit human physical and cognitive capabilities.

6.   *Vocational choice and counselling*: analysis of a person's abilities, interests and values, and their translation into occupational terms.

7.   *Interpersonal skills*: identification and development of skills such as leadership, assertiveness, negotiation, group working and relationships with other individuals.

8.   *Equal opportunities*: monitoring, and if necessary enhancement, of opportunities for minority groups at work.

9.   *Occupational safety and health*: examination of causes of accidents and the introduction of measures to reduce their frequency of occurrence.

10. *Work design*: allocation of tasks so that jobs are as satisfying and motivating as possible.

11. *Attitude surveys*: design, conduct and analysis of surveys (e.g. by questionnaire or interview) of employee opinions and experiences at work.
12. *Well-being and work*: investigation of factors which lead to stress in work and unemployment, and identification of ways to prevent and manage stress. (p. 32)

But given that most managers are trained neither in psychology nor indeed business administration, how is it that for the most part they seem to do a reasonably good job? Could this be an argument for the fact that 'management science' (like occupational psychology) is really no more than common sense – a quality nearly everybody has (see Chapter 1)?

The so-called 'discipline' of management science often has low status in business schools, partly because the hard men of figures (accountants, actuaries, economists) despise the soft waffle of organisational behaviour. Management science is thought to be a trivial, expensive and pointless exercise in describing or proving what we already know. All of its findings are intuitive, unsurprising and uninformative; worse, it is packed with esoteric, mid-Atlantic jargon which clouds common sense in the pretence of clarifying it.

But there are serious problems with the common sense argument. First, common sense is frequently contradictory. 'Clothes make the man' is at odds with 'you can't make a silk purse out of a sow's ear'. 'Out of sight, out of mind' and 'absence makes the heart grow fonder' also seem contradictory. Although it is possible that both are true under different circumstances, common sense does not tell you which.

Second, if all management is common sense, nothing can be counterintuitive or the result of faulty reasoning. Research in the sciences is full of such examples and it would not be surprising if some aspects of management science were the same; that is, the opposite of common sense.

It could be argued that current management knowledge is in fact absorbed from management science as it is frequently popularised in newspapers and magazines. Thus, ironically, common sense could be the result of the ideas of management science being commented upon in the popular press. A frequently discussed finding from research cannot remain non-obvious to managers, any more than a joke can remain funny to people who hear it over and over again.

If all management is common sense and most people supposedly have this curious trait, why is there so much disagreement on management issues, processes and procedures?

When managers try to specify the 'competencies' essential for
high-flyers in a company, many are tempted to include common
sense, despite the fact that it is almost impossible to define, measure
and therefore select. It may indeed be like the search for the Holy
Grail – longstanding, complicated and unsuccessful.

But why not test yourself? Are the following statements true or
false? Mark them accordingly and see how you rate on the common-
sense factor in management.

		True	*False*
1.	In most cases, leaders should stick to their decisions once they have made them, even if it appears they are wrong.	T	F
2.	When people work together in groups and know their individual contributions can't be observed, each tends to put in less effort than when they work on the same task alone.	T	F
3.	Even skilled interviewers are sometimes unable to avoid being influenced in their judgement by factors other than an applicant's qualifications.	T	F
4.	Most managers are highly democratic in the way that they supervise their people.	T	F
5.	Most people who work for the government are low risk takers.	T	F
6.	The best way to stop a malicious rumour at work is to present covering evidence against it.	T	F
7.	As morale or satisfaction among employees increases in any organisation, overall performance almost always rises.	T	F
8.	Providing employees with specific goals often interferes with their performance: they resist being told what to do.	T	F
9.	In most organisations the struggle for limited resources is a far more important cause of conflict than other factors such as interpersonal relations.	T	F
10.	In bargaining, the best strategy for maximising long-term gains is seeking to defeat one's opponent.	T	F
11.	In general, groups make more accurate and less extreme decisions than individuals.	T	F
12.	Most individuals do their best work under conditions of high stress.	T	F

13.   Smokers take more days sick leave than do
       non-smokers.   T   F
14.   If you have to reprimand a worker for a misdeed,
       it is better to do so immediately after the mistake
       occurs.   T   F
15.   Highly cohesive groups are also highly productive. T   F

Answers: 1–5 True, 6–12 False, 13–14 True, 15 False.

If you scored 5 or less, why not try early retirement? Scorers of 6 to 10 should perhaps consider an MBA. A score of 11 or above – yes indeed, you do have that most elusive of all qualities: common sense.

Einstein defined common sense as the collection of prejudices people have accrued by the age of 18, while Victor Hugo maintained that common sense was acquired in spite of, rather than because of education. It might be a desirable thing to possess in the world of management, but don't kid yourself it is very common. Perhaps a close reading of the rest of this book might help low scorers acquire a bit more 'uncommon sense'.

Another go! Why not a little quiz to determine potential management ability? Try the simple true–false quiz to determine your aptitude. Many people believe simple management aphorisms. A considerable number of British managers believe that, for nearly all workers, money is the most important motivating factor at work. They also believe, contrary to the evidence, that happy workers are productive workers, and that great leaders are born with the 'right type' of personality.

Education may not be the panacea for all management evils. It may not be at all helpful to people who lack some basic level of ability. It should, however, discourage people from holding simple, simplistic, naïve and even wrong views about how to get the best out of employees.

Do you have the ability to manage?

		True	*False*
1.	Relatively few top executives are highly competitive, aggressive and show 'time urgency'.	T	F
2.	In general, women managers show higher self-confidence than men and expect greater success in their careers.	T	F
3.	Slow readers remember more of what they learn than fast readers.	T	F
4.	To change people's behaviour towards new		

technology, we must first change their attitudes.   T   F

5.   The more highly motivated you are, the better
      you will be at solving a complex problem.   T   F

6.   The best way to ensure that high-quality work will
      persist after training is to reward behaviour every
      time, rather than intermittently, when it occurs
      during training.   T   F

7.   An English-speaking person with German
      ancestors/relations finds it easier to learn German
      than an English-speaking person with French
      ancestors.   T   F

8.   People who graduate in the upper third of the
      A-levels table tend to make more money in their
      careers than average students.   T   F

9.   After you learn something, you forget more of it
      in the next few hours than in the next several days. T   F

10.   People who do poorly in academic work are
      usually superior in mechanical ability.   T   F

11.   Most high-achieving managers tend to be high
      risk takers.   T   F

12.   When people are frustrated at work they
      frequently become aggressive.   T   F

13.   Successful top managers have a greater need for
      money than for power.   T   F

14.   Women are more intuitive than men.   T   F

15.   Effective leaders are more concerned about
      people than the task.   T   F

16.   Bureaucracies are inefficient and represent a
      bad way of running organisations.   T   F

17.   Unpleasant working conditions (crowding, loud
      noise, high or very low temperature) produce
      dramatic reduction in performance on many tasks. T   F

18.   Talking to workers usually enhances
      cooperation between them.   T   F

19.   Women are more conforming and open to
      influence than men.   T   F

20.   Because workers resent being told what to do,
      giving employees specific goals interferes
      with their performance.   T   F

Answers: 1 = True; 2–7 = False; 8–9 = True; 10–11 = False;
12 = True; 13–20 = False

How did you do?
Score 0–5 Oh dear, pretty naïve about behavioural science.
Score 6–10 Too long at the school of hard knocks, we fear.
Score 11–15 Yes, experience has helped.
Score 16–20 Clearly a veteran of the management school of life.

5.2   The Hawthorne Effect

Occasionally the results of one study may be seminal in the sense that they have a crucial effect on thought in psychology at work. There is one particular study that is most frequently mentioned: the Hawthorne studies.

This nine-year study was begun in 1924 by the Western Electric Company in association with the American National Academy of Sciences. The research was intended to identify lighting levels that would produce optimal productivity. In the first illumination experiment, however, the productivity of the worker increased when illumination was increased but also when it was decreased. Overall, productivity bounced up and down without an apparent direct relationship to illumination level. The results were perplexing.

A second illumination study had an experimental group which experienced illumination changes and a control group for which illumination was held constant. In this experiment, production increased in both groups to an almost equal extent. In yet a third illumination experiment, lighting levels were decreased over time. As a result, productivity levels increased for both experimental and control groups (at least until an extremely low level of illumination was reached). Naturally these results puzzled the experimenters of the time.

To correct some of the control problems in the lighting study, the Relay Assembly Test Room studies were conducted during 13 periods between 1927 and 1932. The experiments progressed from simply recording output under normal conditions to introducing a group incentive programme, rest periods of varying duration, reducing work weeks and providing free lunch. Throughout this time output, morale and attendance rates were shown to increase. It was first thought that relief from monotony, alterations in supervisory styles and the group incentive programme accounted for the increases in measured productivity of staff. Previously, all subjects had worked under conditions such that the overall performance of the group had little effect on individuals. During the experiments, this was changed and individual earnings became closely related to group performance through the group incentive plan. More studies were undertaken to determine exactly how this plan influenced individual performance. What so many results showed was that whatever the researchers did – turn lights up, then down; introduce breaks then take them away – the productivity of those working increased.

Increasingly, the researchers were becoming aware of human attitudes and related behavioural factors. To find out more about these phenomena, between 1928 and 1930, an extensive interviewing programme was conducted among more than 21 000 employees. The interviews made it possible to investigate attitudes about the job, supervisors and working conditions. Finally, in 1931–32, the researchers conducted the Bank Wiring Observation Room studies. In this stage, the importance of the *group and informal relations* were recognised as determinants of individual attitudes toward change. While the experiments had initially started by looking for physical determinants of productivity, they ended up believing psychological factors were more important.

Although the marginal implications of the studies are far-reaching, the value of the Hawthorne studies for researchers and managers lies in its discoveries concerning individuals, individuals in groups and organisational design. Four conclusions were obvious.

1.   *Individual Differences.* The Hawthorne studies emphasised that individuals are different and that these differences can have significant impact on managerial behaviour. The interview programme demonstrated the complexity of attitudes, and how overt behaviour may differ from attitudes. Thus a new wage incentive or vacation policy may be perfectly acceptable to one person and totally rejected by another. Individual differences are systematic, open to investigation and taxonomisable into discrete types or continuous traits.

2.   *Groups.* After the findings of the Hawthorne researchers were publicised, the importance of group processes was realised. During various stages of the experiments it became evident that informal groups not prescribed by organisations can, and do, exert great influence on individuals. Group pressures can cause individuals to work more or less, to accept or resist change, and to behave in a variety of ways that may differ from their own personal preferences. Further, groups outside the organisation can directly reflect behaviour within the organistion.

3.   *Individuals in Groups.* Formal groups are those required and established by the organisation such as production and sales units. Employees also belong to informal or social groups that are not prescribed by the structure. An established group who have worked together for a long time may form a social group who eat or go bowling together. The same is true of 'newcomers' or recent employees. Such groups may be quite important in the formation of individual attitudes and in influencing work behaviour.

4.   *Organisational Design.* The implication of the studies for the formal design of organisations has to do with perceiving the organisation as a social system. Although the structure of an organisation appears very fixed and formal, in reality there is an 'organisation' that does not show up on the chart. This social organisation includes all the social groupings and power alliances that exist in all structures, which include all the friendship groups and political alliances that criss-cross the organisation.

The idea of formal and informal groups, as well as organisations, is an interesting and important one, and may be seen as a result of the Human Relations School. Today people talk about *the Hawthorne Effect* which is like an organisational placebo pill. It refers to the fact that certain changes that occur may be the result not of physical changes (the introduction of IT; a redecoration of the office; new staffing arrangements) but rather the way in which people were treated.

The Hawthorne researchers have been criticised on a number of grounds with regard to the conduct of their studies and their analysis of the results. Their basic assumptions about the cooperative or social nature of man and his ability to be satisfied by changes in his environment have been challenged. They assumed that 'contented' workers were productive workers in much the same way we assume contented cows give more milk.

Perhaps the most serious criticisms made of the Hawthorne studies related to the research methodology employed. Most human relations theory and practice is based on relatively few observations of some small samples of human beings at work. Hawthorne researchers may have minimalised the effects of economic incentives for no apparent justifiable reason and elevated supervision and interpersonal relations to a point of primary importance. Some have argued, in effect, that the Hawthorne studies were scientifically worthless. Others have attempted to counter this criticism by claiming that the Hawthorne studies did make a significant contribution by placing monetary incentives in their proper place within the social context. The defenders of the studies maintain that the researchers did not deny the importance of economic incentives but simply rejected them as an independent factor influencing worker performance.

The most frequently rehearsed criticisms of the Hawthorne studies are that:

1. *They lack scientific validity and tends toward mysticism.* Human relations writers generally spent little time gathering the data necessary to support their claims. When they did, they were rarely obtained in a systematic manner. For this reason they project an aura of mysticism or 'armchair philosophising' which is unacceptable to the modern behavioural scientist.

2. *They overemphasise the group and focuses on group decision making.* In human relations writings the object of concern almost always appears to be the relationship of the individual in a group, with less concern for the behaviour processes of the individual.

3. *They view conflict as fundamentally destructive.* Little concern was given to the positive effects of conflict, such as the stimulation of innovation. Coordination was always the goal.

4. *They are evangelistic.* Advocates were insistent upon the value of human relations concepts in solving organisational problems. It has been shown that human relations, like structural thought, is a creed of the 'establishment' and supports the pre-eminence of management in an organisation.

5. *There was no effect.* Some have agreed that a detailed study of the results in fact provides little evidence of any demonstrable effect at all!

Much of the objection to the human relations perspective has been initiated by modern behavioural scientists who are interested in many of the same phenomena. Behavioural scientists are concerned with the systematic analysis of human behaviour and take pride in the objectivity with which they approach their subject and their adherence to the conventional methods of experimental science. They also view their research as interdisciplinary in character and realise that it is often difficult, if not impossible, to understand the sociology of a group separate from the psychology of the individuals comprising it and the anthropology of the culture within which it exists. However, there have been few subsequent studies, of whatever scientific quality, that have had such an influence on work psychology, as the results of the Hawthorne studies.

5.3   Seven Applications of Occupational Psychology

To illustrate the problems, concepts and issues in occupational or organisational psychology we shall choose six topics.

(1) Why Meetings are (often) a Waste of Time

A meeting is a group of people who keep minutes and waste hours. Yet surveys show that the average middle-to-senior manager may spend as much as 40% of the working day in meetings. The number of committees, subcommittees, task-force groups and board meetings which business people are required to attend grows exponentially with rank.

Meetings are well known to be inefficient for both the dissemination of information and the communication of information. As a result they are indispensable when one does not actually want to do anything but still give the appearance of working. Meetings can stifle ideas, help to postpone and prevaricate over difficult decisions. A committee meeting is often a cul-de-sac down which ideas are lured to their death. No grand idea has ever emerged from a committee meeting which has been described as a group of the unwilling, picked from the unfit, to do the unnecessary!

Given the widespread and justifiable scepticism and cynicism about the usefulness of meetings, why are they so popular? They may be seen as a good way to *pool resources*. Similarly it has been argued that group members may stimulate and encourage each other through their mutual discussions, in what is known as the *synergy effect*. Others talk about them being an efficient and democratic way to *communicate* with people. Still others believe that committees make better decisions and come up with qualitatively and quantitatively better solutions to problems.

These reasons are far from watertight, however, and there is research evidence which leads one to doubt them. Most meetings are held not to make decisions but to avoid them. Further, they are mainly about *diffusion of responsibility*, so that if a wrong, poor, costly or even litigious decision is made, fault is spread among all the committee members. Committee meetings are about covering your back ... not having to take personal responsibility for important decisions.

There are three major problems with meetings that render them inefficient. The first is sometimes called *social loafing*, which refers to the fact that people tend to work less hard (loaf) when in (social) groups than when alone.

This effect was first noted more than 50 years ago by a German scientist named Ringleman, who compared the amount of force exerted by different sized groups of people pulling on a rope. Specifically, he found that one person pulling on a rope alone exerted an average of 63 kilograms of force. However, in groups of three, the force per person dropped to 53 kilograms, and in groups of eight it was reduced to only 31 kilograms per person – less than half the effort exerted by people working alone. In short, the greater the number of people working together on the task, the less effort each one put forth.

The social loafing phenomenon has been studied extensively by American psychologist Bob Latane and his associates. In one of their early experiments, groups of students were asked to perform a very simple task – to clap and cheer as loudly as they could. The participants were told that the experimenter was interested in seeing how much noise people could make in social settings. Comparisons were made between the amount of noise produced by one person relative to groups of two and six people. Although more people made more noise, the amount of noise made per person dropped dramatically as the group size increased. Pairs of people made 82% as much noise as individuals on their own and groups of six produced only 74% as much noise.

Thus, the greater the number of persons in the group, the less the impact of each. Because they are working together, each group member feels that the others will take up any slack resulting from reduced effort on their own part. And because all members tend to respond in this fashion, average output per person drops sharply.

The second problem is called by psychologists *evaluation apprehension*. Basically it suggests that when trying to make decisions in groups, the presence of some group members may intimidate others. Furthermore, disagreement and the voicing of unpopular, if correct, ideas may breed conflict and ill will and may be a 'career-limiting' move.

It should come as no surprise that high-status persons in organisations, such as presidents, chief executives and board chairpersons, are carefully listened to, and what they have to say is given high credence. As a result, high-status persons tend to dominate group situations, and their ideas (right *and* wrong) are frequently accepted without question. The result can easily be a group of 'yes men/women' behind the single dominant force. With an understanding of this phenomenon, former General Motors head Alfred P. Sloan failed to attend the early phase of his group's meetings. He feared that his presence would discourage open and honest discussions of critical problems among other executives, who would insist on pleasing him. Sloan can be complimented on his insight into group dynamics. Indeed, there is every reason to believe that his high status would have had an undue impact on the group by inadvertently encouraging uniformity.

The third problem is quite simply that in creativity-type tasks, groups, rather than individuals working alone, produce qualitatively and quantitatively poorer decisions. In contrast with well-structured tasks that can be divided into several discrete parts and have a definite solution, many everyday management decisions are more poorly structured. Any problem involving creative thinking provides a good example. Suppose an organisation is faced with deciding what to do about the prospect of a declining market for its products in the coming years. There are many possible courses of action, and you would probably expect that a group meeting together would do a better job of handling such a problem than any one individual. However, this is generally not the case. Most of the research has shown that on poorly structured, problem-solving, creative tasks, individuals show superior performance to groups. This generalisation has particularly important – and potentially devastating – implications for organisations, as some administrators spend as much as 80% of their time in committee meetings.

As for business meetings, then, the fewer the better. The weekly staff or board meeting may be useful for sharing information although not useful for problem solving. But it is best to follow some simple rules:

1.   Start on the dot no matter who is missing.
2.   Why not have meetings standing up? The Privy Council chaired by the Queen wisely adopts this rule.
3.   Go around the room to ensure full participation.

(2) Why and Why Not to Use Brainstorming as a Creative Technique

Can creativity be taught? How do we come up with a really innovative idea? What is the best method for generating ideas? For many,

the answer to these problems is brainstorming. The dictionary definition of a brainstorm is curiously 'temporary mental upset marked by
uncontrolled emotion and violent action'. But does it work as a
creative test?

Brainstorming is used most frequently to generate as many solutions to a particular problem as possible and thus quantity is
favoured over quality. The product of a brainstorming session is
ideally a wide range of possible conclusions (options, solutions)
which can be presented to a third party qualified to pick the best one.
The basic assumption is that 'two heads are better than one' and that
together, in groups, innovative solutions can be found. But does
brainstorming work? It can, but only under very special circumstances, and indeed it may have in it the seeds of its own destruction.

The techniques or rules of brainstorming are quite simple. The
first is *free-wheeling*. Participants are encouraged to be different, to
break the mould, to be over-inclusive and allow any crazy idea or
association into the solution. Self-censorship is discouraged and
nothing is unacceptable.

The second rule is *no criticism*. In order to encourage the near-
psychotic activity of wild ideas association, the participants should
not be put off by the disapproval of others. Neither the *sotto voce* hiss
nor the raised eyebrow is tolerated because these are off-putting to
idea producers. At this stage all ideas, however way-out (indeed
because they are unusual) are equally valuable.

The third rule is that *piggy-backing is OK*. This means that it is quite
acceptable to jump on the back of others; to run with their ideas and
to follow someone down an unusual path. Indeed this is precisely
why this activity is group orientated. Groups supposedly give one
synergy and energy, and provide stimulation. But do they? In all
circumstances? The evidence suggests that group-working might not
be the best stimulus to creativity in all conditions. An important
determinant of whether decisions are better made by groups or by
individuals rests in one of the characteristics of the problem: how
well-structured or poorly structured is the issue about which a decision is to be made?

Imagine working on a problem that requires several very specific
steps and has a definite right or wrong answer, such as an arithmetic
problem or an anagram puzzle. How can one expect to perform on
such a *well-structured task* when working alone compared with when
working with a group of people? Research findings indicate that
groups performing well-structured tasks tend to make better, more
accurate decisions, but take more time to reach them than individu-

als. In one study, subjects worked either individually or in groups of five on several well-structured problems. Comparisons between groups and individuals were made with respect to accuracy (the number of problems solved correctly) and speed (the time it took to solve the problems). It was found that the average accuracy of groups of five persons working together was greater than the average accuracy of five individuals working alone. However, it was also found that groups were substantially slower (as much as 40%) than individuals in reaching solutions.

It is interesting to consider the reasons *why* these and other similar results arise. The potential advantage that groups might enjoy is being able to pool their resources and combine their knowledge to generate a wide variety of approaches to problems. For these benefits to be realised, however, it is essential that the group members have the necessary knowledge and skills to contribute to the group's task. In short, for there to be a beneficial effect of pooling of resources, there has to be something to pool. Two heads may be better than one only when neither is a blockhead: the 'pooling of ignorance' does not help at all.

But most of the problems faced by organisations are *not* well structured. They do not have any obvious steps or parts, and there is no obviously right or wrong answer. Such problems are referred to as *poorly structured*. Creative thinking is required to make decisions on poorly structured tasks. For example, a company deciding how to use a newly developed chemical in its consumer products is facing a poorly structured task. Other poorly structured tasks include coming up with a new product name, image or logo; or finding new or original uses for familiar objects such as a coat-hanger, paper clip or brick. Although one might expect that the complexity of such creative problems would give groups a natural advantage, this is not the case. In fact, research has shown that on poorly structured, creative tasks, individuals perform better than groups. Specifically, in one study people were given 35 minutes to consider the consequences of everybody suddenly going blind. Comparisons were made of the number of ideas/issues/outcomes generated by groups of four or seven people and a like number of individuals working on the same problem alone. Individuals were far more productive than groups and arrived at their answers much faster.

The relative ineffectiveness of brainstorming groups has also been demonstrated in a recent study where practising managers and management graduate students worked on a fictitious moon survival problem. Participants were asked to imagine that they have crash-landed on the moon 200 miles from their base. They then ranked, in order of importance to their survival, the 15 pieces of equipment they had intact. It was found that the quality of decisions made by interacting groups was no better than that of the best individual group member. In another study using this same problem, the investigators found that it is essential for the contributions of the most qualified group members to be counted most heavily in the group's decisions in order for the group to derive the benefits of that member's presence. Thus in some groups the people who gave the best, most correct answers were ignored by the group members whose greater insistence but poorer ideas carried the day.

Thus what the research seems to indicate is highly counter-intuitive to many. Most brainstorming is used by creative organisations which care little about the skill composition of the problem-solving groups whose members are then confronted with poorly structured tasks such as thinking of the name for a new product.

How does brainstorming translate into other languages? For a non-native speaker it may be associated linguistically with an epileptic fit or a splitting headache. Certainly, for some people the experience of taking part in this activity to solve a creative, open-ended task leads to a migraine. The paradox of brainstorming is that this technique is most frequently used when research suggests it is least effective.

(3) Why Not to Reward Good Work Performance

Some jobs and some tasks are intrinsically satisfying. That is, by their very nature they are interesting and pleasant to do. They can be enjoyable for a wide variety of reasons and much depends on the preference, predilections and propensities of individuals choosing to do them.

Intrinsic satisfaction implies that merely doing the job is, in itself, its own reward. Therefore, for such activities no reward and no management should be required. But the naïve manager might unwillingly extinguish this ideal state of affairs.

Take the case of the academic writer scribbling at home on a research report. The local children had for three days played extremely noisily in a small park near his study and, like all noise of this sort, it was highly stressful because it was simultaneously loud, uncontrollable and unpredictable. What should be done? (a) Ask (politely) that they quieten down or go away. (b) Call the police or the parents if you know them. (c) Threaten them with force if they do not comply. (d) All of the above in that order.

The wise don used none of the above. Unworldly maybe, but as someone whose job depended on intrinsic motivation, the academic applied another principle. He went to the children on the fourth morning and said, somewhat insincerely, that he had very much enjoyed them being there, the sound of their laughter and the thrill of their games. In fact, he was so delighted with them that he was prepared to pay them to continue. He promised to pay them each £1.00 a day if they carried on as before. The youngsters were naturally surprised but delighted. For two days the don, seeming grateful, dispensed the cash. But on the third day he explained that because of a 'cash flow' problem he could only give them 50p each. The next day he claimed to be 'cash light' and only handed out 10p. True to prediction the children would have none of this, complained and refused to continue. They all left in a huff promising never to return to play in the park. Totally successful in his endeavour the don retired to his study luxuriating in the silence.

This parable illustrates a problem for the manager. If a person is happy doing a task, for whatever reason, but is also 'managed' through explicit rewards (usually money), the individual will tend to focus on these rewards, which then inevitably have to be escalated to maintain satisfaction.

There is considerable research on the types of job which give their holders the most satisfaction. Contrary to popular predictions, it is not merchant bankers or high-flying company executives who report most satisfaction. Many in fact yearn for early but 'comfortable' retirement. Nor is it social workers, nurses or others in the care business. It turns out that craftsmen and women report most job satisfaction. The 'crafts' vary: mathematicians are very job satisfied, as are furniture makers. Goldsmiths, stone-wall builders, and other employed craftspeople report highest intrinsic satisfaction. Even thatchers appear to enjoy their work.

Craftspeople have intrinsic job satisfaction partly because of the pace, timing and control they have over their work but also because of their identification with the final product. However, once a fine furniture builder becomes a successful businessman, he may lose his thrill in design and carving. That is why the best craftspeople have agents who deal with money matters. This is not only because the craftspeople themselves are frequently inexperienced at running a business, but also many do not like doing so despite the obvious monetary rewards.

Intrinsic motivation in part explains why some people continue at poorly paid employment. They do not need motivating in the usual way – through an astute mixture of carrot and stick – because they are intrinsically motivated. But, like all of us, they still respond to praise for the product or service that they supply.

For those limited few who enjoy doing what they do, working (like virtue) is its own reward.

(4) Who Should Appraise Employee Performance?

Managing performance at work involves, by definition, evaluation and giving feedback on that performance. In competitive leisure activities, as in the world of work, judgements of worth, excellence or ability have to be made. Whether the activity is growing and showing roses, disciplining and exhibiting dogs, or blending and tasting wines, judgements of quality and quantity are required. The question is, who is best suited to make the most astute but impartial judgement?

Few jobs or competitive hobbies have a clear, first-past-the-post way of assessing success. The Darwinian rules of survival of the fittest may work, but only over the long term. And because people need feedback on their performance, they have to be evaluated along a range of dimensions.

From a very early age we are given tests of our ability, knowledge and skill which are rated by parents, teachers and peers. School exams, driving tests, and assessment centres all involve the rating of performance.

Performance can be rated in many ways. Sometimes it can be done by machines which can measure strength, fitness etc. Machines can also accurately score multiple-choice answers on a test by laser reading of the pencil marks. But, as we all know, the more subtle, important and higher-level skills, abilities and products cannot be rated by multiple-choice objective tests. No chemistry analysis can discriminate a great wine; no simple selection test can infallibly choose the best CEO.

But given that someone has to make a judgement, the question remains: who should that be? An expert, one's superiors, one's colleagues, one's friends (reference writers)? Traditionally it is a superior – usually the person to whom you report, possibly the boss. But it could equally be a peer. Even more radically it could be a subordinate or, for greater reliability, a whole group of them. Why not be evaluated by your customers – and don't say you don't have any! What about your shareholders? The idea of customers or shareholders judging senior managers sends a shudder up the spines of most people but it could be argued that these groups are making judgements of our performance all the time, even if not explicitly.

Different groups of raters have quite different perspectives and therefore sources of bias. In the jargon of experimental science one needs multi-trait (more than one trait), multi-rater (more than one rater) appraisal. That means evaluation of various traits (or behaviours, or skills) by various people to be most reliably accurate. Consider the advantages to the average middle manager of being rated by his/her boss, peers, subordinates, customers, shareholders (if appropriate) and possibly a self-rating on various work-related behaviours.

For most, self-evaluation is out because it leads to self-aggrandisement and delusional high scores. Some people give themselves unfair and unrealistic positive halos, whereas the depressed and morbidly self-critical do the very opposite and give themselves extremely low scores. Both are inaccurate and poor discriminators.

Most employees are rated by their bosses. He/she supposedly knows their virtues and faults, strengths and weaknesses, abilities and foibles. That may well be true if one has a sensitive, perceptive boss with not too large a span of control. For many people, the quality and quantity of interaction with their boss are so low that there is really no possibility of sensitive and accurate judgements being made.

What about your peers? Some studies have found they are among the most accurate and predictive of judges. Research on officers' training corps and other high-powered assessment centres found, when asked, that the participants were better predictors of success than the judges themselves. Why? Simply because the peers had more opportunity to observe all the antics of their colleagues during both the 'up-front', more public times and also the 'back-stage' activities.

Some organisations are risking using upward feedback for appraisal and development – that is, feedback from subordinates. This may be inaccurate either because subordinates have an axe to grind (leading to very negative evaluations) or are sycophantic (leading to positive evaluation). None the less it is subordinates who experience and therefore know the consequences of a manager's behaviour. And if all subordinates give similar ratings, this is surely a testament to reliability.

Service jobs have external customers and it is not uncommon that they are asked to rate performance. Hotels, banks, airlines and restaurants are used to doing this. How seriously those ratings are taken varies in practice but the principle is a good one.

Much is now made of 360° feedback or ratings from top, bottom and both sides. In theory this must be a good idea as long as the raters are trained and the rating dimensions are relevant to the job. All examiners need to be trained and their criteria need to be salient to the skill or performance evaluated. Given these conditions (often not fully considered), multiple raters help to remove the bias and subjectivity in the whole process.

(5) What Can You Know from an Applicant's CV?

Years ago, CVs were dry, rather formal documents a bit like immigration papers. Without much attention to either presentation style or self-aggrandisement, people simply reported rather mundanely and factually the biographical details of their lives.

This rather quaint, unselfconscious approach has been taken over by the spin doctors, the publicity gurus and the public relations 'experts'. Politicians have learned the meaning and virtue of the sound-bite; the impression of the Italian suit versus the donkey jacket; and the benefit of wearing the (rose) logo so that the hard-of-thinking electorate know whose side they are on. The American influence of 'talking up' nearly all personal achievements means that selectors have to be pretty subtle when reading between the lines. Likewise, ordinary people are now offered the benefits of CV consultants to improve the way they come across. No life is too ordinary, no work history too boring, no pastime too menial to be considered unworthy of the image treatment.

CV consultants are perfect strangers whose job it is to take the details of your rich, varied and complicated life and precis it into a carefully thought out document, laid out on a single page. There are those who believe that this is really money for old rope and that they can quite happily, confidently and money-savingly do it themselves. After all, the individual knows the life history facts and the intended purpose of the CV best of all.

Psychologists call the task of CV consultants 'impression management'. It means quite simply 'attempt to change, alter and shape the impression that others receive'. Through variations in dress, vocabulary and possessions, we all try to create a favourable impression of ourselves to selected others. Given that we put in so much effort at the job interview, it makes sense to spend as much, if not more, time and money on the CV – which in itself may determine whether we ever get to the interview at all.

As a consequence of the professional treatment, the most dreary and ordinary individual with a frankly mediocre, even failed work history can look like a success. No one, it seems, can fail to benefit from the skill of their impression management professional. Read a peer's CV and the way he or she may describe a modest achievement or mundane duty, and one can see the benefits of being 'economical with the truth'.

While this may be good for the job hunter, CVmanship certainly presents a problem for the selection and recruitment specialist. If all students are Einsteinian geniuses, all workers productive Stakanovites, all entrepreneurs neo-Bransons, how can one distinguish between them?

There are three important clues in the modern CV. First what is *left out*. Beware the CV which ignores or fudges chronicity: people may prefer to ignore long periods on the dole, a failed early career, an unwelcome start at one level. All sorts of important information may be omitted in the interests of the applicant. Selectors should perhaps have a checklist of information they really need and obtain it from the applicant if the CV does not provide it.

Second, there are the grand *generalisations*. 'My department had a $2 million budget' does not mean I was in charge of it; 'Coordinated and facilitated staffing issues' could mean anything.

Third, there is the *verifiability* of the information. The more difficult it appears to check, the more likely it is a fudge. Beware the colonial experience where applicants held impressive-sounding jobs, even if they were genuine, in some far-flung outpost where their skin colour and ability to speak English ensured them senior positions. The name and address of organisations on the CV certainly helps a great deal.

The paradox of CVmanship is that there may well be an inverse relationship between the CV and the person behind it. Over-egging the pudding (bound glossy brochures with career histories spanning several pages) screams the cumulative attempts of desperate outplacement consultants. The greater the flourish; the more the prizes; the quicker the promotion – often the more ordinary the individual.

(6) Why Management Training often does not Work

Most big organisations attempt to provide some sort of training for their managers, either in-house or bought-in. Always done with good intention, it can be both extremely expensive and conspicuously ineffective. Very frequently, the people who plan or pay for the training are disappointed because the results are not what they expected or hoped for. Is this because their expectations are inappropriate, their training methods are flawed or their managers are untrainable?

The first problem lies in determining the goals of management training. These may be general or specific; implicit or explicit; realistic or unrealistic; achievable or impossible; measurable or simply determined by gut feel; their results trackable or not. Most management training is about the acquisition of some skill – technical or interpersonal – although it could also be about insight and increasing sensitivity. As such, management training is frequently, but certainly not always, modestly successful. The question, however, remains why the skill is not retained between the classroom and the office.

Apart from skill acquisition, management training can offer other serendipitous benefits. Courses allow people from different parts of the organisation to network, to compare and contrast and to establish lateral links. It may be an expensive way of bringing people together but it can be very effective, particularly if trainees are required to operate on the course in competitive teams or undergo outward-bound-type dangers.

Courses can also help to change the culture of an organisation, either deliberately or not. Taught similar skills, or even concepts/terms, employees develop into a more homogeneous body who, despite the fact that they have different functions and expertise, speak a common language.

Some management training courses may also be perceived as a perk for attendees, not because it is time away from the daily grind but rather because they acquire some highly useful, valuable and transportable skills. In this sense, management training facilitates career development and may be seen by employees as a positive plus.

But most organisations have a training department, or hire in training consultants, in order to make their staff more efficient and effective. A laudable aim but frequently unfulfilled. Why? The following are some of the reasons why many management training courses fail to deliver enough bang for the (frequently large) bucks.

•   The goals of the course are unattainable. Some skills are easier to teach than others; many are not acquired easily; most take lots of practice. What can one realistically expect from a three- five- or even 14-day course? Consider how long it takes and how much practice to master a language or indeed to become fully computer literate. 'Short-sharp-shock' courses may get one started, but need extensive post-course back-up, if skills are to be retained.

- The teaching/instructing method is inappropriate. Not all skills can or should be taught in the same way. There should be a balance between instruction/lecturing, practice, feedback etc. Further, not all individuals like to be taught in the same way. The preferred pace of instructions is also always important. Some like big picture first, then details; others vice versa. Most attenders like to be entertained by a jovial story-telling consultant who can amuse. But do they learn anything?

- The skills are not practised. However steep the learning curve on the course, unless the newly acquired skills are continually practised they decline dramatically afterwards.

- The skills are not necessary and are inappropriate. Although the insight, language and skills acquired on a course may be interesting, they are not strictly relevant to the performance of the job.

- The corporate culture discourages the use of skills. Although the organisation, particularly the human resources department, may be eager for employees to use a particular skill or way of behaving, the strong corporate norms inhibit or even punish it. The skills learned, then, are never used and it is the course which takes the blame.

- The skills were never really acquired on the course. True skill acquisition takes effort and can be hard work. Some trainers prefer a rather old-fashioned chalk-and-talk routine where they are in control. Things can look easy from the participants' point of view and they may bluff themselves that they have acquired the skills, but in actuality they have not.

- The skills are not easily transferable. The atmosphere and context within which one acquires a skill may be very different from those in which it is supposed to be practised. This makes skill transfer less probable and certainly less easy, and may account for course 'failure'.

- The training tasks/situations are unlike the 'real-world' situation. The more similar the practice and the real situation the better the transfer of skills and vice versa. Are plush country hotels or well-equipped training centres similar to the office environment or not?

Using high-trust, low-threat 'learning environments' many middle-management courses focus on personal renewal and the development of skills. These courses play an important (even life-changing) role in their participants' personal and professional lives. Then a typical scenario emerges. After the course the participants return to their organisation. Because no one else from the organisation was on the course the ex-participant gets little reward for their experience. Any notions about change and new ideas are knocked out of their minds by the daily tasks and problems. As a result many course participants report that they are more frustrated by their inability to affect the organisation than they were before they attended the course!

Training courses work in the sense that learning occurs and is retained under specific conditions. People must want to learn and attend the course: one volunteer is worth 10 conscripts. People need reinforcement and rewards for skill acquisition, not to be ignored, despised or punished. Practice of skills is imperative and needs to be distributed over time.

Personnel magazines are full of residential training course advertisements. They promise the earth and a fully changed individual – motivated, insightful, skilled, enthusiastic. Often the person who returns after a training course is exhausted, over-fed and a bit bewildered. Training courses can change people's lives but not always in ways anticipated by those well-meaning employers who sponsor them.

(7) Catching People Lying in Questionnaires

Psychologists have many words for lying: dissimulation, social desirability responding and faking good. They talk of *impression management*, which means lying to make yourself look good and of *aggrandising self-disclosure*, which means telling others untruths about oneself.

People lie for all sorts of reasons: to protect their reputation; to hide highly undesirable facts; simply to portray themselves in a better light. There are lies of omission and commission; of tactical embellishment and of erratic forgetfulness.

But for the manager as disciplinarian, as recruiter and as appraiser they are a problem. How to spot a liar; how to false-foot the dissimulator; how to tumble the bullshitter?

It may be helpful to look at how psychologists attempt to catch people lying in questionnaires. Most lay people believe that the best way to catch the liar is to ask many similar (almost identical) questions and if the person responds erratically (or contradictorily) they are lying. Questionnaires often have numerous similar questions, but this is to boost their internal reliability – it has nothing to do with catching liars. But the more people believe this the better. Psychologists do it differently.

Classically there are four methods used to catch questionnaire liars, each of which may be applied face to face by the wily manager.

The first is the most simple but it is quietly effective. Tell people not to lie. Let them know you expect lies, are used to them and hence are quite good at detecting them when they occur. Although this does not prevent exaggeration, subterfuge or selective memory, it usually serves to reduce many lies and inhibit the majority.

The second method is to have a lie scale. Consider the following questions: 'Do you *always* wash your hands before a meal?'; 'Have you *ever* been late for an appointment?'; 'Have you *ever* taken the credit for something someone else did?' If you answer YES, NO, NO, then, sir or madam, you are a liar. What psychologists have done is devise a series of these questions. Ask a few and see how people do. If they lie on these there is a fair chance they will lie on the others as well!

The third method is great fun in the research phase because it encourages people to lie. Prepare a set of questions and give it to three groups of people: a third are asked to 'fake good' (lie by putting themselves in a positive light); a third are asked to 'fake bad' (lie by putting themselves in a negative light) and the remainder are asked to tell the truth. What one is after is a profile of a liar. This method yields a template of the responses of the fake-good liar (and the fake-bad liar is also occasionally useful), so that one can match up the responses of the employee with those 'known' responses of liars.

The fourth method is the old forced-choice method. People will usually not admit to negative behaviour: absenteeism-related hypochondriasis; pilfering or encouraging stock shrinkage; politicking and back-stabbing. The final way of catching the ingratiator, the liar, the cleaner-than-clean employee is to give him/her a choice. But the method does rely on a careful and judicious assessment of the equivalence of misdeeds. Consider an example: my father said a cad was a man who peed in the bath and slept in his vest. If those two indiscretions are equal, then ask people which they are more likely to do/have done. It is easy to come up with these, thus 'Have you/are you more likely to (a) make a private call on company time/ expenses, (b) take home company stationery?'. This method forces candidates to admit the undesirable side of their behaviour.

We all know about corporate lies – we service what we sell; leave

your CV and we will keep it on file; it's not the money, it's the principle; but personal lying is more difficult to detect. Many contracts
aren't worth the paper they are written on. One advantage of telling
the truth is that you don't need a good memory for what you said
happened. And the liar's punishment is not that he/she isn't
believed, but that *ipso facto* he/she cannot believe anyone else.

Conclusion

Organisational and occupational psychologists study people at work.
They advise on recruitment, selection, ergonomic design, team
development and practically every other issue concerned with
productivity and satisfaction in the workplace. They also study how
non-work behaviours such as leisure, retirement and unemployment
affect individuals. Constant change in the workplace, thanks to
economic events (inflation, stagnation) and the development of
computers, has meant constant evolution in the way people behave.
Occupational and applied psychologists, rather than being done out
of a job, seem more employable than ever.

Chapter 6: Current Controversies in Psychology

6.1 Introduction

There are always controversies in science, and psychology is no exception. Scientists hold their views with passion, although sometimes with more emotion than reason! Some controversies are relatively ephemeral; others never seem to go away. Most controversial issues in psychology are like great subterranean rivers that flow deep and strong underground, emerging only occasionally in a stream, a pool or even a backwater. Controversies likewise bubble up to the surface, sometimes quite unpredictably.

For some thinkers controversy – and its attendant conflict – is inherently unhealthy and to be avoided. For others it is natural, even desirable, as opposition makes one clarify one's position and re-examine one's data.

In this chapter we shall consider various issues which still excite and stimulate controversy among psychologists and lay people. Many of the most controversial issues are those with sociopolitical applications. If the implications of a theory or finding are straightforward but unpopular among some, it is no surprise or accident that the issue raises interest and conflict. Thus it is often the application of theories which causes the conflict, not the theory itself.

6.2 Psychotherapy: What is it and Does it Work?

For many people the prototype psychologist is the psychotherapist: a person who spends his/her time attempting to help those with a variety of difficulties. The goal of contemporary therapy is to change a person's maladaptive behaviours, feelings or thoughts. The many different therapies focus on quite different aspects of a person. Freudian (psychodynamic) therapy emphasises early experiences and clients' conscious and unconscious thoughts about those experiences. Client-centred therapy aims to reconcile people to their authentic or real selves. Cognitive therapies focus more directly on the person's current problematic thought patterns, that is the way they think about and explain the origin of their problems. Behaviour therapies attempt to modify behaviour directly by rewarding appropriate and punishing inappropriate behaviours, while biomedical therapies stress the role of physiological mechanisms in their diagnosis and treatment.

But do these various treatments work for all or any psychological problems? Is it possible that some therapies are good for some problems (i.e. spider phobia) but not for others (depression)? Or does the efficacy of the therapy depend on the particular personality, rather than problem, of the patient? Or is efficacy dependent more on the ability and personality of the therapist than on the patient?

Early treatments for psychological disorders were often based on the assumption that afflicted persons harboured evil spirits. The mentally ill were bad, sad and mad. These treatments frequently were painful, harmful or even fatal. Religious groups in some countries still believe in the devil (or other metaphysical beings) as the main cause of mental illness.

The first mental hospitals were often inhumane places primarily designed to isolate the mentally ill from the community. Many still exist and are throwbacks to another era. A few enlightened doctors argued that 'lunatics' actually suffered from illnesses and should be treated as patients – but this idea did not become widespread until the nineteenth century. And for some sufferers, in some countries, this prospect remains yet a hope.

Modern treatments can be traced to nineteenth-century European applications of hypnosis to the treatment of mental problems. But today we have noticeably different approaches to psychotherapy. Many contemporary therapists identify themselves as being *eclectic* in their approach: they use a variety of methods, either to address different aspects of a person's problem or to treat a wide variety of problems, some of which respond best to a particular approach. Some believe that eclecticism is the enemy of good science because valid and invalid treatments are used together. Yet most therapists are, indeed have to be, pragmatic and use any treatment they are competent to give and which has demonstrated its efficacy at curing or relieving specific problems.

It is worth considering the major schools or approaches to psychotherapy.

Psychodynamic Therapies

Psychoanalysts try to uncover the unconscious reasons behind self-defeating behaviours which render people unhappy. To bring the unconscious to consciousness, they rely on free association, dream analysis and transference.

The goal of traditional Freudian psychoanalysis is to help patients gain insight into the repressed childhood wishes and conflicts which have caused their symptoms. To reveal repressed thoughts, feelings and wishes, the analyst uses such techniques as free association and dream analysis. The patient is encouraged to obey the fundamental rule of psychoanalysis: to say whatever comes to mind, no matter how shocking or seemingly trivial. His or her transference to the analyst and resistance to certain interpretations or topics also provide information about unconscious contents (see below).

Contemporary psychodynamic therapies differ from Freud's in several ways: they require fewer sessions; they are less concerned with the unconscious, with childhood experience and with sexual development; and the therapist takes a more active role in therapy and may relate to the client in a warmer fashion. The following are technical terms used by psychoanalysts.

catharsis	release of pent-up emotions associated with unconscious thoughts and memories
free association	procedure in which a client lies on a couch, starts thinking about a particular symptom, or problem, and then reports everything that comes to mind
manifest content	the content that appears on the surface of a dream
latent content	the hidden content of a dream that is represented only symbolically
transference	extension of a client's feelings toward a parent or other important figure on to the therapist
interpretation	a therapist's explanation of the underlying meaning of what a client says
resistance	according to psychoanalysts, continued repression that interferes with therapy

Client-centred Therapies

Humanistic or client-centred therapists assume that if people accept themselves as they are, they can solve most of their own problems. Person-centred therapists listen with *unconditional positive regard* (no judgement) but seldom offer interpretations or advice.

Client-centred therapy as developed by Carl Rogers assumes that people have an innate ability to heal themselves. The therapy process is designed to free clients from a state of conflict between their personal standards and actual feelings and behaviours. Therapists try to maintain an attitude of genuineness, empathy and unconditional positive regard, and they try to interact with clients in a reflective and non-directive manner. Clearly this therapy works better with some clients and problems than others.

Cognitive Therapies

The rationale behind cognitive therapy is that people's emotions and behaviour are determined by their thoughts about their experiences. The goals of this therapy are to give people insight into their problematic thought patterns and to help them eliminate their problems by changing their thinking. These therapies are particularly popular among educated, western patients, many of whom have been taught to be cerebral.

Rational-emotive therapy, as developed by Albert Ellis, is based on the idea that psychological problems develop because of people's irrational beliefs. The therapist works to change those beliefs by confronting the client about them when they surface in conversation and by assigning homework exercises which combat those beliefs.

Another is Aaron Beck's cognitive therapy which is used for depression and for anxiety disorders. It assumes that psychological disorders are caused by a type of irrational thinking called cognitive distortions. The therapist works to make clients aware of their irrational thinking and to show them how to substitute more constructive thinking and behaviour. Again, in addition to work in the office, homework exercises are common so that patients can practise in the real world.

Behaviour Therapies

Behaviour therapists set specific goals for changing a client's behaviour and use a variety of learning techniques to help a client achieve those goals.

Behaviour therapies are often based on the principles of classical conditioning, the association between two things. In *systematic desensi-*

tisation, for example, the client learns to pair a relaxation response with an anxiety-provoking situation. In *implosive therapy*, the client is required to repeatedly and vividly imagine situations phobic for them until the anxiety response is extinguished. *Flooding* (exposing people to that they fear most – i.e.. making one who is frightened of birds spend an hour among the pigeons of Trafalgar Square) is similar, except that the client actually experiences the anxiety-producing situation rather than imagining it.

Other behaviour therapies are based on operant conditioning principles. In *aversion therapy* a behaviour to be eliminated (nail-biting) is paired with an aversive stimulus (bitter-tasting nail varnish). Shaping and reinforcement have also been used to establish desirable behaviours. *Token economies* (giving people tokens as rewards, such as badges, titles or luncheon vouchers) award tokens as secondary reinforcers in exchange for desirable behaviour (no absenteeism). *Biofeedback training* allows clients to control their physiological responses to avoid a negative stimulus. This gives people aural and visual feedback on their physiological state by letting them hear or see recordings of their emotional arousal (measured physiologically). Getting this clear specific feedback allows them to try to reduce their over-excitement.

Group Therapy

Therapy practised in small groups is less costly than individual therapy. The therapist may have a less prominent directing, controlling or facilitating role than is typical in individual therapy: he or she may serve a facilitating role, encouraging group members to identify with and help one another. The idea is that everyone in the group is both therapist and patient and that by hearing others' stories one can learn a great deal. By getting what psychologists call consensus information people experiencing difficulty get a more realistic insight into the causes and distribution of the problem.

Some unique and advantageous characteristics of group therapy are the installation of hope through the example of others, the recognition of the universality of problems, the opportunity to help others, the recapitulation of family issues through intergroup transference, the improvement of social interaction and the development of group cohesiveness.

Biomedical Therapies

A common form of biomedical therapies is the use of drugs to alter physiological functioning. The principal types of drugs used to treat psychological disorders are anti-psychotics, anti-depressants and anti-anxiety drugs.

Another type of biomedical intervention is electroconvulsive therapy, in which an electric charge is passed through the brain to induce a brief seizure. This controversial procedure is used to treat severe depression, but only when drugs and psychotherapy have been ineffective.

There are, of course, other therapies but these are highly specialised. Therapies can be compared and contrasted (see Table 6.1).

Differences between Therapist and Patients

What do patients think happens when they go to see a therapist? How realistic are they in their beliefs? Furnham, Wardley and Lillie (1992) examined the different beliefs of a general group of adults and practising therapists. They found some fascinating results.

Consider Table 6.2, which shows the results of 22 items (out of 40) which yielded significant differences. The results show very clear patterns. The extent to which adults and therapists agree with the various descriptive statements of the psychotherapy process varies widely. In other words, the impression the general public has about what happens when they go to a psychotherapist is significantly different from what therapists think they do. Most statements were considered by therapists to be 'less true' than the real situation, i.e. adults believe many more things go on in a course of psychotherapy than is actually the case.

What about the prognosis – the prospect of recovery – for mental illness? The two groups – a sample of the adult population and therapists – undertook another exercise where they rated various disorders for their likelihood of recovery (see Table 6.3).

Table 6.3 shows the results for the 22 items (out of 36) which showed significant differences. Generally, the pattern was quite consistent, with lay people believing the prognosis for various disorders to be much better than the therapists did. The exception to this, however, were (5) anxiety/panic attacks, (13) enuresis, (25) impotence, (27) neurosis, (30) phobias, and (31) sleep disorders. It is very difficult to obtain reliable and valid figures on prognosis such that one might be able to say who is right and who is wrong, but it does seem the case that lay people are overoptimistic regarding the prognosis of physically based deteriorating illnesses such as dementia.

The issue of patient/client expectations is an important one because such well-known processes as self-fulfilling prophecies and

TABLE 6.1: Comparison of four major types of psychotherapy

Type of psychotherapy	Theory of the causes of psychological disorders	Goal of treatment	Predominant therapeutic methods	Role of the therapist
Psychoanalysis	Unconscious thoughts and repressed motivations	To bring unconscious thoughts to consciousness; to achieve insight into own behaviour	Free association, dream analysis and other methods of probing the unconscious mind	To interpret associations and find happier ways of existing
Cognitive therapy	Irrational beliefs and unrealistic goals	To establish realistic goals, expectations and attributions	Dialogue with the therapist and 'thinking exercises'	To help client re-examine assumptions
Client-centred therapy	Incongruence between self-concept and ideal self	To enable the client to make personal decisions; to promote self-acceptance and confidence	Client-centred interviews	To focus the client's attention; to provide unconditional positive regard
Behaviour therapy	Learned inappropriate, maladaptive behaviours	To change behaviours	Positive reinforcement and other learning techniques	To develop and direct the behaviour modification programme

From *Introduction to Psychology*, by J. Kalat. Copyright © 1993, 1990, 1986 Wadsworth Publishing Company. By permission of Brooks/Cole Publishing Company, a division of International Thomson Publishing Inc., Pacific Grove, CA 93950.

TABLE 6.2: The beliefs of lay people vs psychotherapists*		
	GROUPS	
	Adults	*Therapists*
1. Most psychotherapists use personality questionnaires	4.40	1.85
2. Psychotherapy often involves resolving sexual conflicts	4.79	4.05
3. Most psychotherapists ask you about your dreams	4.68	3.18
4. Most patients in psychotherapy have to be taught to confront and cope with fearful objects/situations	5.38	4.55
5. Very often psychotherapists prescribe drugs	2.52	1.25
6. A major component of all psychotherapy is teaching about relaxation which helps people cope with anxieties	5.45	2.75
7. Most psychotherapists attempt to teach clients to alter their life-goals to be more realistic	4.50	4.00
8. Psychotherapists believe that the cause of nearly all psychological problems is unconscious	3.87	3.18
9. Psychotherapists teach clients various strategies to reduce conflict or frustrations	5.38	4.03
10. Women tend to make better psychotherapists than men	3.87	2.61
11. Psychotherapists encourage the expression of emotion and feelings that have long been suppressed/repressed	4.27	5.46
12. Some psychotherapists actually expose people to those things (heights, snakes) that they fear most	4.27	5.46
13. Psychotherapy, by its nature, requires surroundings of a relaxing nature	5.26	4.62
14. The establishment of rapport is of major importance during the early phase of therapy	5.73	6.14
15. The work of a psychotherapist consists mainly of listening to clients verbalising their problems	4.86	3.72
16. Most therapies last many months	4.61	4.05
17. Most clients only consult psychotherapists as a last resort	4.81	3.62
18. Most psychotherapy clients lie on a couch	2.42	1.48
19. Most therapies last many years	2.93	2.24
20. Nearly all therapists give clients 'homework exercises' for them to do between therapy sessions	4.53	3.25
21. On average, clients have between two and four 'sessions' a week	3.17	2.07
22. Clients are encouraged to practise new coping skills in the 'session'	4.17	3.94

Note: *The higher the score (1–7), the more they agree with that item; 7 = strongly agree; 1 = strongly disagree.

TABLE 6.3: The means for the two groups		
	GROUPS	
	Adults	*Therapists*
1. Alcoholism	4.48	3.22
2. Anorexia	4.35	3.52
3. Amnesia	4.01	2.95
4. Anxiety/panic attacks	4.81	5.40
5. Childhood autism	3.71	1.84
6. Compulsive behaviours	4.62	3.83
7. Delusions	4.39	2.86
8. Dementia	2.46	1.21
9. Drug dependence	4.04	2.96
10. Enuresis (bedwetting)	5.40	6.05
11. Exhibitionism	4.54	4.00
12. Compulsive gambling	4.36	3.64
13. Hyperactivity in children	4.76	4.24
14. Hypochondriasis	4.56	3.86
15. Impotence	4.93	5.46
16. Manic depressive illness	4.05	3.33
17. Neurosis	4.57	5.62
18. Paranoia	4.02	2.83
19. Phobias	4.76	6.01
20. Sleep disorders	4.74	5.47
21. Senile dementia	2.08	1.15
22. Schizophrenia	3.05	2.64

Note: 7 = good prognosis; 1 = bad prognosis.

placebo (sugar-pill) effects, expectations about the nature of treatment and the efficacy of cure can contribute in a very real way to the client's progress in therapy. Equally, unrealistic and hence unfulfilled expectations can do the precise opposite. Hence, it may be extremely important to obtain clear beliefs and expectations early on in the therapy process (through interview and questionnaire) to determine the client's beliefs about their problem: aetiology, prognosis, the type of therapy that they are expecting to receive and its perceived efficacy. Where necessary, misguided beliefs can be corrected at the beginning of the treatment if thought to be appropriate.

But does Therapy Work?

In 1952 Eysenck published a paper called 'The effects of psychotherapy: an evaluation' that sent shock waves through the therapeutic community. Eysenck compared three groups of people: (1) those who were being treated by psychotherapy; (2) those who were on a waiting list to receive therapy; and (3) those who received no therapy at all. He found that all three groups showed improvement over time, and the therapy group did no better than the others. He interpreted these results as showing that psychotherapy was of little use. Yet his study triggered many additional investigations calculated to answer the question 'Is psychotherapy effective?' or 'Does going to a clinical psychologist help cure psychological problems?'

How do researchers draw an overall conclusion from the results of many different studies which have investigated the same question? This was the problem facing Smith and her co-workers (1980) as they sifted through the results of 475 studies of psychotherapy's effectiveness. Fortunately, a statistical technique called *meta-analysis* (meaning analysis of analyses) made it possible to combine those results. Based on their calculations, these researchers concluded that therapy is generally if modestly effective. By carrying out six calculations for each individual type of therapy, they concluded, however, that there is little difference between the different types of therapy in terms of effectiveness.

Other studies have come to the same conclusion but some studies suggest that behaviour therapy and cognitive therapy may be slightly superior for certain kinds of problems. For example, behaviour therapy is well suited for treating schizophrenia and the phobias, whereas cognitive therapies do well in treating depression.

The fact that the different types of therapy are similarly effective may seem surprising, because of the large differences in both theoretical bases and methods used in the therapy sessions. However, the different therapies do have some features in common. For example, clients generally enter any type of therapy *expecting* improvement, and simply maintaining a positive attitude can have a healing effect. Also, therapists from different schools all offer support, reassurance, suggestions, attention and credibility. Because a number of studies have shown that these qualities are among the variables associated with positive outcomes in therapy, the similarity in effectiveness of the different kinds of therapy becomes less surprising.

The various forms of psychotherapy do share some important features. For example:

•   They all rely on the *'therapeutic alliance,'* – a relationship between therapist and client that is characterised by acceptance, caring, respect and attention. This relationship provides social support which helps clients deal with their problems and acquire social skills which they can apply to other relationships. Presumably the longer and deeper the acquaintance the more powerful the effect on the client.

• In nearly all forms of therapy, clients talk about their beliefs and emotions, how they act, and why they act that way. They examine aspects of themselves that they ordinarily take for granted; in so doing, they gain self-understanding. Just explaining through talk – even to a tape recorder – may therefore have beneficial results.

• The mere fact of entering therapy, whatever the method, usually improves the clients' morale. The therapist conveys the message 'You are going to get better'. Clients begin to think of themselves as people who can cope with their problems and overcome them. Just expecting improvement can lead to improvement, although not of course if expectations are unrealistically high.

• Most importantly perhaps, every form of therapy requires clients to *commit* themselves to making some sort of change in their lifestyle. Simply by coming to the therapy session, they are reaffirming their commitment to attempt to overcome their problems. They are also obliged to work on that change between sessions so that they can come to the next session and report progress. Improvement often depends as much on what clients do between sessions as on what happens in the sessions themselves. This is particularly true if members of their immediate family are also committed to therapy and the patient getting better.

Difficulty in Research

Answering the relatively simple and straightforward question about whether therapy works, or whether one therapy is more successful than another, is by no means simple. Marzillier (1981), a clinical psychologist interested in this area, set out nine reasons why it is difficult to compare the efficacy of therapy.

1. *Length of treatment time.* All groups of individuals having different therapies should have an equivalent amount of treatment time to ensure that differences between them cannot be attributed simply to the number of therapy hours. There are problems because some treatments, such as psychoanalysis, inherently

require more time than others, such as behavioural methods. And thus one cannot know whether it is the type of therapy or the time taken that is most important.

2.   *Selection of subjects/patients.* Groups of patients should be similar or 'homogeneous' in the kinds of patients they contain, especially in terms of any factors likely to affect treatment, such as the level of their initial problems. Homogeneity can theoretically be obtained by random allocation of patients to treatment groups, but this procedure is not always effective with small numbers. In short, if all the patients with a relatively good prognosis are in one group, and those with a bad prognosis in another, this fact alone could account for comparative differences and have little or nothing to do with the specific therapy.

3.   *Measures of change.* Reliable and valid measurement of social adjustment and mental health is extremely difficult. Two main types of measurement have been used: (a) self-report measures – these usually consist of questionnaires which invite the subject to say what he/she would feel or do in response to a hypothetical set of situations before, during and after treatment; (b) ratings of observed behaviour – here actual behaviour of the patient is observed and rated by a panel of judges, which is expensive and difficult. Measures should be comprehensive, yet there has been a tendency in some studies to concentrate exclusively on social behaviour and ignore other important aspects of outcome such as clinical improvement.

4.   *Generalisation and durability of change.* In addition to immediate improvements as a result of treatment, it has to be shown that changes generalise to life outside treatment, and that improvement is maintained over time. Some of the outcome or 'improvement' measures should be designed to test social functioning in situations outside the clinic, with follow-up assessments months or better years after treatment. This is probably the most difficult single problem in outcome studies because some therapies show dramatic and sudden improvements but they don't last, while others have an incubation effect (no improvement immediately but sudden later improvement). The question therefore is when to measure success.

5.   *Therapist effects.* The success of a treatment may be influenced by the personal qualities (good or bad) of the therapist or by his/her own personal beliefs in its efficacy. In comparing two

treatments, therefore, bias may occur if the same therapist gives both treatments or if different therapists give different treatments. This can be partly avoided if at least two therapists are used, each of whom gives each treatment to a proportion of the patients. However, this can be costly, and it may be difficult for therapists of different persuasions to acquire one another's therapeutic skills in a short time. Try getting a Freudian to do behaviour therapy or a behaviourist to interpret dreams!

6.   *Additional therapies.* If patients taking part in a study are receiving other forms of therapy (relaxation, vitamin, thought-stopping), in addition to the treatments being studied, this may affect the results. Thus all other forms of treatment should be withheld for the duration of the experiment. It is surprising how often fairly desperate patients are indulging in a 'cocktail' of therapies at the same time, some of which could easily cancel each other out. Withholding other treatments may not be possible for ethical reasons, particularly if a long follow-up period is incorporated, in which case these other therapies should be specified and controlled for.

7.   *'Contamination' of treatments.* The separate effects of two treatments can be obscured if patients discuss their respective treatments with each other or observe the other treatment in operation. This is most likely to occur with hospitalised patients, and ideally the two treatments should be carried out on different wards or in different parts of the hospital. Even outpatients meet, chat and can contaminate their own treatment.

8.   *Independent assessment of treatment efficacy.* Outcome measures which involve ratings of behaviour should be made by independent judges who are ignorant of or 'blind to' the treatment received. It is also preferable that they be ignorant of whether they are rating pre-treatment or post-treatment behaviour, but this is difficult to achieve unless different judges are used or unless all test behaviour can be filmed and randomly presented. This is therefore a very expensive procedure in terms of time and money.

9.   *Loss of subjects.* Even the most well-designed studies cannot protect themselves against subjects who do not stay the course. This may not be serious if losses occur for reasons unrelated to the treatment, such as death, physical illness or moving away. The effects are more serious if they occur as a result of aversive reactions to one or other treatment or because the patient no

longer wishes to continue. In other words, if those who react worst (or best) to treatment drop out, the treatment may emerge as more (or less) successful than it actually is. There is a temptation to keep the numbers in the study constant by replacing drop-outs with fresh patients, but this can introduce a similar bias.

6.3   Intelligence: What is it and Can it be Measured?

'Intelligence is what an intelligence test measures and that is all.' Many lay people are deeply sceptical about the use of intelligence tests. But are lay people correct?

What, exactly, is intelligence? In 1921, 14 experts were asked this question (Thorndike et al., 1921). Here are some of their answers:

- The ability to carry out abstract thinking.
- The ability to adjust to one's environment.
- The ability to adapt to new situations of life.
- The capacity to acquire knowledge.
- The capacity to learn or to profit from experience.
- Good responses from the point of view of psychological truth or fact.

Although the experts still cannot agree on an exact definition of intelligence, themes common to many of their definitions are that intelligence is (1) the ability to learn from experience and (2) the ability to adapt to the environment.

The experts' difficulty in finding a totally satisfactory definition of intelligence reflects the fact that intelligence is a *psychological construct* – an abstract attribute that is *inferred* rather than observed directly.

Work on lay theories of intelligence goes back over 40 years. Flugel (1947), in a paper entitled 'An inquiry as to popular views on intelligence and related topics', reported a 16-item questionnaire study of 302 persons. He summarised his findings thus:

- The layman distinguishes less clearly than the psychologist between intelligence on the one hand and knowledge or experience on the other, this affecting his views with regard to the influence of education and environment generally upon intelligence.
- He distinguishes less clearly between intelligence and achievement.

- He distinguishes less clearly between intelligence and the genetic factors that enter into character and temperament.
- He overrates the importance of knowledge in intelligence tests.
- He is largely ignorant of the existence of non-verbal tests.
- He is inclined to over-rate the value of tests for vocational purposes as compared with their value for measuring general intelligence.
- He is inadequately informed concerning the wide use of tests for purposes of pure research.
- Though inclined on the whole to the 'monarchic' view of intelligence, he is yet apt to over-rate in some respects the importance of group or specific factors and does not realise fully the implication of the tendency for most forms of ability to correlate positively with one another.
- He is unduly inclined to believe in the inheritance of acquired characteristics and at the same time ignorant or neglectful of the evidence pointing to the inheritability of intelligence as such.
- He is largely ignorant concerning the findings pointing to the cessation of the growth of intelligence after adolescence.
- He is inadequately informed concerning the relative constancy of the IQ. On the other hand the layman is, on the whole, in agreement with most psychologists in believing that:
  (1) Tests can to some extent measure intelligence apart from the effect of education.
  (2) Tests are better than examinations for measuring intelligence.
  (3) Superior intelligence is desirable or necessary for higher education.
  (4) There is no appreciable sex difference as regards intelligence (though he is often inclined to think there may be some relevant qualitative difference, while men are more liable than women to think that the male sex is the more intelligent one). (p. 152)

Twenty-five years later Shipstone and Burt (1973) replicated Flugel's 1947 study using 575 British adults. They compared results statistically on each of the 16 questions and found 12 significant differences. They argue that: over this period, lay and professional views have moved closer to question a one-factor view of intelligence; men and women are seen to be of equal intelligence; laypeople recognise more the environmental influence on test scores; there is increased doubt about the validity of intelligence tests and the high (positive) correlation between tests and occupational performance.

In the 1980s a number of studies appeared which looked at lay theories of intelligence. In a fairly large study Sternberg, Conway, Kelnan and Bernstein (1981) asked nearly 500 laypeople and about 150 psychologists specialising in intelligence to list behaviours they thought characteristic of *intelligence, academic intelligence, everyday intelligence* and *unintelligence*. They found such characteristics as *reasons logically, widely read, open minded* and *displays common sense* were quoted, but that there was a great diversity of often idiosyncratic responses. These characteristics were then rated on a seven-point scale and factor analysed. For both groups three quite clear factors emerged, and although they were similar they were not exactly the same.

Sternberg (1982) notes:

> On the whole, the informal theories of intelligence that laymen carry around in their heads – without even realising that their ideas constitute theories – conform fairly closely to the most widely accepted formal theories of intelligence that scientists have constructed. That is, what psychologists study as intelligence seems to correspond, in general, to what people untrained in psychology mean by intelligence. On the other hand, what psychologists study corresponds to only part of what people mean by intelligence in our society, which includes a lot more than IQ test measures. (p. 35)

In a second series of studies Sternberg (1985) looked at implicit or lay theories of intelligence, creativity and wisdom. When rating attributes of all three qualities, he found that both academic *and* laypeople believe intelligence and wisdom the most similar, and creativity and wisdom the least similar, of three possible pairs of attributes.

Sternberg argues that laypeople's theories overlap with, but also go beyond, skills measured by tests. That is, the intelligent person is believed to solve problems well, reason clearly, think logically, and have a good store of information, but also is able to balance information and show intelligence in worldly as well as academic contexts. Lay theories of creativity overlap with those of intelligence but tend to downplay analytic abilities, stressing rather unconventional ways of thinking and acting. Also, aesthetic taste, imagination, inquisitiveness, and intuitiveness are part of lay theories, most of which go way beyond conventional psychological tests of creativity.

Sternberg (1985) believed that, while lay theories are precursors of academic theories, they are worth studying in their own right. He listed four reasons why the study of lay theories of intelligence, creativity and wisdom are worth pursuing:

(a) the terms – intelligence, creativity, and wisdom – are frequently used in everyday discourse as well as in psychological discourse with no or minimal definition, and it is useful to know what people mean when they use these terms; (b) people evaluate the intelligence, creativity, and wisdom of themselves and others with some regularity, and it is worthwhile to know the psychological bases on which these evaluations are made; (c) as people make these judgements, it is helpful to know to what extent they are correlated with measures derived from explicit theories, such as psychometric tests; (d) the implicit theories may eventually help broaden and change our explicit theories, as we come to realise those aspects of cognition or affect which the current explicit theories of intelligence, creativity, and wisdom do not encompass, but possibly, should encompass. Thus, the study of implicit theories is not merely an easy substitute for the information and study of explicit theories of psychological constructs. Implicit theories deserve to be studied in their own right, and each study is complementary to the study of explicit theories. (p. 625)

Sternberg argues that the test of a lay theory is quite different from that of an explicit academic theory. The former is tested by whether an account is an accurate, comprehensive account of what people 'have in their heads', while the latter is tested through classical empirical methods. These lay theories change over time with fashion, as well as develop and change in people. Furthermore, they are learned and hence culture bound.

In Sternberg's study both laypeople and expert/scientific people were asked to rate academic intelligence, everyday intelligence and general intelligence. They both felt them to be highly correlated, but there were two main differences between the groups. Experts, more than laypeople, stressed the importance of motivation (dedication, persistence), while laypeople stressed social competence more than experts. Laypeople consistently stressed *inter*personal competence in a *social* context (getting on with others) whereas experts stressed *intra*personal competence in an *individual* context (learns quickly, solves problems fast).

Although lay theories of intelligence may have many similarities to expert theories, they are more often descriptive than explanatory. That is, scientific theories must ask what it *means* to reason logically, solve problems, or get on with others; scientists must also devise ways of *measuring* these concepts; more importantly, they must explain individual *variation* in the concepts. Despite the fact that lay theories are descriptive, they are functional in that people use them to assess the ability and competence of others. Most people believe that they are very good at this, although Sternberg has shown that they are only modestly good at assessing or predicting their own personalities. They are, however, much better at self-descriptions, or checklists, of their own abilities that relate more closely to their actual IQ test-derived scores.

Studies on lay concepts of intelligence have not been confined to English-speaking WASPS, and Wober (1972, 1973) examined East African (specifically, Ugandan) attitudes concerning intelligence. He found, for instance, that ideas about intelligence and quickness are not systematically related; indeed they are built into different factors. An earlier study of Keehn and Prothero (1958) in Lebanon showed that teachers' judgements of intelligence covaried with judgements of conscientiousness, thoughtfulness, persistence and emotional stability, but that they were relatively independent of judgements of cyclothymia (rapid mood change) and friendliness. They argue, however, that their results are fairly comparable with those found in America.

A recent Japanese study by Azuma and Kashiwagi (1987) required male and female college students, and mothers of the college students, to rate 67 descriptors of intelligence. Some characteristics, such as *quick thinker, good memory* and *quick judgement*, were common to all groups. Furthermore, compared with American studies, highly rated qualities (descriptors) related to receptive social competence tended to be associated with high intelligence, particularly when the person described was a woman. There was also strong evidence of sex-typing, with women being thought of as more sociable, sympathetic, dextrous and cheerful. They note: 'The overview of our results presents a picture of the Japanese concept of intelligence which has a relatively universal core and culturally defined marginals of which sex stereotyping is an example' (p. 25).

The History of Testing

In 1904 the French Ministry of Education asked psychologist Alfred Binet to devise a method to identify children who would have difficulty keeping up in regular classes. Binet produced a test designed to measure a person's ability to reason and use judgement. He created the test items by identifying questions that could be answered by average children of different ages. This procedure produced six questions for each age level. For example, 3-year-olds would be asked to point to their eyes or nose; 7-year-olds, to describe a picture.

In Binet's test, each child was interviewed individually by an examiner. The child was first asked questions slightly below his or her age level and was then asked questions of increasing difficulty. Testing stopped when the child failed to answer all the questions at a particular specified age level.

Binet's test was scored by noting the age level at which the child answered all the questions correctly and then adding two months' extra credit for each additional answer at the next level. Thus, a child who correctly answered all the questions to the age 9 level test plus three questions above the 9-year-old level was identified as having a 'mental age' of 9 years, 6 months.

Binet's test was introduced to the USA by Lewis Terman (1916) whose revision, the Stanford-Binet test, is still, in its modern form, one of the most widely used intelligence tests in the world. Terman also added a scale for adults and changed the way scores were reported. Instead of calculating mental age as Binet had done, Terman used a measure called the *intelligence quotient* (IQ), which had been introduced by the German Stern in 1912. Stern calculated IQ by dividing mental age by chronological age and multiplying by 100. Thus, an 8-year-old child with a mental age of 10 years would have an IQ of 125 (10 divided by 8 equals 1.25; 1.25 times 100 equals 125). This way of calculating IQ was used until 1960, when it was replaced by a measure called the *deviation IQ*, calculated by comparing a person's score with the distribution of scores obtained by the general population. An advantage of the deviation IQ over the old method, which gave the ratio of mental age to chronological age, is that the deviation IQ shows where a person stands in relation to other people of that age and group (ethnic, religious, national).

Wechsler later devised two tests, the Wechsler Intelligence Scale for Children – Revised (WISC – R) and the Wechsler Adult Intelligence Scale – Revised (WAIS – R). They differ from the Stanford-Binet tests in that they contain a number of subscales, which enable the examiner to construct a profile indicating a person's strengths and weaknesses. The scales can also be combined to obtain two separate scores: a *verbal score*, which depends on knowledge accumulated in the past, and a *performance score*, which depends more on immediate problem-solving ability. These two scores make the WISC – R useful for identifying children with learning disabilities, who may achieve a good verbal score but a poor performance score.

The Facts of Intelligence

Should we describe intelligence with just one number or metric, such as the IQ, or with many numbers, representing different kinds of intelligence? This question has been argued by two groups of psychologists, which Robert Sternberg (1990) describes as the *lumpers* and the *splitters*. The lumpers see intelligence as being global, so that one number should suffice to describe it. If they are correct, a person who is well endowed intellectually should perform equally well in a wide variety of areas.

The splitters see intelligence as made up of a number of specific mental faculties. According to this idea, a person might be intelligent in some areas yet not so intelligent in others. The argument between the lumpers and the splitters is, therefore, about the *basic structure* of intelligence.

One of the first psychologists to address this question was Spearman, who noticed that the scores on most tests of ability correlate with one another. That is, a person who does well on test A is also likely to do well on tests B and C. Based on this observation, he proposed that there is a general factor, *g*, which he called *general mental ability*, that underlies people's performance on all of these tests. However, the correlations between these tests were not perfect, i.e. 1.00. The difference between performance on the various tests must, therefore, be due to abilities specific to each test, so Spearman proposed that in addition to the general factor people also possess specific abilities related to the material in different tests.

Spearman's proposed structure, which is called the *two-factor theory*, contains components of both the lumper and splitter philosophies. Later psychologists proposed structures that more clearly favour the splitters' idea of numerous specific factors. For example, L.L. Thurstone (1928) analysed the results of a number of different intelligence tests using a technique called factor analysis. He concluded that intelligence can be described in terms of the following seven *primary mental abilities*:

1.   *numerical ability*, measured by arithmetic word problems;
2.   *reasoning ability*, measured by analogies ('LAWYER is to CLIENT as DOCTOR is to ____?') or series completions (2, 4, 7, 11, ?);
3.   *verbal fluency*, measured by how fast people can produce words ('What are 50 words that start with the letter s?');
4.   *verbal comprehension*, measured by vocabulary tests and tests of reading comprehension;
5.   *spatial visualisation*, measured by tests requiring mental manipu-

lation of pictorial representations ('How many sides does this solid figure have?');

6.   *perceptual ability*, measured by testing for rapid recognition of symbols ('Cross out the letter s every time it appears in this sentence');

7.   *memory*, measured by testing for recall of words, sentences, or picture-word pairs.

At present there remain quite different approaches, summarised in Table 6.4. Each makes distinctions in types of intelligence. A good question for the psychology student is, of course, to compare and contrast these different theories.

Bias in Testing

Without doubt the 'hottest' issue in intelligence testing is whether tests are biased against certain groups, e.g. females – who nearly always score poorly on tests of spatial ability – and blacks – who frequently score lower than whites on all tests.

Are tests biased in the sense that they systematically and incorrectly *underestimate* (or even overestimate) the scores of people from a particular group?

Many people have raised charges of racial bias in IQ tests and in related ability tests. A large part of their argument is that some of the items ask for factual information or for definitions of words that are more familiar to whites than they are to blacks. To illustrate this point, some critics have developed tests with a 'reverse bias', favouring blacks over whites.

The best way to measure possible bias of standard IQ tests is to determine whether those tests underestimate minority students' likely performance. The evidence indicates that they do not. Minority-group students with a given IQ score generally do about as well in school and at school-related tasks as do middle-class whites with the same IQ score. The unpleasant fact is that, on average, white students get better grades in school than do black students (in the USA). Interestingly, there is also considerable evidence that oriental people – especially the Japanese – actually score higher than do white occidentals. The IQ tests accurately report that fact. Perhaps instead of 'blaming the messenger' (the IQ tests) for the bad news, we should try to address the reasons behind the difference. And this leads on to the next big issue: sex differences.

TABLE 6.4: Four theories of intelligence

Theory	Principal theorist	Key ideas and terms	Examples
Psychometric approach	Charles Spearman (1904)	*g* factor: general abstract reasoning ability common to various tasks	Perceiving and manipulating
		s factor: specific ability required for a given task	Mechanical, verbal, spatial abilities
Fluid and crystallised intelligence	Raymond Cattell (1987)	Divides Spearman's *g* factor into two components:	
		1. Fluid intelligence (reasoning and using information; peaks before age 20)	Fluid: finding a solution to an unfamiliar problem
		2. Crystallised intelligence (acquired skills and knowledge; keeps growing as long as you live)	Crystallised: knowing how to play the piano, build a cabinet, write a novel, calculate the price of 17 pints of milk
Triarchic theory	Robert Sternberg (1985, 1991)	Criticises Spearman's and Cattell's theories for ignoring important non-*g* types of intelligence	
		Says intelligent behaviour depends on three types of processes:	

Theory	Principal theorist	Key ideas and terms	Examples
		1. Metacomponents (abilities used to approach a problem)	Deciding what steps to take and in which order to design a new factory
		2. Knowledge-acquisition components (abilities used to gain new knowledge)	Collecting information on factory design from books and experts in the field
		3. Performance components (abilities used to actually solve a problem or complete a task)	Actually designing the factory, after planning the procedure and collecting the information
Multiple intelligence	Howard Gardner (1985)	People have numerous unrelated forms of intelligence	Music, social sensitivity, maths
		Intelligence is defined as the ability to do something that other people value within your culture	Fill a tooth, sell Chryslers, dance

From *Introduction to Psychology*, by J. Kalat. Copyright © 1993, 1990, 1986 Wadsworth Publishing Company. By permission of Brooks/Cole Publishing Company, a division of International Thomson Publishing Inc., Pacific Grove, CA 93950.

A Summary of What Psychologists think about Intelligence

The publication of a recent highly controversial book on intelligence *(The Bell Curve,* Herrnstein and Murray, 1994) and passionate though not necessarily well-informed debate led over 50 of the world's experts on intelligence to write to the *Wall Street Journal* on 15 December 1994. Their 25-point summary is an excellent and clear statement on what psychologists think about intelligence.

The Meaning and Measurement of Intelligence

1. Intelligence is a very general mental capability that, among other things, involves the ability to reason, plan, solve problems, think abstractly, comprehend complex ideas, learn quickly and learn from experience. It is not merely book learning, a narrow academic skill, or descriptive of test-taking smarts. Rather, it reflects a broader and deeper capability for comprehending our surroundings – 'catching on,' 'making sense' of things, or 'figuring out' what to do.
2. Intelligence, so defined, can be measured, and intelligence tests measure it well. They are among the most accurate (in technical terms, reliable and valid) of all psychological tests and assessments. They do not measure creativity, character, personality or other important differences among individuals, nor are they intended to.
3. While there are different types of intelligence tests, they all measure the same intelligence. Some use words or numbers and require specific cultural knowledge (such as vocabulary). Others do not, and instead use shapes or designs and require knowledge of only simple, universal concepts (many/few, open/closed, up/down).
4. The spread of people along the IQ continuum, from low to high, can be represented well by the bell curve (in statistical jargon, the 'normal curve'). Most people cluster around the average (IQ 100). Few are either very bright or very dull: About 3% of Americans score above IQ 130 (often considered the threshold for 'giftedness'), with about the same percentage below IQ 70 (IQ 70–75 often being considered the threshold for mental retardation).
5. Intelligence tests are not culturally biased against African-American or other native-born, English-speaking peoples in the USA. Rather, IQ scores predict equally accurately for all

such Americans, regardless of race and social class. Individuals who do not understand English well can be given either a non-verbal test or one in their native language.

6.   The brain processes underlying intelligence are still little understood. Current research looks, for example, at speed of neural transmission, glucose (energy) uptake and electrical activity of the brain.

Group Differences

7.   Members of all racial-ethnic groups can be found at every IQ level. The bell curves of different groups overlap considerably, but groups often differ in where their members tend to cluster along the IQ line. The bell curves for some groups (Jews and East Asians) are centred somewhat higher than for whites in general. Other groups (blacks and Hispanics) are centred somewhat lower than non-Hispanic whites.

8.   The bell curve for whites is centred roughly around IQ 100; the bell curve for American blacks roughly around IQ 85; and those for different subgroups of Hispanics roughly midway between those for whites and blacks. The evidence is less definitive for exactly where above IQ 100 the bell curves for Jews and Asians are centred.

Practical Importance

9.   IQ is strongly related, probably more so than any other single measurable human trait, to many important educational, occupational, economic and social outcomes. Its relation to the welfare and performance of individuals is very strong in some arenas in life (education, military training), moderate but robust in others (social competence), and modest but consistent in others (law-abidingness). Whatever IQ tests measure, it is of great practical and social importance.

10. A high IQ is an advantage in life because virtually all activities require some reasoning and decision making. Conversely, a low IQ is often a disadvantage, especially in disorganised environments. Of course, a high IQ no more guarantees success than a low IQ guarantees failure in life. There are many exceptions, but the odds for success in our society greatly favour individuals with higher IQs.

11. The practical advantages of having a higher IQ increase as life settings become more complex (novel, ambiguous, changing, unpredictable or multifaceted). For example, a high IQ is generally necessary to perform well in highly complex or fluid jobs (the professions, management); it is a considerable advantage in moderately complex jobs (crafts, clerical and police work); but it provides less advantage in settings that require only routine decision making or simple problem solving (unskilled work).

12. Differences in intelligence certainly are not the only factor affecting performance in education, training and highly complex jobs (no one claims they are), but intelligence is often the most important. When individuals have already been selected for high (or low) intelligence and so do not differ as much in IQ, as in graduate school (or special education), other influences on performance loom larger in comparison.

13. Certain personality traits, special talents, aptitudes, physical capabilities, experience and the like are important (sometimes essential) for successful performance in many jobs, but they have narrower (or unknown) applicability or 'transferability' across tasks and settings compared with general intelligence. Some scholars choose to refer to these other human traits as other 'intelligences'.

Source and Stability of Within-Group Differences

14. Individuals differ in intelligence due to differences in both their environments and genetic heritage. Heritability estimates range from 0.4 to 0.8 (on a scale from 0 to 1), most thereby indicating that genetics plays a bigger role than does environment in creating IQ differences among individuals. (Heritability is the squared correlation of phenotype with genotype.) If all environments were to become equal for everyone, heritability would rise to 100% because nearly all remaining differences in IQ would necessarily be genetic in origin.

15. Members of the same family also tend to differ substantially in intelligence (by an average of about 12 IQ points) for both genetic and environmental reasons. They differ genetically because biological brothers and sisters share exactly half their genes with each parent and, on average, only half with each other. They also differ in IQ because they experience different environments within the same family.

16. That IQ may be highly heritable does not mean that it is not

affected by the environment. Individuals are not born with fixed, unchangeable levels of intelligence (no one claims they are). IQs do gradually stabilise during childhood, however, and generally change little thereafter.

17. Although the environment is important in creating IQ differences, we do not know yet how to manipulate it to raise low IQs permanently. Whether recent attempts show promise is still a matter of considerable scientific debate.

18. Genetically caused differences are not necessarily irremediable (consider diabetes, poor vision and phenylketonuria), nor are environmentally caused ones necessarily remediable (consider injuries, poisons, severe neglect and some diseases). Both may be preventable to some extent.

Source and Stability of Between-Group Differences

19. There is no persuasive evidence that the IQ bell curves for different racial-ethnic groups are converging. Surveys in some years show that gaps in academic achievement have narrowed a bit for some races, ages, school subjects and skill levels, but this picture seems too mixed to reflect a general shift in IQ levels themselves.

20. Racial-ethnic differences in IQ bell curves are essentially the same when youngsters leave high school as when they enter first grade. However, because bright youngsters learn faster than slow learners, these same IQ differences lead to growing disparities in amount learned as youngsters progress from grades one to twelve. As large national surveys in the USA continue to show, black 17 year olds perform, on average, more like white 13-year-olds in reading, maths and science, with Hispanics in between.

21. The reasons that blacks differ among themselves in intelligence appear to be basically the same as those for why whites (or Asians or Hispanics) differ among themselves. Both environment and genetic heredity are involved.

22. There is no definitive answer to why IQ bell curves differ across racial-ethnic groups. The reasons for these IQ differences between groups may be markedly different from the reasons why individuals differ among themselves within any particular group (whites or blacks or Asians). In fact, it is wrong to assume, as many do, that the reason why some individuals in a population have high IQs but others have low IQs must be the same reason why some populations contain

more such high (or low) IQ individuals than others. Most experts believe that environment is important in pushing the bell curves apart, but that genetics could be involved too.

23. Racial-ethnic differences are somewhat smaller but still substantial for individuals from the same socioeconomic backgrounds. To illustrate, black students from prosperous families tend to score higher in IQ than blacks from poor families, but they score no higher, on average, than whites from poor families.

24. Almost all Americans who identify themselves as black have white ancestors – the white admixture is about 20%, on average – and many self-designated whites, Hispanics and others likewise have mixed ancestry. Because research on intelligence relies on self-classification into distinct racial categories, as does most other social science research, its findings likewise relate to some unclear mixture of social and biological distinctions among groups (no one claims otherwise).

Implications for Social Policy

25. The research findings neither dictate nor preclude any particular social policy, because they can never determine our goals. They can, however, help us estimate the likely success and side-effects of pursuing those goals via different means.

6.4   Sex Differences

Are the sexes psychologically different in terms of ability, personality, motives and so on. Are men more intelligent than women who, in turn, are more emotional than men? This area is now so controversial that few psychologists wander into it with simple, naïve questions hoping to have them answered. Sex differences have been politicised and arguments, as well as data, are given an ideological, rather than empirical, screening.

There are those who, believing that biology is destiny, are quite unsurprised by the sex differences they and others report and attribute them mainly to biological differences. The biological determinist view is that culture and society amplify nature which has ensured through a natural division of labour that males develop skills for hunting and protection. So men should be better at spatial location, stronger and more aggressive than women. Diametrically opposed are the group that refuse to acknowledge any evidence of sex differences, attributing certain minor variations they might find to upbringing. This group in the debate suggests that it is predominantly cultural factors that shape sex differences. In traditional patriarchal societies, from a very early age, young male babies are taught certain attitudes and behaviours quite different from those taught to girls. Some psychologists argue that it is crucially important that we conduct disinterested, impartial, empirical research into the question, while others are only happy to report results if they demonstrate no differences.

The problems, even for the reviewer, arise not simply because the results of the studies are so equivocal and inconsistent. They have always been so. The first major, well-quoted, review was published 20 years ago by Maccoby and Jacklin (1974) (see Table 6.5) who said:

> Returning to one of the major conclusions of our survey of sex differences, there are many popular beliefs about the psychological characteristics of the two sexes that have proved to have little or no basis in fact. (Maccoby and Jacklin, 1974, p. 355)

But less than two years later the distinguished American psychologist Jack Block (1976) wrote:

> I suggest that many of the 'popular beliefs' and 'myths' about sex differences to which Maccoby and Jacklin refer are not easily explained by pointing to the pervasiveness and persuasiveness of stereotypes. (p. 285)

> While stereotypes may only embody 'myths,' they may have encoded also certain culturally discerned and repeatedly validated truths. (p. 295)

TABLE 6.5: Summary of Maccoby and Jacklin's findings concerning psychological differences between the sexes

Unfounded beliefs about sex differences:
1. That girls are more 'social' than boys
2. That girls are more 'suggestible' than boys
3. That girls have lower self-esteem
4. That girls are better at rote learning and simple repetitive tasks, boys at tasks that require higher-level cognitive processing, and the inhibition of previously learned responses
5. That boys are more 'analytic'
6. That girls are more affected by heredity, boys by environment
7. That girls lack achievement motivation
8. That girls are auditory, boys visual

TABLE 6.5: Contd.

Sex differences that are fairly well established:
1. That girls have greater verbal ability than boys
2. That boys excel in visual-spatial ability
3. That boys excel in mathematical ability
4. That males are more aggressive
Open questions:
1. Tactile sensitivity
2. Fear, timidity and anxiety
3. Activity level
4. Competitiveness
5. Dominance
6. Compliance
7. Nurturance and 'maternal' behaviour

Lippa (1994) has provided a more recent meta-analysis of many studies which accomplishes three goals: (1) it tells us when a sex difference is reliably found; (2) it informs us how large the average sex difference is; (3) it tells us whether sex differences depend on other variables.

TABLE 6.6: Meta-analyses of sex differences

Behaviour	Mean value of d (positive values denote females higher)	Number of studies from which d was computed
SOCIAL BEHAVIOURS		
Non-verbal behaviours:		
Decoding skill	0.43	64
Social smiling	0.63	15
Amount of gaze	0.68	30
Personal space (distance of approach in natural settings)	−0.56	17
Expansiveness of movements	−1.04	6
Filled pauses ('ahs' and 'ums' in speech)	−1.19	6
Aggression	−0.50 (median d value)	69
Group conformity	0.28	35
Helping		
Overall	−0.34	99
When being watched	−0.74	16
When not being watched	0.02	41
Behaviour in small groups:		
Positive social-emotional behaviours	0.59	17
Task-orientated behaviours	−0.59	10

Behaviour	Mean value of d (positive values denote females higher)	Number of studies from which d was computed
TABLE 6.6: Contd		
Leadership:		
Overall in lab groups	−0.32	74
Task leadership	−0.41	61
Social leadership	0.18	15
Democratic vs. autocratic style	0.22	23
Self-disclosure	0.18	205
COGNITIVE ABILITIES		
Verbal	0.11	165
Maths	−0.43	16
Visual-spatial	−0.45	10
PHYSICAL ABILITIES AND CHARACTERISTICS		
Throw velocity	−2.18	5
Throw distance	−1.98	11
Grip strength	−0.66	4
General motor activity	−0.49	127

From *Introduction to Social Psychology* by Richard A. Lippa. Copyright © 1994, 1990 Brooks/Cole Publishing Company, a division of International Thompson Publishing Inc., Pacific Grove, CA 93950. By permission of the publisher.

The bigger the d the bigger the sex difference; a positive sign means women more than men; a negative sign indicates men score higher than women.

Table 6.6 shows the results of a number of meta-analyses of studies on sex differences. Listed are the mean values of d from all studies that examined a particular variable and the number of studies from which the mean values of d were computed.

The d statistic allows us to study sex differences systematically. For any study that measures the means and standard deviations of women's and men's scores on a given variable (height, aggression, mathematics ability, and so on), we can compute d. But the existence of a sex difference cannot be proved by a single study alone.

As a general rule of thumb for psychology research, it is suggested that a d value of 0.2 is small, a value of 0.5 is medium, and a value of 0.8 is large (enough to be readily perceived in everyday life). Women and men display a number of differences in behaviour, but are by no means 'opposite' sexes. The means of the measures of certain characteristics simply differ between the sexes to various degrees. In general, there is considerable overlap between the distributions of women's and men's social behaviours, and thus sex accounts for only a fraction of the total variation in these measures.

On the other hand, even if the difference between the means of two distributions is relatively small, differences can become quite large at the ends of the distributions. For example, although the mean *d* value for the difference in women's and men's ability is only 0.43, sex differences at the extremes of the distributions are much larger. Sex differences in maths ability of the magnitude just described could influence the number of men and women who become mathematicians, engineers and scientists – professions that require maths ability in the upper tail of the distribution.

The trouble with the research on sex differences is that the literature is voluminous, the findings often contradictory, the issues frequently value-laden and emotionally volatile, and the conclusions of potential importance for social policy. These problems include ambiguities concerning the concept being measured, contradictory results according to different measures used (e.g. observations, ratings, self-reports), varying results according to characteristics of the population sampled (e.g. age and social class), and varying results according to the task and situational context used. These problems in research are not unique to the area of the psychology of sex differences.

One way to proceed is to look at different results – such as cognitive or intellectual differences, and affective or emotional differences between the sexes – and actual behavioural differences (Pervin, 1988).

What Table 6.6 means is this. The non-verbal behaviours of women and men differ in a number of interesting ways. Women on average are superior to men in decoding non-verbal cues, particularly facial expressions. Women smile more and engage in more eye contact during social interactions than men do. Men maintain greater personal space and are more expansive in their body movements and postures. Men make more errors in speech than women do and use more 'filled pauses' ('ahs' and 'ums') when they talk.

Smaller sex differences emerge in studies on such social behaviours as aggression, helping, susceptibility to social influence and self-disclosure. On average, men are more aggressive than women. On average, men help more in emergencies than women do; this finding is qualified by the fact that men help more particularly when they are being watched and when the victim is female, which suggests that men may be motivated by the opportunity to display their masculine valour to an audience as much

as by the need to be helpful. Women on average are more susceptible than men to social influence in attitude change and conformity studies. This sex difference tends to be strongest in
group-conformity experiments in which subjects are under the
surveillance of other people. Finally, women tend to disclose
more about themselves in conversations than men do, particularly when talking to other women. Overall, women and men
show small to medium differences in aggression, helping behaviour, susceptibility to influence and self-disclosure; however, these
differences are often moderated by situational factors.

(Lippa, 1994, p.346)

Women seem to show more positive social-emotional behaviours
(acting friendly, agreeing with others, offering emotional support);
men show more task-orientated behaviours (giving and asking for
opinions, trying to solve the group task). These differences may indicate that women are more effective than men in group tasks requiring considerable discussion and negotiation, and that men may be
more effective in those requiring focused, task-orientated behaviour.
The question remains as to not only whether these findings are reliable and valid but why they occur.

As leaders, women and men show small to moderate differences,
at least in western cultures. Men are somewhat more likely to emerge
as leaders of artificial groups studied in labs than women are, and
men are more likely to be the task-orientated leaders of groups.
Women in leadership positions are also more likely than men to
employ democratic as opposed to autocratic methods, although with
all these findings there are dramatic exceptions.

Men and women on average display a number of differences in
cognitive or mental abilities. For example, men tend to perform
better than women on tests of maths and visual-spatial ability, but
there is overall female superiority in verbal ability. However the most
recent evidence suggests that this difference in general verbal ability
no longer exists but there may be sex differences favouring women in
certain specific verbal skills such as fluency. Some scientists have
argued that spatial tasks require bigger brains which explains the
reliable finding that men have bigger brains than women.

Women and men of course display a number of consistent physical differences. Men are stronger than women, particularly at tasks
requiring upper body strength. Men show higher levels of general
motor activity than women do, and women generally have more
flexible joints than men do.

The realm of affective or emotional functioning has been particularly difficult to study. Boys seem more active and more variable in temperament than girls. Many research studies show greater fear and timidity in girls, but these results tend to be more associated with studies using ratings and self-reports than with those using observational data. After the age of 18 months boys also tend to show greater outbursts of negative emotion in response to frustration than do girls. Boys quite simply are (and remain) more aggressive than girls. Differences in affective functioning are equivocal, but enough studies have reported differences in activity level, fearfulness and emotional responses to frustration to suggest that basic differences in affective functioning may exist. Such differences would not be surprising in the light of hormonal differences between the sexes and the association between temperament and hormone functioning.

In overt behavioural functioning, the evidence suggests that men are higher in aggression and dominance while women are higher in dependence and nurturance-type behaviour. The evidence concerning some of these differences is not conclusive but is most reliable for differences in aggression as it comes from a variety of sources: evolutionary, cross-cultural, developmental and biological-hormonal. However, the level and form of aggression expressed are highly susceptible to sex role influences.

When assessing the role of biological factors, researchers usually ask four main empirical questions:

1. Do sex differences occur early in development, before considerable learning has a chance to take place? (If so, the case for biological explanations of sex differences is strengthened.)
2. Do sex differences occur consistently across cultures? (Cross-cultural variability would suggest sex differences are learned, whereas cross-cultural universality would be consistent with biological causes.)
3. Do sex differences occur consistently across species, particularly species closely related to human beings (for example, other primates)? (If so, the case for biological causes is strengthened.)
4. Do physiological variables related to gender (such as sex hormones) have an effect on the behaviours in question? (If so, this provides direct evidence that sex-linked biological variables may contribute to behavioural sex differences (Lippa, 1994, p.347).)

Using these four kinds of evidence, can we make a convincing case that some sex differences result in part from biological factors? The strongest case for biological origins can be made with respect to aggression. Boys are more aggressive than girls as early as age 2 or 3; but aggression may decrease with age. In most societies and cultures, men are more aggressive than women; this difference is reflected in virtually all social indexes of aggression, including participation in warfare, violent crimes, murders and suicides, as well as aggressive language. From an early age, male non-human primates are more aggressive than females. There is also evidence that sex hormones, particularly testosterone, are related to aggression in humans and animals. But these biological predispositions may be amplified or dampened by culture and social learning depending on how the culture has evolved and what it values.

Another sex difference that may have a biological foundation is that of visual-spatial ability. One theory holds that this difference results from varying degrees of brain lateralisation in women and men. For most people, language skills depend more on the left hemisphere of the brain, whereas visual-spatial skills depend more on the right hemisphere. The lateralisation hypothesis assumes the separation of the functions of the two hemispheres is more complete and extreme in men than in women. While the evidence for this hypothesis is complex and inconsistent, it seems likely that biological factors are responsible to some degree for the frequently observed sex differences in visual-spatial ability. Again, such a conclusion does not preclude the possibility that these differences are also influenced by cultural factors and learning.

Different Theories for Sex Differences

By now it should not surprise any reader to find that psychologists hold rather different (and contradictory) theories about the origin of sex differences – which most but not all even acknowledge. However, it may be sociopolitical issues as much as theoretical persuasions or even evidence that lead psychologists to favour one theory over another.

1. Psychoanalytic Theories

Freud argued that children's early sexual feelings and their emotional ties to their parents lead them to develop masculine or feminine identities. Both boys and girls begin life with their mother as their primary love object. But after age 3, boys' and girls' development diverges. Boys first experience genital pleasure around this time and the boy's love for his mother takes on a sexual tinge. He becomes aware that his father is a major competitor for his mother's affection.

Boys also notice the genital differences between men and women and learn that women lack penises. Frightened and bewildered, little boys assume that women once possessed penises but somehow lost them, which intensifies the boy's fear of his father and of his own sexual desires, for he reasons that his possible vengeful father may remove ('cut off') his penis as punishment for his incestuous desires for his mother. This intense *castration anxiety* leads the boy ultimately to give up his sexual wishes for his mother and to identify with his father.

The *Oedipus complex* refers to the boy's unconscious feelings of sexual attraction to his mother and the rivalry with his father. This supposedly universal problem is the major determinant of sex differences at least with respect to attitudes and emotions.

Girls, according to the theory, presumably notice the genital differences between males and females between ages 3 and 6; however, rather than fearing the loss of their genitals, girls (unconsciously) assume that their penises have already been cut off.

According to classical Freudian theory, girls are unconsciously weakened because of their genital 'inferiority', and *penis envy* is the prime motivation of the feminine personality. Throughout life, women strive to regain their missing penis by having love relations with men and by having children, particularly male children. Hence the 'feminine' desire for close emotional relationships and for children.

Because of their genital 'inferiority', women supposedly often feel contempt for other women, specifically for their own mothers. For this reason, girls give up their mothers as primary love objects, and instead court their fathers, taking on an 'inappropriate' male love object. The self-disparagement (due to genital 'inferiority') and the desire to please their fathers (and indirectly all males) leads women to be masochistic in their love relationships. Needless to say it takes courageous psychoanalysts these days to state belief in these classical Freudian ideas.

2. Biological Theories

Biological theories argue that innate differences exist between women and men. This is obviously true for certain physical characteristics and physiological processes. Women produce ova and men produce sperm. Men are bigger and stronger than women.

Wilson (1978), probably the father of modern sociobiology, argued that because women were responsible throughout the evolutionary history of our species for bearing, nursing and caring for children, they evolved to be more nurturing and communicative. Further, because men were responsible for hunting and fighting, they evolved more aggressiveness and better visual-spatial ability to find their way home. Furthermore, women and men have different optimal reproductive strategies: women must guarantee that the relatively few offspring they bear will survive and flourish, whereas men, who produce millions of sperm, can father an indefinite number of offspring. As a result, women have evolved to be more sexually coy and desirous of committed relationships that provide stable resources, and men have evolved to be more sexually aggressive and promiscuous. For these theorists biology is destiny.

3. Social Learning Theory

Self-evidently this theory explains sex differences in terms of classical learning theory concepts – conditioning (by rewards and punishments) and modelling (observing and copying others). Operant conditioning, which occurs when girls' and boys' behaviours are rewarded and punished in systematically different ways, can also lead to sex differences.

Children, it is suggested, also acquire sex-typed behaviours through observational learning. Children often learn about 'female' and 'male' behaviours without being directly rewarded or punished, simply observing their friends, parents, relatives and the portrayal of various characters by the mass media, especially television. Such models (parents) are particularly influential when they have a nurturing relationship with the children, are powerful, and control salient rewards for children.

Social learning theory makes an important distinction between the acquisition of behaviour and the performance of that behaviour; people can learn behaviours through observation, but that does not mean they necessarily behave in accordance with that learning.

The theory argues that women and men are capable of performing the same behaviours, but they don't because of past conditioning, rewards, punishments, observational learning and all the situational contingencies (special circumstances) that exist in a society that treats women and men differently.

Much research supports social learning theory's basic contention that environmental factors help create and sustain sex differences. A number of studies suggest that parents treat girls and boys differently from birth. Parents provide different toys for their girls and boys and decorate their rooms in different ways. Parents treat girls as 'women-in-training' and boys as 'men-in-training'. Both parents and peers encourage sex-typed behaviours in children, and they discourage behaviours, sometimes vigorously, that are not sex-typed. Television, radio and the print media often portray women and men in stereo-typical ways, and children often view media characters as models for behaviour. For learning theorists, then, sex differences are learned and can therefore be unlearned.

4. Cognitive Theory

These theories (there are a few within the same general area) suggest that children progress through a number of discrete cognitive stages in becoming psychologically 'male' or 'female'. Children's concep-tions of gender develop in step with their more general levels of cognitive growth.

Although they are aware of sex differences as a 'social category', young children do not think about gender as adults do. For instance, they do not realise that 'male' and 'female' are defined most funda-mentally by genitalia; instead, they define gender by its surface manifestations, such as clothing, hair length and the kinds of games one plays. At 3 and 4 years of age, children will often state that they could be the other sex if they wanted to – all they have to do is change their clothing, hairstyle, name, toys and bedroom. By age 6 or 7, children consistently realise that sex and gender are constant and linked to male and female genital differences.

Cognitive developmental theories argue that the act of self-cate-gorisation ('I'm a girl' or 'I'm a boy') leads the child to develop stereotypically female or male behaviours. Cognitive theory assumes this sequence: I'm a boy, therefore I want to do boy-type things, therefore the opportunity to do boy things is rewarding, therefore it is better than being a girl.

Discomfort with cross-sex behaviour seems to be stronger for boys than girls, perhaps because most societies punish boys who are 'sissies' more than girls who are 'tomboys'.

There is evidence for both social learning theories and cognitive theories of gender: children first come to behave in 'male' and 'female' ways through modelling, reinforcement and social pres-sures; however, in time they internalise these gender standards and strongly positively evaluate their own behaviour according to these internalised standards.

Other researchers in the 'gender-scheme' tradition believe children and adults learn a complex network of gender-related concepts and symbols from their cultures. For example, 'tender' and 'flowers' may be seen as feminine, whereas 'aggressive' and 'guns' are masculine. Once people have acquired gender schemata, they perceive their own and others' behaviour through the filter of those schemata. As one gets older these schemata become more elaborate and sophisticated.

People who are strongly gender-schematic tend to perceive the world in terms of 'male' and 'female', and they try to keep their own behaviour consistent with stereotypical standards for their sex. They may feel very threatened when these schemata are challenged. More conservative, often less intelligent, people tend to hold more rigid and unambiguous schemata.

5. 'Cultural' Theory

In most cultures, women and men occupy quite different roles: Women are more responsible for child-rearing and domestic duties; men are more responsible for hunting, fighting and, in modern industrial societies, income-producing work (although this has clearly changed substantially in recent years). This sex-based division of labour, which occurs in virtually all societies (although it can be reversed), leads necessarily to sex differences in behaviour and to the stereotypical perceptions that women and men are different. Women who are constrained by their social roles to rear children and take care of the home, therefore, show more nurturing behaviours. Equally guided by their social roles in the competitive world of work, men display more competitive, assertive behaviours, and as a result people perceive men to be more competitive and assertive. Cultural norms and rules therefore dictate sex roles. Hence one may expect generational differences, which are all too apparent today.

6. 'Self-presentation' or 'Constructionist' Theory

According to the main theories outlined above, sex differences are dictated either by biology, by early relations with parents, by conditioning and modelling, by cognitive labelling and schemata and by social roles.

More radical views hold that gender is a cultural invention, a social construction, and a self-presentation we enact in certain settings and with certain people. It is not fixed but switched on and off at certain periods.

We play our roles as men and women depending on our own concepts of gender, others' expectations and the setting in which we happen to be. For example, the same woman may be a no-nonsense, assertive executive at work but quite 'feminine' when on a date. Equally the cold, stand-offish male boss may be a warm and caring father of his children.

One study demonstrated that women will change the amount of food they eat depending on the man they are with. This means women are presenting themselves quite differently to different men.

Another study documented yet another self-presentational strategy women use to display their femininity: modifying their voices. Mrs Thatcher was famous for her different voices ranging from stridently assertive to coy and demure. Women's phone conversations in one research project were recorded with either intimate or casual male friends. When women spoke to their boyfriends, their speech displayed significantly more 'feminine' characteristics: their voices were higher in pitch, more 'baby-like', more pleasant and more variable in tone. The women's speech was also rated as more 'submissive' and 'scatterbrained' when they conversed with their boyfriends. Many of these women were consciously aware of the change; some observed that their voices became more 'babylike', 'endearing', 'girlie' and even 'slightly whiny'. Clearly, women display different vocal characteristics depending on the social setting and on the image they want to project.

Overall the different theories may be labelled as listed in Table 6.7.

6.5   Nature or Nurture: What Determines Human Nature?

One of the most enduring and passionate debates in the whole of psychology concerns the nature–nurture question: that is, the extent to which hereditary/genetic and/or environmental/educational characteristics determine human characteristics. The debate and controversy is perhaps most passionate when discussing a genetic basis to intelligence or the causes of psychological differences between the sexes. However, with a rise of interest in the person–situation debate, social and personality psychologists have executed and reviewed studies on person (internal) vs situation (external) determinants of a wide range of social behaviours.

This is a very old issue as the following quotes illustrate:

TABLE 6.7: Theoretical perspectives on sex differences and gender

Theory	Main focus
1. Psychoanalytic	Early emotional and sexual attachments to parents
2. Biological theories	
Evolutionary theories	Evolutionary pressures on prehistoric women and men
Physiological factors	Hormonal and brain differences between the sexes
3. Social learning theories	
Classical conditioning	Labels such as 'sissy' or 'drip' acquire strong emotional connotations
Operant conditioning	Different behaviours rewarded and punished for boys and girls
Observational learning	Children imitate male and female parents, peers and media models
4. Cognitive theories	
Cognitive-developmental theory	Self-labelling as male or female leads to gender-related behaviours
Gender schema theory	Gender schemata comprise cultural beliefs about gender; gender schematic individuals monitor their own and others' behaviour with respect to masculinity and femininity
5. Cultural theory	Different social roles occupied by men and women lead to gender stereotypes and different behaviours in men and women
6. Self-presentation theory	Gender is a social 'performance' that varies depending on gender schemata, the setting and the social audience

The thief and the murderer follow nature just as much as the philanthropist. T. H. Huxley, *Evolution and Ethics* (1873)

Nature has always had more power than education. Voltaire, *Vie de Molière* (1739)

Education makes a greater difference between man and man, than nature has made between man and brute. J. Adams, *Letter to a Relative* (1776)

I should like to go one step further now and say, give me a dozen healthy infants, well-formed, and my own specified world to bring them up in and I'll guarantee to take any one at random and train him to become any type of specialist I might select – doctor, lawyer, artist, merchant-chief, and, yes, even beggar-man and thief, regardless of his talents, penchants, tendencies, vocations and race of his ancestors. J.B. Watson, *Behavioursim* (1930)

Political writings express both explicit and implicit beliefs as to the origins of human nature and it is often assumed that all political doctrine must be founded on a theory of human nature. Thus it seems that communism assumes that selfish, competitive and self-aggrandisement aspects of human nature are not natural but the product of social, economic and political conditions. Likewise liberalism seems to assume that all people have a strong desire for total freedom, while conservatives have a negative view of man, believing people to be naturally selfish, aggressive and anarchic. As the orientations of modern political parties have their bases in different political philosophies, it might be expected that these orientations reflect different views as to the determinants of human characteristics, and that voters for different parties would thus hold different views on human nature.

Although there has never been a close rapprochement between empirical psychology and political science, there have been a number of salient studies on the personality of different party supporters and on differences in their beliefs and values. For instance, Rokeach (1973) has argued and others have demonstrated in America that political beliefs are based essentially on the two unrelated values of freedom and equality. Thus whereas socialists value both freedom and equality positively, conservatives will value freedom positively and equality negatively, communists will value equality positively and freedom negatively, whereas fascists value both freedom and equality negatively.

More recently, studies have concentrated on the relationship between moral reasoning and political beliefs and attitudes. For instance, Emler, Renwick and Malone (1983) set out to test whether individual differences in adult moral reasoning reflect differences in the content of politico-moral ideology. They found, as predicted, that Scottish students who classified themselves as left-wingers gained higher scores on a principled moral reasoning test than moderates or right-wingers, but that both of the last groups' scores increased if they responded from the perspective of a radical.

Perhaps the most extensive research on nature–nurture beliefs has been on the personality of people from different political persuasions, particularly conservatism. Wilson (1973) reviewed over 20 studies on the determinants of conservative attitudes and beliefs and described it as a syndrome that represents a generalised susceptibility to experiencing threat or anxiety in the face of uncertainty. The concept of uncertainty refers both to stimulus uncertainty (innovation, complexity, novelty, ambiguity, risk and anomie) and response uncertainty (freedom of choice, conflicting needs and desires etc.):

> The theory suggests that certain genetic factors such as anxiety proneness, stimulus aversion (sensitivity to strong stimuli), low intelligence, lack of physical attractiveness, old age and female sex, and certain environmental factors such as parental coldness, punitiveness, rigidity and inconsistency, and membership of the lower classes, will give rise to feelings of insecurity and inferiority (low self-esteem).... Feelings of insecurity and inferiority may be expected to result in a generalized fear of uncertainty, the insecure individual fearing stimulus uncertainty because in his inability to control events in his environment or make autonomous decisions regarding his own behaviour. (Wilson, 1973, pp. 259–261)

Because political ideology has been thought to be associated with general social attitudes, values and behaviours it has also been argued that the way in which scientists go about their work (problems and methods chosen) is governed by their politics. For instance, several commentators on science believe that modern or bourgeois ideology is responsible for the acceptance of ideas of human nature. Eysenck (1982) has recently offered current and historical evidence to justify his position that the 'alleged conformity of political ideology and scientific stance is, in fact, completely erroneous and historically untenable' (p. 1288). In a reply Albee (1983) has claimed that biological determinism is a major ideological weapon against Marxism, although he omitted the inverse implication that environmental determinism is a major ideological weapon against bourgeois ideology and social Darwinism. Yet a study by Pastore (1949) which investigates the relationship between an individual's views about the nature–nurture controversy and his/her attitudes to social, political and economic questions, found upon examining the works of famous scientists (Galton, Rutherford) that there was a strong correlation between beliefs in the influence of heredity and the degree of conservatism in sociopolitical attitudes.

In a British study Furnham, Johnson and Rawles (1985) found strong relationships between political orientation and beliefs concerning the origins of human nature – the more right-wing (conservative) a person is in his/her voting pattern (and political beliefs), the more they tend to believe in genetic determinism for all human characteristics, including personality, psychological problems and physical characteristics.

However, the results of this study do not necessarily resolve the debate between Albee (1983) and Eysenck (1982) over political ideology and science, although they may shed light on it. Eysenck had maintained that as regards scientific psychological writing, and indeed the writings of major political figures (Lenin, Engels, Marx) in the former Eastern Bloc countries, there is no rejection of a biological or genetic view of human differences in favour of totalitarian environmentalism. Albee (1983) has however argued that:

> One of the most fundamental tenets of Marxism and of communist doctrines is that the personalities of people are shaped by their economic class and by their role in the class struggle which is about as environmentalistic a position as can be imagined. (p. 965)

This argument may, however, be fairly easily resolved: Eysenck is probably correct when he argues that Marxist scientists are by no means total environmentalists, stressing the importance of biological differences, while Albee is probably correct when he argues that lay Marxists are more environmentalist than most in their beliefs about human nature. That is, the difference is a matter of degree and who one is talking about. Furthermore, it is quite possible, and indeed established with regard to politics (particularly socialism) that people neither know nor necessarily believe in the tenets of their political party's doctrine. In fact the issue of cross-voting (the electors and elected having different beliefs) is well known in political circles and may account for the fact that lay Marxists or those who vote for western communist parties do not necessarily hold precisely the same views as orthodox (or even current) Marxist philosophers or scientists.

Furnham's study has also demonstrated that to discuss the politics of nature and nurture one should distinguish which human characteristics are being considered. Although some human characteristics (cognitive abilities, sex-related differences) provoke so much passion as to be almost impossible to discuss rationally, there are a number of characteristics about which there is a fair amount of agreement between people of different political persuasions. Thus, for instance, everyone taking part in the study believed physical characteristics are more genetically determined than physical problems, although even here left-wingers believed them significantly more environmentally controlled than right-wingers. It is also interesting to note that conservatives felt, more than communists, that psychological abilities, psychological problems, personality and beliefs were genetically determined. Indeed, it is personality – especially innate aggressiveness and independence – that is currently most debated in terms of sociobiology. Certainly there are a number of other characteristics, especially cooperativeness, competitiveness and collectivism/individualism, that may be included in future studies of this sort. It appears that the more social-psychological the human characteristic considered, the more it teases apart people of different political persuasions.

Twins, Siblings and Adopted Children

Identical twins reared apart in very varied environments provide the best test of the nature–nurture dilemma, for in this rare incidence we have genetically identical children reared in different environments. Similarities can thus be directly related to nature and differences to nurture.

Galton (1869/1978) was the first to offer evidence that a tendency toward high intelligence is hereditary. As evidence, he simply pointed out that eminent and distinguished men – politicians, judges, etc. – generally had a number of distinguished relatives. But distinguished people share environment as well as genes with their relatives and becoming distinguished is only partly a matter of intelligence. Furthermore nepotism, élitist education and other social factors may account for achievements in families.

The question of how heredity affects intelligence has persisted to this day and has turned out to be difficult to answer scientifically. If we could treat people as we treat experimental animals, we could answer the question conclusively. We could take hundreds of offspring from high-IQ parents and hundreds from low-IQ parents and then randomly assign half of each group to either high-IQ or low-IQ adoptive parents. We could see to it that none of the parents would 'adopt' their own child and that none would know whether their adoptive child was from high-IQ or low-IQ parents. Later we could test the children to see whether their IQs matched those of their biological parents or those of their adoptive parents, or neither!

This maybe an ideal experiment but it is of course unethical. Instead, some researchers have spent years trying to find identical (monozygote) twins reared apart.

People interested in the nature–nurture debate, particularly with reference to that highly controversial topic intelligence, have focused typically on six groups of subjects. Table 6.8 is the work of two American researchers, Bouchard and McGue (1981).

Table 6.8: Relationships and rearing	
Relationship	Average correlation in intelligence
MZ twins reared together	0.86
MZ twins reared apart	0.72
DZ twins reared together	0.60
Biologically related siblings reared together	0.47
Non-biologically related siblings reared together	0.31
Biologically related siblings reared apart	0.24

These data contain the following evidence supporting the role of genetics in determining intelligence:

* The correlation between the IQs of MZ twins reared together is 0.86; that of DZ (dizygotic) twins reared together is 0.60. The higher correlation for MZ twins reflects their genetic similarity.
* The correlation between the IQs of biologically related siblings reared together is 0.47, of non-biologically related siblings, 0.31. The shared genes of the biologically related siblings increase the correlation between their IQ scores.

The correlation for MZ twins is 0.86, but it would be 1.00 if heredity were the only factor controlling intelligence, because MZ twins are genetically identical. When MZ twins experience different environments by being reared apart, the correlation between their IQs drops from 0.86 to 0.72. Similarly, the correlation for siblings drops from 0.47 if they are reared together to 0.24 if they are reared apart.

We can also compare DZ twins with non-twin siblings. Although they all share 50% of their genes, the DZ twins' IQs are more closely related – presumably because twins, whose ages match, experience more similar environments than do non-twin siblings, whose ages are different. If children are biologically unrelated, just growing up in the same household results in a correlation of 0.31 – evidence that environment affects intelligence.

The importance of environment to intelligence has also been demonstrated in studies in which children are moved from a deprived environment to an enriched one. For example, Scarr and Weinberg (1976) found that a group of African-American children who were adopted by white middle-class families had average IQs of 110, about 15 to 20 points higher than children raised in the deprived community from which they were adopted.

The interpretation of these results is also confounded to some extent by the policies of adoption agencies. Many adoption agencies place children of high-IQ parents with the brightest available adoptive parents. Thus, adopted children with high-IQ parents may develop high IQs themselves not just because of their heredity but also because of their environment. Nevertheless, the fact that adopted children resemble their biological parents in IQ more than their adoptive parents implies a significant role of heredity in IQ scores. All but the most politically committed and scientifically naïve admit this fact.

These results are usually interpreted to mean that identical twins resemble each other more in IQ scores than fraternal twins do because their genes are the same. Some psychologists have challenged this interpretation, saying that identical twins resemble each other more than fraternal twins do only because their parents and others probably treat identical twins more similarly than they treat fraternal twins. Careful research has found that identical twins who always thought they were fraternal twins resemble each other as much as other identical twins; fraternal twins who always thought they were identical twins resemble each other only as much as other fraternal twins, not as much as identical twins. That is, the main determinant of similarity in IQ is whether twins are actually identical, not whether they think they are identical. The reason for the similarity is more likely genetic than environmental.

Extensive and careful reviews of the literature have concluded that both hereditary and environmental differences do contribute to variations in human intelligence and presumably all other human characteristics. The important question is no longer do they contribute, but how do they contribute? That is, how do various genes and various experiences alter the way we develop and the way we eventually respond to certain experiences?

The fact that heredity contributes to variations in IQ scores does not mean that people are somehow stuck with the IQ score they were born with. 'Hereditary' does not mean 'unmodifiable'. Heredity does not control IQ (or anything else) directly; it controls how the individual reacts to the environment. It is possible that the 'best' environment for one group of children may not be the best for some other group.

What are the implications of the fact that both genetics and the environment influence intelligence? Every individual inherits a set of genes that determines her or his abilities. There is not, however, a single 'intelligence gene'. Intelligence is determined by a large number of different genes that determine a person's basic potential. The person's actual level of intelligence is, however, determined by the interplay of this potential with the environmental conditions the person experiences during development. Early malnutrition, a poor environment, little formal education and many other factors may inhibit intelligent behaviour.

Intelligence is one of the determinants of a person's ability to obtain schooling and jobs and therefore helps determine the person's position in society. Thus, when people grow up in a deprived environment, they are handicapped not only by their lack of money, possibly dangerous living conditions and poor health care, but also by the lack of opportunity to develop their full intellectual potential.

The environment in which a person lives can have other implications for intelligence as well. Someone who grows up in a culture other than the one in which an intelligence test was developed may have normal intelligence but perform poorly on the test because of a lack of knowledge of the test's 'culture'. In such situations, intelligence tests will not accurately reflect people's capabilities.

Conclusion

Only four of the many controversies in modern psychology have been examined. There are many others: the cause of anorexia or schizophrenia, the nature of subliminal perception, the measurement of personality and the existence of extrasensory perception. It is possible that as we get to know more and more about the science of behaviour these problems will be solved and the debates become of only historical interest. But when policy implications are associated with psychological findings debate and dispute are sure to follow.

Chapter 7:
The Psychology of
Everyday Life

7.1 Introduction

It comes as a surprise to many that psychologists study the very stuff of everyday life: why, when and how people fall in love, why certain telephone numbers are difficult to remember and equally why in big cities passers-by often ignore cries for help.

Nothing from the world of art, drama, literature or poetry has escaped psychologists. Although the novelist and the psychologist may be interested in the same thing, they approach the problem in quite different ways. Art and literature offer an intensive focus on specific issues: through paint and words powerful emotions and great truths can be stated. It is not the aim of the novelist (usually) to develop and test a theory or to posit universal truths. Novels can and do offer great and profound insights into the human condition: so much so that it has been proposed – by academic psychologists themselves – that students may learn more about life from novels than from psychology textbooks.

That branch of psychology probably most concerned with the vicissitudes of everyday life is social psychology, which is the study of human interaction. One of the first studies published in 1897 nicely illustrates the concerns of this discipline.

Triplett (1897) was interested in finding what effects the social environment had on human performance. Would people perform various tasks more effectively if other people were present or if they were absent? And how would competition with other people affect a person's performance? Triplett first explored these questions by scanning the records of bicyclists – his personal hobby – who had completed a 25-mile course under one of three conditions: (1) competing against a clock, (2) riding with a companion who paced them, and (3) competing with other riders. Under which condition would the cyclist perform with the greatest speed? The results showed that the presence of another person facilitated performance greatly. When riding alone against the clock, the cyclists averaged approximately 24 miles per hour. However, when a pacer was present the average speed was 31 miles per hour. Competition failed to improve this speed very much (the average was about 32½ miles per hour). Triplett continued his work by demonstrating that similar effects occurred when subjects in the laboratory carried out such tasks as counting, jumping up and down, or winding fishing reels.

Through experimentation and observation social psychologists develop theories – logically coherent, general propositions that explain the cause and manifestation of human behaviour. Theories sensitise one to the most important causative factors in everyday life and how they operate.

Social psychologists document everyday life and attempt prediction of behaviour in particular circumstances. The topics that are both a source of fascination for lay people and a topic of genuine research for social psychologists include the following:

1.   the causes of happiness;
2.   non-verbal or bodily communication;
3.   stereotyping and prejudice;
4.   love and attraction;
5.   conformity, compliance and obedience;
6.   altruism and helping behaviour;
7.   advertising and propaganda;
8.   sexual behaviour.

As a final test there are three short quizzes for you to try. Each has been taken from the multiple-choice tests devised by authors of American first-year social psychology textbooks (Baron and Byrne, 1981; Forsyth, Kelley and Nye, 1984; Tedeschi, Lindskold and Rosenfeld, 1985). They show not only the range of topics covered by social psychologists but also the extent of your knowledge of the psychology of everyday life!

PSYCHOLOGICAL COMMON SENSE QUIZ (1)

Test your knowledge of psychology in this multiple-choice test. Circle the letter you believe is correct.

1. A smile is recognisable as a sign of happiness and a frown as a sign of sadness:
    a. only among Britons
    b. among all people except those living in remote regions
    c. among all people
    d. at no greater than chance levels

2. With regard to sex differences in the use of non-verbal communication, ... are better at reading non-verbal messages and ... are better at sending them.
    a. men; women
    b. women; men
    c. men; men
    d. women; women

3. A high level of eye contact is interpreted as a sign of ..., a low level is interpreted as a sign of ..., and staring is interpreted as a sign of ... .
    a. friendliness; hostility; unfriendliness
    b. unfriendliness; friendliness; hostility
    c. hostility; friendliness; unfriendliness
    d. friendliness; unfriendliness; hostility

4. The fact that only six emotions are represented by distinct facial expressions means that we are capable of only six different emotional expressions. Is there anything incorrect about this statement?
    a. yes, more than six emotions have their own distinct facial expressions
    b. yes, while there are only six distinct expressions, they occur in many combinations
    c. yes, less than six emotions have their own distinct facial expressions
    d. no, the statement is true

5. Sitting so as to face us, leaning toward us and nodding in agreement to what we say are all interpreted as signs of:
    a. liking
    b. disliking
    c. hostility
    d. uneasiness

6.   Persons high in ... are generally more easily persuaded than
      persons who are low on this characteristic.
      a. the need for social approval
      b. self-esteem
      c. intelligence
      d. all of the above

7.   People are best able to withstand attempts to persuade them
      when they have had prior exposure to:
      a. no defensive arguments
      b. a supportive defensive argument
      c. a refutational defensive argument
      d. b and c would be equally effective

8.   When persons attending a fair were asked to rate their confi-
      dence in winning at various games of chance, who was most
      confident of winning?
      a. persons who had not yet placed their bet
      b. persons who had already placed their bet
      c. persons who did not intend to bet
      d. none of the above, there is no difference between them

9.   Asked to recall attitude statements that they rated a day
      earlier, people tend to recall those statements that they:
      a. agreed with
      b. disagreed with
      c. either strongly agreed with or strongly disagreed with
      d. spent the most time considering

10.   Why is it that people's written responses to questionnaires
      often do not predict their behaviour?
      a. individuals are often prevented from acting in accordance
          with their attitudes by external factors
      b. attitudes often fluctuate over time
      c. researchers often measure general attitudes and then try to
      predict specific behaviours
      d. all of the above are factors

11.   Prejudice refers to:
      a. any kind of bias or inclination toward anything
      b. positive attitudes of a special kind
      c. negative actions directed toward the persons who are its
      objects, the victims of prejudice
      d. negative attitudes of a special kind

12.   Discrimination refers to:
      a. any kind of bias or inclination toward anything
      b. positive attitudes of a special kind

  c. negative actions directed toward the persons who are its objects, the victims of prejudice

  d. negative attitudes of a special kind

13. One reasonable solution to preventing the development of prejudice is:

  a. take children away from parents who are socialising them to be prejudiced

  b. call parents' attention to the influence of parental attitudes and behaviours on their children

  c. send psychologists into homes to reinforce (reward) anti-prejudicial behaviours when they naturally occur

  d. teach parents to punish expressions of prejudice by their children by administering physical punishment

14. Contact between groups may increase rather than decrease prejudice if the contact is in a ... atmosphere.

  a. equal status

  b. religious

  c. competitive

  d. both a and b

15. In comparing the stereotypes of men and women it is evident that:

  a. the stereotypes of men are more favourable

  b. the stereotypes of women are more favourable

  c. the stereotypes of men and women are equally favourable

  d. the stereotypes of women and men are equally unfavourable

16. Given that males and females perform the same job highly and equally successfully:

  a. they will be evaluated equally (success wipes out the bias effect)

  b. females will be evaluated more favourably (the underdog becomes top dog when it finishes first)

  c. the successful females will be considered lucky

  d. the successful males will be considered lucky

17. Statement A. With regard to pictures of our own face, we prefer pictures that present a mirror image rather than a true image that others see.

  Statement B. With pictures of our friends, we prefer the true image rather than a mirror image.

  a. statement A is true; statement B is false

  b. statement B is true; statement A is false

  c. both statements are true

d.   both statements are false

18.   Which of the following aspects of the situation has (have) been
      shown to affect liking for a stranger encountered in that situa-
      tion?
      a.   whether or not the temperature is uncomfortably hot
      b.   whether or not the subject has just viewed a sad or a funny
      movie
      c.   whether the subject has just heard good vs bad news on a
      radio
      d.   all of the above

19.   Statement A. When waiting to take part in a fear-arousing
      experiment, people prefer to wait for the experiment by them-
      selves.
      Statement B. When waiting to take part in an embarrassing
      experiment, people prefer to wait for the experiment with
      other people.
      a.   both statements are true
      b.   both statements are false
      c.   statement A is true; statement B is false
      d.   statement B is true; statement A is false

20.   Which of the following is true?
      a.   within a given culture in a given era people learn to agree
      as to what is attractive
      b.   standards of beauty remain virtually constant across time
      in a given culture
      c.   standards of attractiveness are quite standard from one
      culture to the next
      d.   people place little value on physical attractiveness

21.   Statement A. Essays are judged to be of a higher quality when
      they are written by an attractive member of the opposite sex.
      Statement B. Students seeing a videotape described as a male
      and his girlfriend rated the male more positively if his girl was
      attractive than if she was unattractive.
      a.   both statements are true
      b.   both statements are false
      c.   statement A is true; statement B is false
      d.   statement B is true; statement A is false

22.   Statement A. We like people who evaluate us positively and
      dislike people who evaluate us negatively.
      Statement B. Being ignored by other group members causes a
      person to talk less and to describe himself in negative terms.
      a.   both statements are true

b.   both statements are false

c.   statement A is true; statement B is false

d.   statement B is true; statement A is false

23.   Conformity is:

a.   changing behaviour in response to direct commands from others

b.   changing behaviour in response to direct requests from others

c.   changing behaviour as a result of simple observation of the behaviours of others

d.   changing behaviour to adhere to widely accepted beliefs or standards

24.   Compliance is:

a.   changing behaviour in response to direct commands from others

b.   changing behaviour in response to direct requests from others

c.   changing behaviour as a result of simple observation of the behaviours of others

d.   changing behaviour to adhere to widely accepted beliefs or standards

25.   Among the reasons that females may have 'conformed more than males' in past experiments would be:

a.   most experimenters have been male

b.   females are inherently compliant

c.   the tasks of past experiments have been of greater interest to females

d.   females are typically coerced into compliance

26.   It appears that people will obey orders:

a.   even if the authority figure has no real power over them

b.   only if the authority figure has real power over them

c.   only if the authority figure is a real-life 'boss' of the people being given the orders

d.   both b and c

27.   When strangers witnessed a fellow person faint they were ... likely to help compared with people who had previously been introduced to one another.

a.   less

b.   more

c.   equally

d.   either a or b depending on circumstances

28.   Which of the following influences the likelihood that the

victim of a calamity will receive help?

a. whether the victim is wearing a uniform

b. familiarity of the potential helper with the setting

c. whether the victim has just donated some money to the potential helper

d. whether it is lunch time or dinner time

29. When a person is distressed in some way 'on the motorway' what determines whether that person has a good likelihood of being helped?

a. the person's age

b. the person's sex

c. whether the person has previously given aid

d. whether the person has a flat tyre or motor trouble

30. If a medical emergency occurs, which of the following is most likely to inhibit helping?

a. the presence of a person in a white coat with medical insignia

b. nothing, people always help in such situations

c. an abundance of medical skill

d. fear of getting dirty in a necessarily messy situation

31. Aggression is any form of ... directed toward the goal of harming or injuring another living being who is motivated to avoid such treatment.

a. emotion

b. thought

c. behaviour

d. instinct

32. Which of the following is most likely to counteract the influence of TV violence on children?

a. expose all children to physical punishment just after they view a violent TV show

b. be careful not to comment on TV violence, because it might draw the children's attention to that violence

c. speak disapprovingly about violent acts as these are being depicted on the TV screen

d. both a and c

33. Which of the following is a reason why people engage in competitive behaviour?

a. sometimes competition is unavoidable

b. in many cases competition is exciting

c. sometimes competition is a basis for social comparison

d. all of the above

34. Among male persons playing a competitive game it has been found that:
    a. the higher the persons' heart rates before the game, the more they won from their opponent
    b. the lower the persons' heart rates before the game, the more they won from their opponent
    c. there is no relationship between heart rate and winning
    d. arousal is a poor predictor of success

35. The best strategy to use in social exchange and negotiation seems to be:
    a. offer many concessions
    b. offer a few large concessions
    c. offer a few concessions, and keep them small in magnitude
    d. offer no concessions

36. We tend to perceive successful behaviour as stemming from ... causes; we tend to perceive unsuccessful behaviour as stemming from ... causes.
    a. internal; internal
    b. external; external
    c. internal; external
    d. external; internal

37. Which of the following is (are) a rule that people use in making judgements of fairness:
    a. equity – output in proportion to input
    b. relative needs – judging the needs (not input or output)
    c. equality – equal output irrespective of input
    d. all of the above

38. Statement A. In any given situation, the dominant response tendency (the first answer people give) is always the correct response.
    Statement B. The presence of others will improve performance when the person's dominant response tendencies in the situation are correct.
    a. both statements are true
    b. both statements are false
    c. statement A is true; statement B is false
    d. statement B is true; statement A is false

39. How is the performance of cockroaches affected by the presence of other cockroaches?
    a. there is no effect
    b. cockroaches' performance is improved
    c. cockroaches' performance is impaired

    d. either c or b, depending on whether the cockroaches'
        dominant response is correct or incorrect
40. What happens when people discuss their attitudes with a
    group of persons who share their views?
    a. peoples' attitudes become more moderate
    b. nobody changes, because people already agree
    c. peoples' attitudes become more extreme
    d. the outcome of the discussion is impossible to predict
41. 'Personal Space' is?
    a. the exact space that each person occupies when, for
    example, a person sits in a chair
    b. the physical space that legally belongs to each person (e.g.
    house and accompanying drive)
    c. the space that exists between any two persons
    d. the area immediately around persons' bodies that they
    regard as an extension of themselves
42. How friendly is your professor? Which of the following would
    give you a prediction of her/his friendliness?
    a. whether the professor is a he or a she
    b. whether the professor has office hours
    c. whether the visitors' chair in his/her office is next to the
    desk
    d. whether he/she will allow students to violate her/his
    personal space
43. When pedestrians were waiting to cross an intersection and
    were approached by a stranger who stood at varying distances
    from them:
    a. the closer the stranger stood, the slower the pedestrians
    crossed the street
    b. the closer the stranger stood, the more negatively he was
    evaluated when the pedestrians were subsequently inter-
    viewed
    c. the closer the stranger stood, the quicker the pedestrians
    crossed the street
    d. both b and c
44. Women tend to sit ... someone they like.
    a. diagonally to
    b. across from
    c. beside
    d. at an obtuse angle to
45. When people have the opportunity to help a stranger either in
    the presence of noise or in the absence of it, in which case are

they most likely to help?

a. it depends on whether the person in question has had a history of generosity

b. presence: the individual who needs help is more in need when noise is present

c. absence: noise apparently distracts people away from altruistic thoughts and makes them want to escape the scene

d. presence: noise makes people feel badly and they help someone else to restore good feelings

46. What general belief do people hold with regard to the relationship between heat and aggression:

a. the hotter it is the more the aggression

b. the hotter it is the more the aggression up to a point; when it really gets hot aggression begins to go down

c. the hotter it is the less the aggression

d. the hotter it is the less the aggression up to a point; when it really gets hot the aggression begins to go up

47. The relationship between job satisfaction and general self-satisfaction with life is:

a. self-satisfied people tend to be satisfied on the job

b. self-satisfied people tend to be dissatisfied on the job

c. curvilinear relationship (results in a curved line when plotted on a graph)

d. there is no relationship

48. Statement A. Jurors who are in favour of capital punishment are more likely to convict a defendant.

Statement B. When a law is generally unpopular members of the jury are less likely to vote for a conviction.

a. both statements are true

b. both statements are false

c. statement A is true; statement B is false

d. statement B is true; statement A is false

49. Which one of the following factors influences the decisions made by juries?

a. the degree of attitude similarity expressed by the defendant

b. the defendant's positive versus negative personality characteristics

c. how much the defendant is liked

d. all of the above

50. The attractiveness of the ... influences the jury's decision.

a. defendant
b. witness
c. both a and b
d. neither a nor b

51. Advertisements that ... are more likely to gain the attention of
the consumer.
a. are large
b. are black and white, rather than in colour
c. avoid humour
d. avoid sex

52. Which statement is true?
a. nursing home patients given greater responsibility for
themselves show an increased mortality rate
b. the nursing home patient who reacts to his environment
with apathy is better off psychologically than the prisoner
who reacts to his with anger
c. nursing home patients given plants to care for simply allow
them to die
d. memory loss in the elderly can be reversed if they are
encouraged to engage in cognitive activity and are
rewarded for doing so

53. Physically (that is sexually) attractive as opposed to unattractive people are more likely to be rated as:
a. 'sluts' if they are females
b. 'conmen' if they are male
c. more desirable to date and marry
d. sexy but 'off the wall'

54. Contrary to popular belief, alcohol:
a. is unrelated to sexual arousal or behaviour
b. enhances sexual arousal and behaviour
c. inhibits sexual arousal and behaviour
d. does not increase the ability of performing sexually, but
increases the pleasure derived from performance

55. Negative beliefs and expectations about a sexual behaviour:
a. usually are accompanied by avoidance of that behaviour
b. usually are accompanied by an irresistible urge to perform
that behaviour
c. usually are accompanied by some factual information
about that behaviour
d. both b and c

56. On the one hand attitudes toward sexual matters appear to
have changed over time. On the other hand the practice of

sexual behaviours:
a. appears to have remained the same over time
b. appears to have decreased for most behaviours
c. appears to have increased for most behaviours
d. appears to have increased for most behaviours in the case of males but not in the case of females

57. The more knowledge a teenager has about sex,
a. the more favourable his or her attitude toward contraception
b. the earlier he or she engages in intercourse
c. the more likely he or she is to become pregnant during adolescence
d. both a and b

ANSWERS TO PSYCHOLOGICAL COMMON SENSE QUIZ (1)

1, C; 2, D; 3, D; 4, B; 5, A; 6, A; 7, C; 8, B; 9, C; 10, D; 11, D; 12, C; 13, B; 14, C; 15, A; 16, C; 17, B; 18, D; 19, B; 20, A; 21, A; 22, A; 23, D; 24, B; 25, A; 26, A; 27, A; 28, B; 29, B; 30, A; 31, C; 32, C; 33, D; 34, A; 35, C; 36, C; 37, D; 38, D; 39, D; 40, C; 41, D; 42, C; 43, D; 44, C; 45, C; 46, A; 47, A; 48, A; 49, D; 50, C; 51, A; 52, D; 53, C; 54, C; 55, A; 56, C; 57, A

PSYCHOLOGICAL COMMON SENSE QUIZ (2)

Test your knowledge of psychology in this multiple-choice quiz. Circle the letter you believe is correct.

1. Researchers in psychology generally use deception in order to:
a. maintain an individual's alertness
b. increase external validity
c. reduce experimenter bias
d. conceal the true purpose of the experiment from individuals

2. Ethical concerns in conducting research are evidenced by:
a. the use of deception
b. safeguarding confidentiality of participant responses
c. safeguarding against unnecessary anxiety
d. all of the above

3. The mere physical appearance of a psychological researcher can affect the responses of individuals:
a. true, and it is likely to occur in all experiments

b.   true, but it seldom occurs
c.   false, no empirical evidence has supported this notion
d.   false, individuals are not affected by such superficial cues

4.   A policeman stopped a motorist who was very obviously speeding. The gentleman behind the wheel claimed that he was a new doctor in town and was just checking out how long it would take him to get to the hospital in case of an emergency. The doctor:
a.   was presenting an excuse
b.   was presenting a justification
c.   was presenting an apology
d.   none of the above

5.   Presenting oneself as attractive:
a.   increases the probability of rewards
b.   promotes an image of predictability and stability
c.   promotes an image of being a rule-abiding individual
d.   all of the above

6.   Evidence about stereotypes indicates that they:
a.   generally involve unfavourable evaluations
b.   are never true
c.   are sometimes correct
d.   are usually correct in judging ethnic groups
e.   none of the above

7.   When I think of Russians, I think of ignorance, secrecy and deceitfulness. My impression of Russians is:
a.   produced by stereotypes
b.   flawed with logical error
c.   based on limited information or interaction with Russians
d.   all of the above

8.   Superstition is associated with:
a.   lack of control over events
b.   fear
c.   anxiety
d.   ignorance of causes of events
e.   all of the above

9.   Psychologists study attitudes because:
a.   attitudes are excellent predictors of behaviour
b.   attitudes are assumed to be related to behaviour
c.   they are learned through social interactions
d.   they rarely change

10. Assume that you are a subject in a laboratory experiment and you are hooked up to a pupilographic device (measures the

size of your pupils). Every time you are asked about smoking
marijuana, your pupils dilate. This reaction occurs because:
a.   you probably have a negative attitude toward grass
b.   you probably have a positive attitude toward smoking pot
c.   you probably are nervous and tension is related to pupil
dilation
d.   you are somewhat surprised by the question and pupil size
is highly correlated with unexpected events
e.   b or c

11.   You see a photograph of a grotesquely mutilated human
corpse, and a pupilograph shows that your pupils are
constricted. What could a psychologist conclude about your
attitude toward the photograph?
a.   you have a positive reaction to it
b.   you have a negative reaction to it
c.   you have neither a positive or a negative reaction to it
d.   none of the above

12.   Which of the following can enhance the effectiveness of
persuasive communications (i.e. advertising or propaganda) ?
a.   drawing a conclusion for the audience
b.   increasing the number of people supporting the message
c.   increasing the frequency of arguments
d.   all of the above

13.   Persuasive communications may be enhanced by:
a.   a steady gaze by the source
b.   a fluent speaking style by the source
c.   the use of humour by the source
d.   all of the above

14.   Social influence occurs when one person brings about a
change in another person's:
a.   beliefs
b.   attitudes
c.   values
d.   behaviour
e.   all of the above

15.   People who possess positive characteristics, such as status,
esteem, prestige and attractiveness:
a.   tend to attempt influence less often than other people
b.   tend to attempt influence more often than other people
c.   are no more likely to attempt influence than other people
d.   are reluctant to use their power over other people

16.   Which person would be perceived as most persuasive?

a.   an attorney who argues in favour of the court system
b.   a criminal who argues against the prison system
c.   a criminal who argues in favour of the court system
d.   a social worker who argues for welfare programmes
e.   a biologist who argues in favour of cancer research

17.   A person is likely to use threats and/or punishments:
a.   in self-defence
b.   when there is no confidence other forms of influence will work
c.   in competition for scarce resources
d.   to establish a reputation for being tough
e.   all of the above

18.   The probability that a child will be abused:
a.   is directly related to the amount of stress experienced by the parents
b.   is increased if the child is retarded or handicapped
c.   increases with the number of children, up to five, in the family
d.   all of the above

19.   Viewing pornographic materials has been clearly shown to:
a.   increase aggression
b.   decrease aggression
c.   both increase and decrease aggressiveness
d.   have no effect on aggressiveness

20.   Anger:
a.   typically leads to acts of physical aggression
b.   is an emotion which may lead to aggression occasionally and in special cases
c.   never leads to aggressive tendencies
d.   is a form of self-punishment

21.   When researchers staged a fight between a man and a woman, 65% of male passers-by intervened if:
a.   the woman screamed for help
b.   the woman was being physically attacked
c.   the woman yelled 'I don't know you!'
d.   the man screamed for help

22.   An individual takes less responsibility in emergency situations:
a.   when others are present
b.   when people with special expertise are present
c.   when the individual perceives him/herself as more competent than others

    d. a and b

    e. all of the above

23. Which of the following is an important factor in whether or not action will be taken by bystanders in an emergency situation?

    a. the crisis is life-threatening

    b. the bystander's relation to the victim

    c. the presence of an individual who offers help

    d. b and c

24. People appreciate help from a relatively ... person more than they do from a relatively ... person.

    a. poor, wealthy

    b. intelligent, stupid

    c. expert, non-expert

    d. wealthy, poor

    e. non-expert, expert

25. Assume that you are a white male bystander who witnesses another person fall down on the street. Of the following, which victim would receive the most help?

    a. a black male

    b. a person who appears to be drunk

    c. a person who is bleeding profusely

    d. a person who appears to be ill

    e. not enough information to make a prediction

26. Stereotypes about physically attractive people include the belief that attractive people are:

    a. kinder than unattractive people

    b. more interesting than unattractive people

    c. better in character than unattractive people

    d. happier in their marriages than unattractive people

    e. all of the above

27. People who are alone are almost always:

    a. lonely

    b. unhappy

    c. bored

    d. helpless and invisible

    e. none of the above

28. The largest group of lonely people are:

    a. old people

    b. young married women

    c. people between the ages of 18 and 25

    d.   people between the ages of 40 and 55

    e.   teenagers

29.   People prefer to affiliate (attach to) with:

    a.   another person who is depressed

    b.   a person who is happy

    c.   others who have higher status than themselves

    d.   none of the above

30.   As compared with unattractive people, physically attractive people:

    a.   are perceived as more successful

    b.   are believed to be better parents

    c.   receive less sympathy from others after a misfortune

    d.   are seen as more maladjusted

    e.   a and c

31.   Boys are more likely to play with guns and girls with dolls because:

    a.   males are genetically stronger and more aggressive than girls, and so prefer to play with more aggressive toys

    b.   parents encourage different forms of play in boys and girls

    c.   girls have a maternal instinct to practise mothering and so prefer to play with dolls

    d.   a and c

    e.   all of the above

32.   Analyses of male–female conversations reveal:

    a.   women talk more often and for longer intervals than men

    b.   women talk to men about 'female' topics whilst men talk to women about 'male' topics

    c.   males more frequently interrupt females than females interrupt males

    d.   females more frequently interrupt males than males interrupt females

    e.   a and b

33.   Which factor may be responsible for an increase in reported rapes?

    a.   increased education about rape

    b.   feminist groups organised to facilitate the reporting of rape

    c.   changing attitudes among law enforcement officials

    d.   a and b

    e.   a, b and c

34.   People are likely to make the judgement that a rape occurred when:

a. force was used
b. resistance was strong
c. protests were made early before the encounter
d. b and c
e. all of the above

35. Analyses of male–female conversations show that:
    a. females talk more
    b. males talk more
    c. females smile and laugh more often
    d. a and c
    e. b and c

36. Most rapes:
    a. are unplanned and impulsive actions
    b. are carried out by a person acting alone
    c. occur in alleys, car parks and other dimly lit areas
    d. involve victims who are young and attractive
    e. none of the above

37. A rape victim:
    a. can be anywhere from 3 to 90 years of age
    b. is more likely to be white than black
    c. tends to dress or act in a manner that precipitates an attack
    d. is more likely to be a member of lower socioeconomic classes
    e. all of the above

38. When a member dissents (expresses different opinion) against a majority in the group, members:
    a. express approval of his/her courage
    b. are likely to perceive him/her as a leader
    c. are likely to reject and dislike the person
    d. a and b
    e. none of the above

39. As compared with members of small groups, members of large groups:
    a. are more satisfied
    b. participate in more group activities
    c. are more friendly toward one another
    d. b and c
    e. none of the above

40. Eyewitnesses:
    a. remember the details of a violent crime better than one that is non-violent
    b. typically underestimate the duration of a crime

    c. who are more confident also tend to be more accurate
    d. a and b
    e. none of the above

41.   Attractive defendants are:
    a. less likely to be found guilty in jury trials
    b. are given lighter jail sentences when found guilty
    c. less likely to be found guilty of swindling
    d. more likely to take the witness stand in their own defence
    e. a and b

42.   As compared with white defendants, black defendants are:
    a. more likely to be found guilty by white jurors
    b. less likely to be found guilty by black jurors
    c. more likely to be found guilty by black jurors
    d. less likely to be found guilty by white jurors
    e. none of the above

43.   Among people who oppose the death penalty:
    a. there are more blacks than whites
    b. there are more men than women
    c. there are more whites than blacks
    d. there are more orientals than blacks

44.   Adolescents who smoke:
    a. realise that smoking has negative effects on health
    b. underestimate the number of other adolescents who smoke
    c. overestimate the number of other adolescents who smoke
    d. do not realise that smoking has negative effects on health
    e. a and c

45.   Research conducted on the institutional elderly found that ... was associated with better health and longevity.
    a. attractiveness of the nurses
    b. availability of psychiatrists
    c. feeling of control
    d. visits from family members

46.   In seating arrangements:
    a. people who sit close together tend to like one another
    b. people indicate their power by sitting further away from the leader of the group
    c. a person who sits at the head of the table probably is disinterested in the group
    d. people tend to sit near a leader they dislike
    e. a and b

ANSWERS TO PSYCHOLOGICAL COMMON SENSE QUIZ (2)
1, d; 2, d; 3, b; 4, b; 5, d; 6, c; 7, d; 8, e; 9, b; 10, e; 11, b; 12, d; 13, d;
14, e; 15, b; 16, c; 17, e; 18, d; 19, c; 20, b; 21, c; 22, d; 23, d; 24, d;
25, d; 26, e; 27, e; 28, c; 29, b; 30, a; 31, b; 32, c; 33, e; 34, e; 35, e;
36, e; 37, a; 38, c; 39, e; 40, e; 41, e; 42, a; 43, a; 44, e; 45, c; 46, a

PSYCHOLOGY COMMON SENSE QUIZ (3)

*Test your knowledge of psychology in this multiple-choice quiz. Circle the letter
you believe is correct.*

1. A study concludes that A is correlated with B. Therefore:
    a. A causes B
    b. B causes A
    c. either A causes B or B causes A
    d. A is related to B
2. The impact of feedback from others is most powerful when it
    comes from:
    a. acquaintances
    b. significant others
    c. relatives
    d. the opposite sex
3. Androgynous individuals:
    a. are as masculine as they are feminine
    b. display behaviours and abilities of both sex-roles
    c. are masculine if female, feminine if male
    d. display behaviours that match their sex-role
4. People tend to assume that physically attractive people:
    a. possess many positive attributes
    b. are very self-centred
    c. possess many negative attributes
    d. possess the same qualities as less attractive people
5. Which statement is true?
    a. some facial expressions convey a universal meaning
    b. emblems (hand gestures) are interpreted similarly in all
    cultures
    c. touching a person is always a good way to show
    friendliness
    d. the longer you look at people, the more they tend to like
    you
6. To create a sense of involvement and friendliness when inter-
    acting with another person, you should:

     a.   cross your arms across your chest
     b.   never break eye contact
     c.   smile
     d.   all of the above

7.   If you are introduced to someone whom you believe is dumb (not very bright), you are likely to ask questions that:
     a.   will disconfirm your beliefs
     b.   will support your beliefs
     c.   avoid reference to intelligence
     d.   test that person's intelligence

8.   Studies of eyewitness testimony argue that witnesses are:
     a.   as accurate as they are confident
     b.   more accurate than they are confident
     c.   confident even when they are inaccurate
     d.   not confident when they are inaccurate

9.   Following a close game, your school wins by scoring a last-second, risky shot. You are likely to attribute the victory to ... and Fred, a fan of the losing team, is likely to attribute the victory to ... .
     a.   ability; luck
     b.   luck; ability
     c.   luck; luck as well
     d.   ability; ability as well

10.   Attitudes:
     a.   are types of behaviour
     b.   are very unstable
     c.   can't be accurately measured
     d.   sometimes determine behaviour
     e.   once formed, don't change

11.   Opinion polls:
     a.   are valid provided they are properly conducted
     b.   do not need to be based on a representative sample
     c.   are a good indictor of private attitudes
     d.   rarely yield valid results

12.   Newspaper and magazine polls that generalise their findings to a large population (i.e. the whole country) should have a minimum sample size of:
     a.   500
     b.   1500
     c.   3000
     d.   10 000

13.   Pupil dilation usually indicates:

    a.   a positive reaction
    b.   a negative reaction
    c.   a strong emotion
    d.   sexual arousal

14.   Racism in America seems to be decreasing according to ...,
      but not according to ... .
    a.   psychologists, blacks
    b.   blacks, whites
    c.   whites, opinion polls
    d.   opinion polls, behavioural measures

15.   Our attitudes are more closely linked to our behaviour if they
      are:
    a.   extreme
    b.   available
    c.   formed through direct experience
    d.   relevant
    e.   all of the above

16.   Stereotypes, while not intrinsically prejudicial, tend to:
    a.   encourage overgeneralisation about the out-group
    b.   act in ways that fulfil their out-group
    c.   be negatively toned
    d.   be inflexible and hard to change
    e.   all of the above

17.   The outcome of persuasion depends on the:
    a.   nature of the communication itself
    b.   the source of the communication
    c.   the characteristics of the audience
    d.   all of the above

18.   In the study conducted in a paint store, the salesperson was
      more influential when he had:
    a.   done a good deal of painting with the brand
    b.   recently used the same amount of paint that the customer
       was planning to buy
    c.   had not tried the brand
    d.   was viewed as trustworthy
    e.   smiled and seemed pleasant

19.   Research suggests that you should use a ... speech rate if you
      want to increase your credibility when making a speech.
    a.   rapid
    b.   slow
    c.   moderate
    d.   variable

20.   Which statement is true?
       a.   people who speak slowly are more persuasive than fast
       talkers
       b.   rhetorical questions are most effective when listeners are
       involved with the topic
       c.   people we like tend to be more persuasive than people we
       dislike
       d.   all of the above are true

21.   Rhetorical questions are most effective when your:
       a.   audience is uninvolved and your argument is strong
       b.   audience appears uninvolved
       c.   argument is strong and your audience is involved
       d.   audience is involved with the issue
       e.   arguments are weak

22.   Fear appeals are effective only when:
       a.   the appeals are quite strong and fear provoking
       b.   the receiver thinks the negative consequences are very
       likely
       c.   the receiver thinks the recommendations for avoiding the
       negative consequences will work
       d.   all of the above are true

23.   ... of the studies conducted to date suggest that women are
       more easily persuaded than men.
       a.   virtually all
       b.   a majority (80%)
       c.   a small number (16%)
       d.   almost none (2%)

24.   Shyness:
       a.   causes people to feel that their personal relationships are
       too few
       b.   is one of the most common forms of social anxiety
       c.   is a disabling fear of situations where one is exposed to the
       scrutiny of others
       d.   involves psychological rather than physiological symptoms

25.   In one study where male subjects talked briefly with a woman
       by telephone:
       a.   the subjects' behaviour varied in accordance with their
       imagined attractiveness of their partner
       b.   the subjects rated their partner more positively when they
       thought she was attractive
       c.   the women behaved more positively when talking to men
       who thought their partner was attractive

     d. all of the above
26.   Which statement is least accurate?
     a. we tend to like people who live close to us
     b. exposure to a stimulus tends to increase attraction for that stimulus
     c. we like people who provide us with rewards
     d. we are attracted to people with qualities that complement our own qualities
27.   Compared with women, men:
     a. are more idealistic about sex
     b. adopt more responsible attitudes about sex
     c. are less accepting of premarital sex
     d. are more sexually permissive
28.   Research suggests that for someone to help a person-in-need/victim depends on:
     a. the nature of the situation
     b. the characteristics of the helper
     c. the characteristics of the victim
     d. all of the above
29.   Which of the following is true?
     a. people help more in ambiguous situations
     b. helping rates are higher in urban settings than in rural areas
     c. people tend to help people who are similar to them in some way
     d. none of the above
30.   Evidence indicates that:
     a. on average, women help more than men
     b. on average, men help more than women
     c. androgynous people help less than feminine people
     d. androgynous people help more than men
31.   Evidence indicates that exposure to ... pornography leads to ... in violence against women.
     a. erotic; increases
     b. aggressive; increases
     c. aggressive; decreases
     d. erotic; no change
32.   Studies indicate that if you want your fellow group members to like you, you should start off the discussion ... and end up ...
     a. neutral; agreeing
     b. agreeing; neutral
     c. agreeing; agreeing

    d. disagreeing; neutral
33. Evidence indicates that smaller juries ... than larger juries.
    a. take less time to deliberate
    b. reach harsher decisions
    c. reach more lenient decisions
    d. listen to high-status members more
34. Which statement is true?
    a. people can't be trained to be good leaders
    b. good leaders make friends with their subordinates
    c. group members are often biased against women leaders
    d. leadership effectiveness depends on the situation rather than the leader's traits
35. Which statement is true about personal space?
    a. generally, individuals' personal space requirements are constant across situations
    b. different individuals require different amounts of personal space
    c. personal space needs are the same no matter what your cultural background
    d. all of the above are true
36. Men, more than women:
    a. have smaller personal space needs
    b. react positively to space invasions
    c. allow others to approach them closely
    d. react negatively when intruders sit across from them
    e. all of the above

ANSWERS TO PSYCHOLOGICAL COMMON SENSE QUIZ (3)

1, d; 2, b; 3, b; 4, a; 5, a; 6, c; 7, b; 8, c; 9, a; 10, d; 11, a; 12, b; 13, c; 14, d; 15, e; 16, e; 17, d; 18, b; 19, a; 20, c; 21, b; 22, d; 23, b; 24, b; 25, d; 26, d; 27, d; 28, d; 29, d; 30, b; 31, b; 32, c; 33, a; 34, c; 35, b; 36, d

How did you do on these three social psychological tests? Our research shows that most people get about one-third to a half correct, even psychology students themselves.

Social psychologists are interested in how the actual or imagined presence of others influences individuals' behaviour, emotions and thoughts. They have been responsible for showing to the world a picture of a typical person that is not the caring, altruistic, independently minded character we may have hoped to see. Various famous studies in psychology have shown the average human being to be selfish, conforming and brutal.

In order to provide some examples of research in social psychology its three perhaps most important study areas will be discussed. They are typical of social psychological research but show only a very small part of the extensive research programme of social psychologists.

7.2   The Bad Samaritan

Over 20 years ago a single, horrific, but all too common incident that was widely reported started a research programme in psychology. Late one night in March 1964 Catherine Genovese was attacked by a lone male as she returned to her home in Queens, New York. Her screams drove the assailant off at first, but he quickly returned when it became apparent that her shouts were to no avail. Again and again he tore at the woman with his knife, but her frantic cries brought only silence from the surrounding apartment houses. In the half hour or so it took to kill Kitty Genovese, no one came to her aid. The next day when the police interviewed the residents of the nearby buildings, 38 admitted hearing Miss Genovese's screams. Although they might well have been afraid of confronting the murderer, no one had even bothered to pick up the telephone to call the police.

Why hadn't anyone done anything? Were the onlookers so callous that they didn't even care what was happening? Shortly after Miss Genovese's death, a writer for the *New York Times*, A.M. Rosenthal, wrote a book about this tragic event and blamed the neighbours' inaction on the sense of alienation produced by life in a huge city. Only in limited cases, he thought, would 'a person step out of his or her shell toward his brother'. But isn't this too simple – and too sweeping – an indictment of modern urban life? City dwellers do help each other on occasion, even when they don't know each other. How can we account for the apparent lack of concern shown by Miss Genovese's neighbours? Is one individual always a hero and another always indifferent to the welfare of his fellows? It is very likely that at least some of the people who turned their backs on Miss Genovese's screams had given money to charity or donated blood on behalf of an anonymous patient. When are we likely to be helpful, and when aren't we willing to aid those in need?

For nearly a quarter of a decade social psychologists have done studies on what they call the *unresponsive bystander*. This is not the good but the bad samaritan who, according to the biblical story (Luke 10), was the levite, who seeing the robbed man, 'passed by on the other side'.

Dozens of studies have been done on this topic including a classical study called 'From Jerusalem to Jericho' which actually studied seminary students as they walked from a theological lecture on the good samaritan (Darley and Batson, 1973).

The studies, nearly always in the field research tradition (see Chapter 3), frequently require a stooge or experimental confederate supposedly requiring help and measuring passer-by reactions. Thus psychologists can investigate whether the presence of blood, physical disfigurement, alcohol intoxication etc. affects whether or not people help.

Generally the theories in this area try to explain why people do help yet the research has concentrated almost exclusively on why people do not help. Study after study does not reveal us as caring, altruistic and helpful but as unresponsive. And, curiously, the more people there are to witness an emergency, the less likely any are to help.

So, why don't we help each other? There appear to be at least four reasons:

- *The ambiguity of emergencies*: Surprising as it may seem, it is not always clear what is going on in an emergency or who needs what kind of help. As Sabini (1995) notes with regard to the Genovese case: 'Emergencies aren't things one can measure with a ruler; we have no chemical tests for emergencies. The most obvious thing for the onlookers to do was to find out what other people were thinking. But how could they do that? Well, they could look at what other people, who also must have heard the screams, were doing. They could look at, and through, other windows that faced the courtyard. In those windows, what they saw were other people. And what were those other people doing? They were looking back at them. This suggested to the witnesses that all was well. After all, those other people in the windows weren't running downstairs to see what was happening. Apparently those other people didn't think there was an emergency going on beneath them. Thus, the witnesses misread each other's passivity as a sign that they were convinced that nothing was very wrong, when, in fact, it was just a sign that no one was *sure* something *was* wrong' (p. 40).
- *Pluralistic ignorance*: This is a related phenomenon whereby

people misinterpret others' behaviour. A good example of this can be found in the lecture room. The teacher going through a difficult problem notices blank stares so asks 'do you understand; is this clear?'. But nobody says no, not wanting to be the first to admit ignorance. Thus nobody owns up although all are confused and this may lead many to believe they are the only people not understanding. In emergency situations people respond (or do not respond) to what they believe everybody thinks is appropriate rather than to the actual consensus of beliefs. That is, you might feel the situation requires your help but as nobody else is helping, or seems to believe the situation is one that requires you to behave as a good samaritan, you don't.

- *Diffusion of responsibility*: This helps explain why the more people there are at accidents, the fewer help and vice versa. The logic is this. If someone had decided that there really was an emergency, then that person surely would have known that *someone* should do something – come to the victim's aid or at least call the police. But that still wouldn't help decide that question of just *who* should do something. There is an important difference between knowing that *someone* should act and knowing that *you* should act. The problem is that everyone watching may have believed that someone was responsible to act, but everyone may also have believed that *someone else* was the someone who was responsible.

- *Fear of* faux pas *and social embarrassment*: Anyone who has genuinely offered help only to be rebuffed by someone who felt patronised by a social misinterpretation knows the shame, hurt and discomfort this causes. Few people are trained sufficiently in first aid and other relevant skills required in emergencies. Some in fact fear their clumsy attempts at help may aggravate rather than alleviate crisis situations. So, rather than volunteer their help which they may feel quite necessary, they do nothing.

- *De-individuation*: Big cities where bystander unresponsiveness is at its highest are anonymous places. The more people remain anonymous, dressed like others doing similar things, the more they are de-individualised and unlikely to help. Conversely, the more they can be identified the more likely they are to help.

The number and actions of bystanders seem the single strongest determinant of whether people help others in need. Simply observing others help makes one more likely to help. The more familiar the situation, the clearer the cry for specific help, the stronger the cultural norms of social responsibility and reciprocity – the more likely people are to help.

What of the characteristics of the 'victim'? Usually females receive more help than males; people tend to favour people of their own ethnic, religious or occupational group; non-bleeding people are helped more than bleeding; and those not at personal fault (i.e. drunk) are helped more.

And the characteristics of those who are altruistic? People with high self-esteem help more; so do those in a good mood. Pervin (1988) has offered an unusual perspective on why people are altruistic. According to psychoanalytic theory, people may behave in an altruistic way either as an expression of an impulse or as a defence against the expression of an impulse. In the former case, a person may behave in a helpful, altruistic way as an expression of love based on the early mother–child relationship. The altruistic person identifies with the giving, helping mother and offers assistance to those in need. This is identification with a helping figure which can take place with other helping figures in the person's past. Yet as a defence against an impulse, extreme helping behaviour or altruism can be part of a neurotic effort to cope with anxiety, guilt and hostility. The person who felt deprived of help as a child may be extremely helpful and charitable as an adult as part of an effort to deal with earlier anxieties. Instead of feeling helplessly in need of assistance from others, they can become the active giver and at the same time identify with the recipient of their assistance. They are both giver and recipient of their assistance: they are both giver and recipient at the same time. An example is of the person who copes with feelings of guilt about his or her own greed and envy by constantly giving to others. In some cases the guilt can lead to a kind of masochism in which the person is charitable to the extent of putting him/herself into debt or needlessly risking injury to the self in the service of assistance to others.

Finally, there is the kind of behaviour that is generous and kind as a defence against underlying hostility. Such a person uses the defence known as reaction formation, masking any expression of aggression with an ever-present helpful attitude. Altruism and other forms of helping behaviour can come from at least two different routes, the routes being almost opposite in their underlying basis. The one involves a healthy identification with an altruistic figure, the other a neurotic effort to cope with feelings of guilt, anxiety and hostility. Although the latter behaviour generally takes on a more rigid quality, and generates more anxiety when helping behaviour is blocked from expression, the two bases for altruism are often hard to distinguish in terms of the manifest behaviour. Furthermore, many expressions of altruism express both healthy and neurotic components in terms of their deeper meanings for the individual.

The research in social psychology has shown quite clearly that we are not often good samaritans. There are particular conditions under which we help our fellow man but too frequently we are content to pass by on the other side.

7.3   Only Obeying Orders

When Adolf Eichmann was tried for his part in the Holocaust, his defence was that he was only obeying orders. The American soldiers at Mi Lai in Vietnam who followed Lt Calley's orders said likewise. It is easy to argue that insane men during wartime perform such acts but that it would never happen to people like you and me. But psychologists have shown that it can and does!

Sociologists who focus on groups and who take conformity and obedience for granted are interested in deviance (labelling, stigma, discrimination). Psychology, whose unit of analysis is the individual, takes deviance and idiosyncrasy for granted and focuses on conformity. Why do people comply, conform and obey the orders of others? We should point out that obedience and conformity are not the same, and differ in the following four ways:

1.   *Hierarchy*: Conformity regulates the behaviour of equal status subjects while obedience links one status to another.
2.   *Imitation*: Conformity is imitation, while obedience is not.
3.   *Explicitness*: In obedience the prescription for action (an order) is explicit, while in conformity the requirement of going along with the group is implicit.
4.   *Voluntarism*: Because conformity is a response to implicit pressure the subject interprets his/her own behaviour as voluntary. However, the obedience situation is publicly defined as one devoid of voluntarism and thus the subject can fall back on the public definition of the situation as the full explanation of his/her action.

Perhaps the most dramatic experiment in psychology this century was that of Stanley Milgram (1974) whose book, published over 20 years ago, caused a storm. Indeed, it is now impossible to replicate his study for ethical reasons. What the study showed was that nice, normal, middle-class Americans were prepared, for a $4.00 fee, to shock to death an innocent man who wasn't too hot on memorising paired words. In essence the study went like this: Milgram attracted people to the experiment, through an advertisement in a local paper, in a laboratory. He told them they were there to take part in an experiment on human learning. Their particular job, supposedly determined by drawing lots (but actually fixed), was to consist of delivering electric shock to a learner – a jolly middle-aged man – each time he made an error in learning associations between paired words. The subject saw their fellow volunteer strapped into a chair; they saw electrode paste and electrodes attached to his arm. The experimenter, a white-coated autocrat, said that the paste was to avoid blisters and burns. In some cases, they heard their pupil-to-be tell the experimenter that he had a slight heart condition, but the experimenter reassured them that although the shocks might be painful, they would cause no permanent tissue damage.

The experimenter conducted 'the teacher' (our naïve volunteer subject) to another room and showed him/her the machine with which he/she was to deliver the 'punishment'. It was an impressive-looking device with 30 switches marked from 15 to 450 volts in 15-volt increments. Below the numerical labels were others characterising the shocks. These ranged from 'SLIGHT SHOCK' at the low end to 'INTENSE SHOCK' in the middle, through 'DANGER: SEVERE SHOCK', and finally to a simple, stark 'XXX' beneath the last two switches. The experimenter, a psychologist, gave him/her a sample shock of 45 volts, which was within the slight shock range and was only one-tenth of the shock that would be delivered by the final lever.

The experimenter then explained what to do. The 'teacher' was to read the learner lists of word pairs. Then he or she was to read the first word of each pair back to the learner with four other words, one of which was the correct completion of the pair. The learner was to answer this multiple-choice test by pressing one of four buttons to indicate his impression of the right answer.

The 'teacher' was to give the learner a 15-volt shock for his first wrong answer, and was to shock him again every time he made a mistake. The 'teacher' was to increase his punishment one shock level (15 volts) for every wrong answer. The learner was a friend of the experimenter; the only real shock delivered was the sample shock given to the 'teacher'. But the teacher didn't know this.

The experimental sessions began innocuously enough; the

learner got some of the pairs right, but he soon made an error and was 'given' a mild 15-volt shock. Until 75 volts, the 'teacher' had no indication that he/she was causing the learner much pain. But at 75 volts, the learner grunted in pain. The 'teacher' could hear the grunt through the wall separating them. At 120 volts, the learner shouted to the experimenter that the shocks were becoming painful. At 150 volts, the 'learner' screamed, 'Experimenter get me out of here! I won't be in the experiment any more! I refuse to go on!' This response made it clear to both that the shocks had become very painful and, perhaps more important, that the learner was no longer a willing participant. He was now a captive of the experimenter (Milgram, the psychologist) and his agent – the 'teacher' (our neighbourly subject).

The learner continued to cry out in pain, with his cries increasing in intensity, becoming agonised screams once the shocks reached 270 volts. The experimenter and 'teacher' were now engaged in torture!

At 300 volts, the learner shouted in desperation that he would no longer respond to the word pairs. The experimenter – our, cold, steely authority figure – matter-of-factly informed the subject to treat no response as if it were an error, and to go on administering shock. From this point on, the subject heard no more from the learner; he/she did not know whether the learner was alive. The subject could certainly see that the torture had become pointless torture, whatever else was true; because the learner was no longer answering, he/she was surely no longer taking part in a learning experiment. When the subject reached the end of the shock board, he/she was told to continue using the last lever for all subsequent 'mistakes'. The subjects were, of course, physically free to leave the experiment, to relieve the victim's suffering; the victim was strapped in, but nothing barred the subject's escape.

Twenty-six of the 40 male subjects who took part in the experiment continued to the end; exactly the same number of women, 26 out of 40, continued to the end. The fully obedient subjects stopped administering the 450-volt shocks to the victim only when *the experimenter* told them to stop.

There have been several replications of the experiment in other countries. The rates of obedience vary from place to place, but the general fact is that, in all countries, subjects obey at rates most would never expect.

Ordinary people seemed happy to obey the orders of a torturer! One of the fascinating aspects of the study was the close record

Milgram kept of how his individual subjects reacted. It is worth recording the reactions of one: a divinity Professor:

> A somewhat gaunt, ascetic man, this subject could be taken for a New England minister. In fact, he teaches Old Testament liturgy at a major divinity school. In this Proximity condition, he adjusted his seat to look at the learner while administering shocks. While reading the word pairs, he employs exaggerated precision in his pronunciation, and seems curt and officious in saying 'Correct.' Whenever the learner makes an error, he appears almost to be chastising him for his failing. Each time he administers a shock, his lips are drawn back, and he bares his teeth. An excessive fastidiousness characterizes all his actions. After administering 150 volts he balks at going further. The experimenter states that the learner's protests are to be disregarded, and the experiment must continue:

EXPERIMENTER: It's absolutely essential to the experiment that we continue.
SUBJECT: I understand that statement, but I don't understand why the experiment is placed above this person's life.
EXPERIMENTER: There is no permanent tissue damage.
SUBJECT: Well, that's your opinion. If he doesn't want to continue, I'm taking orders from him.
EXPERIMENTER: You have no other choice, sir, you must go on.
SUBJECT: If this were Russia maybe, but not in America.
(The experiment is terminated.)

In his discussion with the experimenter, the subject seems in no way intimidated by the experimenter's status but rather treats him as a dull technician who does not see the full implications of what he is doing. When the experimenter assures him of the safety of the shock generator, the subject, with some exasperation, brings up the question of the emotional rather than physiological effects on the learner.

SUBJECT (spontaneously): Surely you've considered the ethics of this thing (extremely agitated). Here he doesn't want to go on, and you think that the experiment is more important? Have you examined him? Do you know what his physical state is? Say this man had a weak heart (quivering voice).
EXPERIMENTER: We know the machine, sir.

SUBJECT: But you don't know the man you're experimenting on.... That's very risky (gulping and tremulous). What about the fear that man had? It's impossible for you to determine what effect that has on him ... the fear that he himself is generating.... But go ahead, you ask me questions; I'm not here to question you.

He limits his questioning, first because he asserts he does not have a right to question, but one feels that he considers the experimenter too rigid and limited a technician to engage in intelligent dialogue. One notes further his spontaneous mention of ethics, raised in a didactic manner and deriving from his professional position as teacher of religion. Finally, it is interesting that he initially justified his breaking off the experiment not by asserting disobedience but by asserting that he would then take orders from the victim.

Thus, he speaks of an equivalence between the experimenter's and the leaner's orders and does not disobey so much as shifts the person from whom he will take orders.

After explaining the true purpose of the experiment, the experimenter asks, 'What in your opinion is the most effective way of strengthening resistance to inhumane authority?'

The subject answers, 'If one had as one's ultimate authority God, then it trivializes human authority.'

Again, the answer for this man lies not in the repudiation of authority but in the substitution of good – that is, divine – authority for bad. (pp. 47–49)

In this study and others that followed, various factors were examined to see how they increased or decreased the obedience of experimental subjects. A summary of these findings is given in Table 7.1.

But the central question remains: Why do people do it – obey orders to kill? To a large extent these findings can be explained in terms of the social psychology of the experience.

1.   *Evaluation apprehension.* When people take part in a research project, they often feel that the investigator, a psychologist, is evaluating them. This concern over evaluation is particularly strong in research settings, because people assume that the investigators are insightful appraisers who will notice any flaws they fail to hide. If Milgram's subjects experienced evaluation apprehension, they may have worried about the impression

TABLE 7.1: Summary of variables that affect obedience	
Variable	Effect
Proximity to victim	Subjects obey less the closer they are to a suffering victim
Proximity to authority	Subjects obey less the further away the authority who gives commands is
Institutional setting	Conducting Milgram's obedience experiments in a run-down office building away from Yale University reduced obedience only slightly
Conformity pressures	Obedient peers increase subject's obedience; rebellious peers greatly reduce obedience
Role of person giving commands	People obey others most when others are perceived to be legitimate authorities; in Milgram's studies, subjects generally obeyed the experimenter but did not obey other subjects
Personality traits	In Milgram's studies, assessed traits correlated weakly with obedience
Gender	Milgram found no difference between men and women in their average levels of obedience
Cultural differences	Cross-cultural replications show some variation across cultures, but obedience in Milgram-type studies tends to be high regardless of culture
Attitudinal and ideological factors	Religious people are more likely to obey in Milgram-type experiments; attitudes toward individual responsibility and toward obedience influence whether people hold individuals responsible for crimes of obedience

they were making. To appear helpful and 'normal', they did whatever the experimenter asked.

2. *Subject roles.* Research participants also behave differently depending on the *subject role* they enact when they enter the study. Some people, for example, try to fulfil the *good subject role* by carefully following instructions and by conscientiously performing all requirements (yes-sayers, sycophants). People who are motivated to be good subjects also try to figure out the purpose of the research. Then they change their responses to

confirm the hypothesis they think is being investigated. In contrast with the good subject role, others may adopt a bad or *negative subject role*: they complain that the research is trivial and uninteresting, and therefore refuse to cooperate with the researcher at every turn. Negativistic subjects may even evidence what has been termed the 'screw you' effect by actively trying to distort the findings; they respond at random or in other ways that they hope will disconfirm the researcher's hypothesis. Negativistic subjects are often very suspicious. But presumably because most subjects are volunteers, educated, middle-class and stable (non-neurotic) they are more likely to adopt the positive, passive role.

3.   *Experimenter effects*. Demand characteristics (Chapter 3) are those features of the situation that subjects believe demand (or require) they behave in a particular way. In the Milgram study these are the subtle cues given by the experimenter. Milgram's experimenter was supremely matter-of-fact. If the real subject protested against the order to shock (and many subjects did), the real experimenter said, 'Please continue'. If the subject protested again, the experimenter said, 'The experiment requires that you continue'. Further protest was met by 'It is absolutely essential that you continue', and if necessary the experimenter finally said, 'You have no choice, you must go on'. Replies are cold, factual, impersonal.

Obedience in the Milgram experiment is *not* a matter of the subject's giving over his/her will to the experimenter; rather, it is a matter of the experimenter's persuading the subject that he/she has a *moral* obligation to continue. This moral aspect of the experimenter–subject relationship is sustained in part by the impersonal nature of the experimenter's behaviour. The experimenter, the scientist, is objective; he presents himself to the subject as an unbiased, disinterested observer concerned only to interpret the experiment's requirements for the subject. The experimenter acts as if he is simply presenting the social-moral world to the subject as he sees it. The expert, the officer, the scientist often plays this role.

Naturally, having at least (in part) understood the nature of obedience researchers have turned their attention to understanding and teaching how and why certain people resist. The Milgram experiment remains perhaps the most famous in the whole of psychology and it is not difficult to see why!

7.4   The Brutal Jailer

A third study which revealed our less noble character took part in the
basement of one of the world's best psychology departments. The
American authorities had been worried by a number of serious
prison riots and an imaginative psychologist called Zimbardo
decided to do a role-play study. Its consequences, like its findings,
were dramatic, not only for the prison (correction) service but for
how we see ourselves.

Zimbardo constructed a mock prison that was to be the site of a
two-week study of the effects of prison on the behaviour of subjects
pretending to be prisoners and other subjects pretending to be
guards. To 'populate' his prison, Zimbardo placed an advertisement
for male college students willing to participate in a two-week study of
prison life. They were to be paid $15.00 per day. Seventy applicants
answered and were carefully screened for evidence of psychological
disorder. Twenty-four college students from all over the United
States and Canada who passed these tests remained.

Twelve of these young men were assigned at random to be prisoners; 12 were assigned to be guards. Remember these were student
role-players and all knew they were being paid to take part in an
experiment. All knew that chance alone separated guards from prisoners. Most features likely to produce real brutality in real prisons
were missing here: the subjects were normal; they were only role
playing. But the role play was very realistic.

The 'prisoners' were picked up from their homes in real police
cars. They really were lined up spread-eagled against the police cars
and frisked. They were carried off in a car with a siren that wailed.
They were fingerprinted, stripped and de-loused. Zimbardo's
prison, like all total institutions, degraded its prisoners. They were
sprayed with a deodorant, searched, issued with an identification
number, and outfitted in a dress-like shirt but no underwear, heavy
ankle chain and stocking cap to hide their long hair. Guards were
issued khaki uniforms, billy clubs, whistles and reflective sunglasses
reminiscent of those worn by the guards in the film *Cool Hand Luke*.
The guards were told to maintain security and order in the prison
(Haney, Banks and Zimbardo, 1973; Zimbardo, 1975).

A brief description of what went on is set out in Table 7.2.

The question that arises from this study is not so much why the
'guards' were so brutal, but rather what stopped or did not stop them
being brutal. Why were these normal students not inhibited from
their various actions? In a prison, guards are entitled, and know they

TABLE 7.2: What happened in Zimbardo's simulated prison?*	
Time	Description of event
Day 1	Prisoners are brought to the 'Stanford County Prison'
Day 2	The guards awaken the prisoners at 2:30 a.m. and make them shout out their prison identification number, which is sewn to their shifts
	The prisoners rebel, remove stocking caps and numbers, and barricade themselves in their cells. Guards counter by hosing them down with a chemical fire extinguisher
	To prevent rebellious incidents, the guards set up a privilege cell and a solitary confinement cell
Day 3	Using the bathroom becomes a privilege. After 10:00 p.m. prisoners must urinate in a bucket in their cells
	Prisoner No. 8612 is released because of 'acute emotional disturbance'
	Visiting day: all parents, relatives and friends agree to the prison's arbitrary visitation rules
Day 4	A priest visits the prisoners, encourages them to contact a lawyer or public defender
	Prisoner No. 819 is released after breaking down and crying hysterically
Day 5	Parole board meets; all subjects say that they will forfeit all the payment they have earned as subjects up to this time if paroled
	Prisoner–guard relations stabilise; prisoners join guards in an attempt to force one subject to end a hunger strike
	Several factors – the increasing malice of the guards, the depression levels of the prisoners, and the reaction of a colleague to the prisoners' degradation – prompt Zimbardo to consider ending the study
Day 6	Experiment terminated

*The behaviours indicated suggest that the subjects were working hard to conform to the rules of the game. In doing so, they unwittingly slipped into the social roles of prisoner and guard.

are entitled, to use (at least minimal amounts of) force to restrain unruly prisoners. The rule they must follow is to use 'minimal force', not 'no force'. But how much force is appropriate? Thus, each guard must answer the question: How far should I go in 'disciplining' these truculent prisoners? Guards in the Zimbardo experiment slid from reasonable force to brutality. And they do so in many prisons.

Two factors seem to have caused this to happen:

1. *Degradation.* Once a person has been degraded, it is far easier to do whatever one wants to him/her, to ignore his/her

humanity and even basic human rights. We are ordinarily unaware of the degree to which our being treated as civilised, decent, autonomous, moral agents depends on our ability to look and act like such agents. To the degree that we make it impossible for other people to look and act that way, we make it easy to treat them as less human. Prison dress is the start of the degrading experience.

2.   *Moral drift.* Bad guards, a minority, served as a model for the others and their brutality increased. One of the bad guards turned a fire extinguisher on the prisoners. He did two things at once: he assaulted the prisoner; he also expressed his moral view of such behaviour. He announced that such behaviour was acceptable. He didn't do this in words, but his behaviour made it clear. This behaviour could have been countered by its opposite, or by an expression of the view that such behaviour was unacceptable. Some of the good guards felt this way, but they didn't say so. The good guards, then, contributed to a sort of pluralistic ignorance. Not objecting to brutality, this is a form of compliance.

Why didn't the good guards cut through the pluralistic ignorance by telling the bad guards that what they were doing was wrong? Possibly the good guards felt they had no right to tell other people what to do. Most people seem to be quite inhibited about saying to someone, 'What you are doing is wrong'. Yet remaining silent in the face of immoral action contributes to that immorality. And a failure to express disapproval of an immoral action means that our disapproval doesn't enter into the formation of a shared, objective social consensus.

The study does, however, provide us with a dramatic illustration of the power of pressures to conform in social life. Almost from the start, subjects tried to conform to the implicit norms of the situation. A *norm* is a social standard that describes what behaviours should and shouldn't be performed in a social setting. Even though the situation created by Zimbardo was ambiguous, it was not normless. All of the subjects had a general idea of what it meant to act like a prisoner or like a guard. As the study progressed, they became more and more comfortable in their roles. Eventually, to be a guard meant to control *all* aspects of the prison, and to use force to protect this control if necessary. Prisoners, on the other hand, were supposed to accept this control and try to get through the experience as easily as possible by obeying all the prison's rules. Subjects who refused to obey these norms were pressurised by the other subjects until they brought their behaviour back in line; nonconformity was not tolerated.

One wonders then what sort of people are attracted to the prison service. More importantly, one wonders how they should be trained.

Chapter 8:
The State of the Art in Psychology

Psychology is one of the most popular degree topics at universities around the world. Its popularity and popularisation may be one reason why its results seem commonsensical, precisely because so many people study and read about it. There are more trained and practising psychologists than ever before. And we are making headway in understanding behaviour, although not always in banishing myths and superstition.

The topics of interest and research methods are growing apace in psychology. Some of the approaches to behaviour – like the psychoanalytic and humanist – once so popular have smaller and smaller followings. Psychology is becoming more biological and cognitive and new methods are being developed to test new theories and measure new aspects of behaviour.

Inevitably some of the more difficult and multidetermined applied problems that psychologists study and attempt to solve remain much the same as ever. Applied psychologists in hospitals, prisons and business organisations are, however, called upon more and more to provide their expertise in multidisciplinary teams.

But what of the future? Furnham (1994b) has speculated on the present and future state of psychology.

It has been nearly 20 years since psychologists celebrated the centenary of the establishment of their discipline as an experimental science in Germany. Historians and futurologists have looked back and forward respectively attempting to ascertain whether psychology has lived up to its promise, what the most important discoveries have been, and where the discipline is going.

In some circles, and in some countries more than others, psychology has always received indifferent to bad treatment in the press. Never fully accepted as a natural science, yet somehow not exclusively a social science, sceptics have often adopted a wait-and-see attitude to psychology. For some, over 100 years have revealed very little either we did not know, or that was not ultimately derived from other disciplines such as physiology, statistics or philosophy. This disillusionment has occurred within the discipline as much as it has outside.

Yet vigorous debates occur both inside and outside and discipline concerning, for example, the role of theory in psychology or the link between the behavioural and natural sciences.

There are all sorts of dangers haunting those who peer into psychology's crystal ball. Perhaps the most salutary warning about the foibles of such an enterprise is to be seen in examining the writings of past futurologists. Frequently there is an embarrassing gulf between what was predicted and what actually occurred. Nearly always, futurological speculators have been trapped into believing that the theories, concerns and methodologies of their time will somehow, although possibly transformed, dictate future concerns. Divergent thinking in terms of major paradigm shifts, interventions or responses to social and economic crisis seldom occurs. In this sense it is almost impossible to speculate accurately at any detailed level although it might be possible to anticipate broad trends.

In addition, there is the danger of creating a self-fulfilling prophecy. Speculation about the future may encourage young researchers and funding bodies to support certain, quite specific areas of research while ignoring others. Although advantageous for some, this inclination could lead other researchers to eschew, to their detriment, other equally important areas of research.

Finally, and because speculators are neither omniscient nor totally disinterested, there may be a degree of wish fulfilment in their speculations. They cannot know all the developments in all areas of psychology, and no doubt have a fairly well-developed personal epistemology; their speculations are a function of their personal interests and personal philosophy of science. One way of dealing with this problem is to canvass the opinions of a fairly large group and then examine systematically the determinants and correlates of their beliefs.

In 1988, a distinguished working party of the British Psychological Society (BPS) considered in detail the future of psychology. They argued that psychological questions may be legitimately asked in any sphere of human activity, and that the breadth of both pure and applied psychology is very wide. Although they recognised the diversity of psychology and its possible fragmentation, differences of opinion were seen by some to be destructive and demanding, but by others as providing creative tensions potentially capable of providing a worthwhile synthesis. Their report began with a dozen examples of psychology's contribution to well-being, but noted the tension that remains between the pure and applied researchers. In many ways the report is parochial, dealing narrowly with British concerns about funding, government recognition etc., but it also considers issues of importance to the wider community. The BPS noted, for instance:

> While we see considerable benefits in establishing groups of individuals with common interests within the psychological sciences, we believe the psychological community should seek to establish mechanisms which ensure mutual communication between such groupings and opportunities for synthesis. We believe that the disciplines should resist splintering of psychological knowledge into groups which identify themselves as separate from the mainstream of psychology, and seek to deny their psychological origins.... Psychologists when talking of psychology in the public domain should be encouraged to show how a variety of viewpoints is inevitable given the complexity of the human condition and that diversity is a sign of intellectual strength. While it may be a useful teaching strategy to set up one 'school' of psychology against another, such a confrontational approach creates a distorted view of knowledge. (pp.48–49)

Of course, not everyone would agree with this observation. Further it is unclear to which 'view of knowledge' or philosophy of science reference is being made. Apart from working parties, several groups have speculated about the current and future status of psychology. These include laypeople, employers of psychologists, philosophers and sociologists of science.

The relatively rapid, demand-led ascendance of professional psychology (applied, clinical counselling, education, occupational, organisational and school) has resulted in some interest in what employers (clients) want and expect of psychologists. One US study found employers distinguishing sharply between practitioners and scientists, favouring the former (Dole, Levitt, Baggaley and Stewart, 1986). They note:

> ... if our responses are valid, the job applicant who gives evidence that she is a flexible, genuine, intelligent, caring, empathic, smil-

ing, team player, who manages stress with innovation, is far more likely to be hired than a person who reads the journals and attends professional meetings. If she is tough-minded, hard-nosed, and publishes, her chances of a job often are somewhat less. (p. 654)

A similar British study also revealed some surprising findings. Fletcher, Rose and Radford (1991) had 132 completed questionnaires returned from potential employees participating in a graduate recruitment interview round. Respondents were asked the extent to which they believed that psychology, humanities and science graduates had various attributes. More than both of the other disciplines, psychology graduates were seen as being good at dealing with people's problems, having face-to-face communication skills, knowing what makes people tick, able to sum up people well, sensitive to others and having counselling skills. Curiously they received the lowest ratings on business knowledge, having values sympathetic to business, ambition and career orientations, and knowing what they want from life. Whereas psychology graduates could have been seen as getting the best of both the arts and science worlds, in fact the respondents seem to have thought that they had the strengths of neither.

Kimble (1984), in a similar but somewhat more sophisticated and extensive study, set out to discover how psychologists differed on a 12-item epistemic differential that represented bipolar positions on major issues. He gave his questionnaire to undergraduates, but did not report their responses, preferring to discuss the results from 81 officers of various APA divisions and, perhaps most interestingly, with regard to his hypothesis, 164 members from rather different APA divisions. He received a 58% response from the experimental psychologists, a 45% response rate from those interested in the study of social issues, a 30% response rate from the psychotherapists, and a 31% response rate from the humanistic psychologists. His results showed a clear scientist–humanist distinction in relation to research which highlighted the two cultures of psychology. He argues:

People with biases in either the humanist or scientist direction find their way into organizations where these values are dominant. Once they are there a process of socialization takes over. The biases that made the organization attractive in the first place are nurtured and strengthened. In short, the dual processes of selection and emphasis, rather than a pre-established epistemological typology are the bases for psychology's two cultures. (p. 838)

For Kimble, this fundamental difference explains why one group might take the vehemently held beliefs of the other to be trivial. The two groups in psychology differ in important values, beliefs about the sources of basic knowledge and the generality of psychological laws. However, it is not clear why he thinks that bias pre-dates membership of particular societies.

Krasner and Houts (1984) were particularly interested in perceptions of the value of neutrality of science. They surveyed two groups – one of 82 (63% response rate) who were interested in behaviour modification, and another of 37 (37% response rate) who were randomly selected from APA journal authors. Respondents were asked to complete three questionnaires: a theoretical orientation survey, an epistemological style questionnaire and a value survey. The two groups differed dramatically, consistently and predictably, especially on the theoretical orientation. The 'behavioural', more than the mixed comparison group endorsed a factual, quantitative, empirical and objective approach to understanding human behaviour. However, the two groups did not differ on values concerned with political and social philosophy. In arguing for more 'case studies' of this kind, the authors conclude:

> It is both propitious and pragmatic that such a science of scientists should begin with psychologists, scientists whose discipline requires them to be at once subject and object of their own research. (Krasner and Houts, 1984, p.849)

Other studies have examined psychologists' speculations about the future of their discipline. Smith (1975) asked 50 British psychologists from a variety of backgrounds to complete a 40-item questionnaire which asked them to predict the date of various happenings; e.g. 'Learning theory will be of historical interest only; Psychology as a discipline will disintegrate.' The respondents felt a number of things would never happen; for example, that there would never be a formal split between humanistic–philosophical psychologists and mechanistic–behavioural psychologists. Factor analysis yielded seven clear, interpretable factors concerning a scenario for the future. These included belief in a period of expansion, and belief in a breakthrough in neuropsychology by the end of the century. The respondents also expected an increased emphasis on behavioural control, and a trend toward greater social relevance.

> The decline and fall of psychology is unlikely to set in until after the year 2040. Traditional theories such as learning theory will

still be hallowed in 50 years' time. Psychology will have neither disintegrated nor split. The psychology that we know will only begin to decline when our present assumptions begin to crumble as events that we consider impossible – for example extra-terrestrial psychology, reliable ESP and thought transference with animals – become possible. (p.9)

More recently Furnham (1994b) attempted a snapshot of how academic psychologists see their discipline. He got 202 academic psychologists working worldwide to complete questionnaires.

Table 8.1 contains the overall results. Very few questions elicited strong agreement except those relating to the ability of psychologists to diagnose and assess reading difficulties and intellectual deficits. On the other hand, the total population strongly disagreed with eight of the statements. They tended not to believe that psychological questions will be reduced to neurophysiology; that the public is well informed about psychology; that there have been no developments in the treatment of the mentally ill; that psychologists should decrease the emphasis on teaching experimental design; psychology is not a science; studies with $N = 1$ can never really be scientific; social behaviour can be understood without considering cultural and economic factors; and measurement procedures do not influence what is measured. The standard deviations and means indicate that few questions elicited floor or ceiling effects or extremely skewed data/responses.

Keynote speakers and psychological society presidents (Conway, 1992) have recently focused on not so much the state of the art but the possibly fragmented future of the discipline. Conway, for example, posed the fascinating and difficult question 'How is it that we psychologists come to hold such contrasting meta-theoretical positions about the discipline? What leads some of us to believe that mind is brain, that human behaviour is completely determined, or that humans can be explained by the laws of a natural science of behaviour, while others of us reject such beliefs in favour of contrasting positions?' (p.1). Rather surprisingly, perhaps, he argues that metaphysical values are essentially cognitive styles which are related to personality variables.

Different researchers have highlighted the two approaches of psychologists. Kimble (1984) called them the humanist and the scientist, and Conway (1992) the analytic and holistic, while others have talked about the correlational vs experimental approach. Other ways of looking at overall attitudes to the disciplines are optimistic vs pessimistic, or unifiers vs fragmenters (Scott, 1991).

TABLE 8.1: Means and standard deviations of responses to the 91 questions (N = 202)*

Items	Mean	SD	Response
1. Psychology as a unified discipline is bound to break up in the near future	3.55	1.77	Disagree
2. There is likely to be a 'major breakthrough' in psychology in the near future	3.43	1.64	Disagree
3. Cognitive psychology has almost no ecological validity	3.04	1.46	Disagree
4. The 'softer' areas of psychology (social, personality) have shown precious little advance over the past 50 years	2.96	1.70	Disagree
5. Most psychological questions will ultimately be answered by neurophysiologists	2.42	1.68	S.Disagree
6. Psychology is a social science	4.68	1.72	Agree
7. Research psychologists tend to study their own problems	3.12	1.77	Disagree
8. The public is very well informed about the discipline of psychology	2.16	1.12	S.Disagree
9. Psychology is a natural science	4.05	1.81	Disagree
10. Cognitive science will shortly replace psychology as the major behavioural science	2.58	1.46	Disagree
11. The animal liberation movement will eventually stop psychological studies on animals	2.97	1.56	Disagree
12. There have been no major developments in the treatment of the mentally ill for 50 years	2.38	1.51	S.Disagree
13. To all intents and purposes, psychoanalysis as a theory and method is dead in most countries	3.43	1.81	Disagree
14. Within the next 20 years computers will be able to simulate cognition	3.64	1.77	Disagree
15. We should encourage the decline in the importance of statistical experimental design in teaching	2.47	1.38	S.Disagree
16. Learning theory is of historical interest only	2.59	1.52	Disagree
17. Compared to medicine, psychology has made very little progress	3.50	1.79	Disagree
18. Most of the patients of clinical psychologists do not get better	3.16	1.79	Disagree
19. Mothers know more about child development than most educational psychologists	2.90	1.59	Disagree
20. There are far too many 'quacks' that call themselves clinical psychologists	4.19	1.80	
21. A surprisingly large number of practising psychologists appear to have psychological problems themselves	3.82	1.68	
22. Most members of the public in this country are surprisingly ignorant about psychology	5.03	1.56	Agree
23. Clinical psychologists are of much lower status than psychiatrists in the eye of the public	4.59	1.61	Agree

24. Psychologists tend to place too much emphasis on genetics and the inheritance of human abilities and problems	3.10	1.57	Disagree
25. It is a pity psychologists are not called upon more by government committees	5.05	1.52	Agree
26. 'Pop Psychology' as shown in self-help paperbacks and popular magazines and books is harmless nonsense	3.38	1.53	Disagree
27. University psychology courses attract rather unstable people	2.37	1.42	Disagree
28. Most personality tests are hopeless, unreliable and invalid	3.15	1.63	Disagree
29. Intelligence tests do not measure intelligence	3.56	1.78	Disagree
30. Psychologists can be very helpful in diagnosing/assessing the following problems:			
a. marital problems	5.41	1.23	Agree
b. organisational issues	5.44	1.21	Agree
c. reading difficulties	5.73	1.04	S.Agree
d. intelligence deficits	5.60	1.18	S.Agree
31. Psychologists can be helpful at curing the following problems:			
a. learning problems	4.71	1.48	Agree
b. reading difficulties	4.75	1.44	Agree
c. marital problems	4.62	1.46	Agree
d. neurotic illness	4.69	1.45	Agree
e. intelligence deficits	3.31	1.68	Disagree
f. personality problems	4.13	1.56	
g. organisational issues	4.90	1.39	Agree
h. psychosis, schizophrenia	3.20	1.62	Disagree
32. The major aim of psychology is to increase knowledge	4.75	1.66	Agree
33. All psychologists have an obligation to apply their findings	3.77	2.01	
34. Human behaviour is basically lawful	4.85	1.63	Agree
35. We can only increase psychological knowledge by experiment and observation	4.43	1.84	
36. Psychology is heavy on data but light on theory	4.02	1.74	
37. It is better to sacrifice ecological validity for experimental generalisability	3.23	1.41	Disagree

TABLE 8.1: (Contd.)*

Items	Mean	SD	Response
38. Field studies with naturalistic observation are preferable to experimental manipulation	3.77	1.37	
39. Psychology is not a science	2.22	1.44	S. Disagree
40. Psychologists have underplayed the importance of genetic factors in human behaviour	3.61	1.62	
41. Studies with $N = 1$ can never really be scientific	2.47	1.68	S.Disagree
42. Psychologists have tended to work at a too molecular level of analysis to understand complex human behaviour	4.09	1.68	
43. Cognition precedes affect in most cases	3.51	1.69	
44. The major aim of psychology should be to improve the human condition	4.54	1.67	Agree
45. Most complex human behaviour is essentially unpredictable	3.38	1.67	Disagree
46. The vast majority of findings in psychology are commonsensical	3.21	1.57	Disagree
47. The explanatory power of psychological theories is very poor	3.66	1.62	
48. Nearly always longitudinal research is preferable to cross-sectional research	4.20	1.58	
49. It is a mistake to assume that man is a rational animal	4.14	1.75	
50. Correlational psychology has achieved far less than experimental psychology	3.75	1.55	
51. Most normal adults are trustworthy, moral and responsible adults	4.44	1.47	
52. Personality does not change much over time	4.17	1.43	
53. Most people are able to maintain their beliefs in the face of group pressure to the contrary	3.18	1.28	Disagree
54. There is no such thing as genuine altruism	3.23	1.68	Disagree
55. Normal adults have sufficient insight into their own behaviour never to need a psychologist	3.25	1.62	Disagree
56. Psychology is more of a science than economics.	4.47	1.57	
57. Most adults are untrustworthy, immoral and irresponsible	2.87	1.56	Disagree
58. America leads the world in psychological research	4.47	1.75	
59. Single case studies in psychology are useless	2.33	1.40	Disagree
60. Psychology requires more quantification to become a better science	3.46	1.71	Disagree

#	Statement			
61.	Psychologists spend too much time discussing the philosophy of their subjects	3.09	1.58	Disagree
62.	Psychology students should be taught more genetics and evolution theory	3.86	1.77	
63.	It is a mistake to think of memory as a 'store house'	4.32	1.58	Agree
64.	Studies of animal behaviour have made an invaluable contribution to psychology	4.92	1.57	Agree
65.	Psychologists would profit from a better education in philosophy	4.72	1.60	Agree
66.	Psychologists use too much jargon	4.64	1.64	
67.	Most psychological theories radically underestimate the influence of emotion on cognition	4.28	1.36	
68.	Evolutionary theory does more harm than good when it is used to 'explain' psychological phenomena	3.78	1.60	Agree
69.	Social, personality and clinical psychology is easy to research but hard to research well	4.77	1.70	Disagree
70.	Psychology is a 'pre-science' that changes but does not progress	3.06	1.49	Disagree
71.	Most publications in psychology are useless because they report findings that cannot be replicated	3.11	1.54	
72.	It will soon be impossible to work as a cognitive psychologist without a thorough understanding of connectionist/PDP models	3.86	1.46	
73.	Connectionist models of cognitive functions are preferable to 'serial' models because they are more consistent with what we know about neural action	3.95	1.37	Disagree
74.	In the future, sophisticated computers will have conscious experience	2.83	1.64	S.Disagree
75.	Social behaviour can be understood without considering cultural and economic factors	2.03	1.39	Disagree
76.	Psychology is objective	3.72	1.47	Disagree
77.	Psychological knowledge is absolute and cumulative	2.77	1.47	
78.	Psychology is capable of discovering universal laws that govern the external world	3.50	1.75	
79.	Psychologists usually subject their theories to potential falsification through rigorous empirical testing	3.60	1.59	S.Disagree
80.	Measurement procedures do not influence what is measured	2.48	1.60	S.Disagree
81.	Data provide objective, independent bench marks for testing theories	4.11	1.75	
82.	The processes by which theories are created, justified and diffused throughout a research community are needed to understand science	5.26	1.32	Agree

TABLE 8.1: (Contd.)*

Items	Mean	SD	Response
83. All behaviour is a social process and cannot be understood without considering cultural, social, political and economic factors	5.27	1.54	Agree
84. Psychological knowledge is relative to a particular context and period of time in history	4.95	1.55	Agree
85. Psychology creates theories that are context-dependent, i.e. relative to a frame of reference	4.98	1.52	Agree
86. Truth is a subjective evaluation that cannot be properly inferred outside of the context provided by the theory	4.43	1.40	
87. Psychology is rational to the degree that it seeks to improve individual and societal well-being by following whatever means are useful for doing so	4.34	1.57	
88. There are many ways of doing psychological research validly that are appropriate in different situations	5.71	1.41	S.Agree
89. Psychologists seek supportive, confirmatory evidence in order to market their theories	4.63	1.55	
90. Nothing can be measured without changing it	3.96	1.72	
91. Data are created and interpreted by psychologists in terms of a variety of theories, and thus are theory laden	4.97	1.46	Agree

Note: *A mean of less than 2.5 was considered strongly (S.) disagree; 2.51 to 3.50 disagree, 4.50 to 5.50 agree and above 5.51 strongly (S.) agree. Genetic, Social and General Psychology Monographs **120**, 409–434 (1994). Reprinted with permission of Helen Dwight, Reed Educational Foundation. Published by Heldref Publications ,1319 18th Street, N.W. Washington, D.C 20036-1802.

The subjects in the study seemed to reject the *pessimistic* argument that psychology had made little progress (items 4, 12, 17, 71) over the years. Furthermore they (not unnaturally) rejected the *common sense* argument (items 19, 46). But they were not optimistic about a breakthrough in the near future (item 2), nor confident that all psychological questions will be answered by neuro-physiology (item 5) or cognitive science (item 10) or artificial intelligence (AI) (item 74).

To a large extent the lecturers who answered this questionnaire were very traditional: they believed that psychology is a social science, not a natural science (items 6, 9, 39, 70); they were in favour of cognitive psychology and learning theory (items 3, 16) (although it has only 'been around' for about 30 years), and in favour of statistics (item 15), genetics (item 24), single case studies (items 41, 59) and the study of philosophy (item 65). They believed that human behaviour is lawful (item 34), and disagreed with the idea that complex human behaviour was essentially unpredictable (item 45). They rejected the idea that psychologists are unstable (items 7, 27), and appeared in favour of animal studies (items 11, 64). They tended to believe the general public to be woefully ignorant about the topic of psychology (items 8, 22, 26).

The respondents seemed optimistic about applied aspects of psychology such as personality testing (item 28) and diagnosis (item 30). With few exceptions, they believed psychology was good at solving problems arising in a range of contexts from organisations to marriages (item 31).

However, when examining questions on the nature of human beings and the nature of science it seems that the sample leaned towards a humanist/holistic, rather than a scientific/analytic, tradition. Thus, the subjects wanted more philosophy (items 61, 65) and less quantification (item 60), and believed that knowledge is relatively context-dependent (items 75, 82, 83, 84, 85, 91), rather than objective, absolute and cumulative (items 76, 77, 80).

Although not directly comparable with studies reviewed in the introduction, there are some obvious overlaps and similarities. However, the respondents in this study did not expect as much change as those of Smith (1975). Finally, the neat division between psychologists from a humanistic vs scientistic perspective as described by Kimble (1984) was not apparent.

University professors' views have been canvassed before (Donald, 1990). They are not an especially accessible or a cooperative bunch, but they are important to the extent that they shape both pure and applied psychology. But there are a high number of psychologists working in education, industry, the clinical sector and the armed forces whose views on their discipline are important.

Audits of the state of the art, and crystal-gazing into the uncertain future, tend to be either empirical in the case of the former (Smith, 1975; Nederhof and Zwier, 1983) or individually speculative in the case of the latter (Conway, 1992). Few attempt a combination, as did Kimble (1984), whose work is a fine model. The ease of communication and the growth of psychology worldwide suggests that ethnocentric, one-country studies on topics such as this are misguided.

To look at academic psychologists' views of psychology of course ignores the views of the many practitioners in clinical, educational and occupational psychology, along with those working in many other different fields (e.g. prisons and the military). These applied psychologists may have radically different views about the discipline of psychology.

The state of the art is, of course, always in flux. Major breakthroughs in behavioural genetics, cognitive neuro-psychology and other 'high-tech', biologically based areas mean the future is likely to be very exciting indeed for all psychologists. There is no doubt that for psychologists at the turn of the millennium, and barely 120 years since the start of the discipline, we now live in very interesting times.

References

Aiken, L. (1994). Some observations and recommendations concerning research methodology in the behavioural sciences. *Educational and Psychological Measurement* **54**, 848–860.

Albee, G. (1982). Political ideology and science: a reply to Eysenck. *American Psychologist* **38**, 965–966.

Arnold, J., Robertson, I. and Cooper, C. (1991). *Work Psychology*. London: Butterworth.

Azuma, H. and Kashiwagi, K. (1987). Descriptors for an intelligent person: a Japanese study. *Japanese Psychological Research* **29**, 17–26.

Baron, R. (1986). *Behaviour in Organisations*. Boston: Allyn & Bacon.

Baron, R. and Byrne, D. (1981). *Instructors' Manual to accompany Social Psychology*, 3rd edn. Boston: Allyn & Bacon.

Barrass, R. (1978). *Scientists Must Write*. London: Chapman & Hall.

Ben-Shaktar, G., Bar-Hellel, M., Belen, F., Ben-Abba, B. and Fling, A. (1986). Can graphology predict occupational success? Two empirical studies and some methodological ruminations. *Journal of Applied Psychology* **71**, 615 653.

Beyerstein, B. and Beyerstein, D. (Eds) (1992). *The Write Stuff*. Buffalo, NY: Promotions.

Block, J. (1976). Issues, problems and pitfalls in assessing sex differences. *Merrill–Palmer Quarterly* **22**, 283–308.

Bouchard, T. and McGue, M. (1981). Familial studies of intelligence: a review. *Science* **212**, 1055–1059.

BPS (1979). *Report of the Society's Working Party on Corporal Punishment in Schools*. Leicester: BPS.

Brown, R. and Brown, N. (1982). Bias in psychology and introductory psychology textbooks. *Psychological Reports* **51**, 1195–1204.

Conway, J. (1992). World of differences among psychologists. *Canadian Psychologist* **33**, 1–22.

Clare, A. (1979). The causes of alcoholism. *British Journal of Hospital Medicine* **4**, 103–110.

Coleman, J., Butcher, J. and Carson, R. (1980). *Abnormal Psychology and Modern Life*. London: Scott Foresman.

Colman, A. (1988). *What is Psychology? The Inside Story*. London: Hutchinson.

Conklin, E. (1919). Superstitions, beliefs and practices among college students. *American Journal of Psychology* **30**, 83–102.

Conway, J. (1992). World of differences among psychologists. *Canadian Psychology* **33**, 1–22.

Cook, M. (1988). *Personnel Selection and Productivity*. Chichester: Wiley.

Darley, J. and Batson, C. (1973). From Jerusalem to Jerico: A study of situational and dispositional variables in helping behaviour. *Journal of Personality and Social Psychology* **27**, 100–108.

Dole, A., Levitt, D., Baggaley, A. and Stewart, B. (1986). What do employers want: functions, knowledge areas and characteristics desired of professional psychologists. *Psychological Reports* **58**, 643–658.

Donald, J. (1990). University professors' views of knowledge and validation processes. *Journal of Educational Psychology* **82**, 242–249.

Emler, N., Renwick, S. and Malone, B. (1983). The relationships between moral reasoning and political orientation. *Journal of Personality and Social Psychology* **45**, 1073–1080.

Eysenck, H. (1952). The effects of psychotherapy: an evaluation. *Journal of Consulting Psychology* **16**, 319–324.

Eysenck, H. (1957). *Sense and Non-Sense in Psychology*. Harmondsworth: Penguin.

Eysenck, H. (1982). Political ideology and science. *American Pyschologist* **37**, 1288–1289.

Eysenck, M. (1990). *Happiness: Facts & Myths*. Hove: LEA.

Fletcher, C., Rose, D. and Radford, J. (1991). Employees' perception of psychology graduates. *The Psychologist* **36**, 105–109.

Flugel, J. (1947). An inquiry as to popular views on intelligence and related topics. *British Journal of Educational Psychology* **17**, 140–152.

Forsyth, D. (1987). *Social Psychology*. California: Brooks/Cole.

Forsyth, D., Kelley, K. and Nye, J. (1987). *Instructors' Resource Manual for Social Psychology*. California: Brooks/Cole.

Furnham, A. (1988). Write and wrong. The validity of graphological analysis. *Skeptical Inquirer* **13**, 64–69.

Furnham, A. (1993). A comparison between psychology and non-psychology students' misperceptions of the subject. *Journal of Social Behaviour and Personality* **8**, 311–321.

Furnham, A. (1994a). The Barnum effect in medicine. *Complementary Therapies in Medicine* **2**, 1–4.

Furnham, A. (1994b). Reflections on the state-of-the-art in psychology. *Genetic, Social and General Psychology Monographs* **120**, 409–434.

Furnham, A., Johnson, C. and Rawles, R. (1986). The determinants of beliefs in human nature. *Personality and Individual Differences* **6**, 675–684.

Furnham, A. and Oakley, D. (1995). *Why Psychology?* London: UCL Press.

Furnham, A. and Pendleton, D. (1991). The academic consultant. *Journal of General Management* **17**, 13–19.

Furnham, A., Wardley, Z. and Lillie, F. (1992). Lay theories of psychotherapy. *Human Relations* **45**, 839–858.

Galton, F. (1978). *Hereditary Genius*. New York: St Martins Press.

Gregory, C. (1975). Changes in superstitious beliefs among college women. *Psychological Reports* **37**, 939–941.

Hall, J. (1984). *Instructor's Manual to accompany Rosenthal/Rosnow: Essentials of Behavioural Research*. New York: McGraw Hill.

Haney, C., Banks, C. and Zimbardo, P. (1973). Interpersonal dynamics in a simulated prison. *International Journal of Criminology and Penology* **1**, 69–97.

Herrnstein, R. and Murray, C. (1994). *The Bell Curve*. New York: Free Press.

Hogan, R. and Schroeder, D (1981). Seven biases in psychology. *Psychology Today* **15**, 8–14.

Huxley, T. (1902). *Collective Essays*. London: Methuen.

Hyman, R. (1977). Cold reading: how to convince strangers that you know all about them. *The Zetetic* **1**, 18–37.

Jahoda, G. (1971). *The Psychology of Superstition*. Harmondsworth: Penguin.

Kalat, J. (1993). *Introduction to Psychology*. Pacific Grove, CA: Brooks.

Keehn, J. and Prothero, E. (1958). The meaning of 'intelligence' to Lebanese teachers. *British Journal of Educational Psychology* **58**, 339–342.

Kimble, G. (1984). Psychology's two cultures. *American Psychologist* **39**, 833–839.

Klein, P. (1984). *Psychology and Freudian Theory: An Introduction*. London: Methuen.

Krasner, L. and Houts, A (1984). A study of the 'value' symptoms of behavioural scientists. *American Psychologist* **39**, 840–850.

Levitt, E. (1952). Superstitions: twenty-five years ago and today. *American Journal of Psychology* **65**, 443–449.

Lippa, R. (1994). *Introduction to Social Psychology*. Pacific Grove, California: Brooks/Cole.

Maccoby, E. and Jacklin, C. (1974). *The Psychology of Sex Differences*. Stanford: Stanford University Press.

Marks, D. and Kammann, R. (1980). *The Psychology of the Psychic*. Buffalo, NY: Prometheus.

Marzillier, J. (1981). Outcome studies of skills training: a review. In P. Trower, B. Bryant and M. Argyle (Eds), *Social Skills and Mental Health*. London: Methuen.

McClutcheon. (1986). A new test of misconceptions about psychology. *Psychological Reports* **65**, 443–449.

McKeachie, W. and Doyle, C. (1966). *Psychology*. Reading, MA: Addison Wesley.

Medawar, P. (1969). *Introduction and Intuition in Scientific Thought*. London: Methuen.

Milgram, S. (1974). *Obedience to Authority*. London: Tavistock.

Nachmias, C. and Nachmias, D. (1986). *Research Methods in the Social Sciences*. London: Edward Arnold.

Nederhof, A. and Zwier, A. (1983). The 'crisis' in social psychology: an empirical approach. *European Journal of Social Psychology* **13**, 255–280.

Nicholson, J. and Lucas, M. (1984). *All in the Mind: Psychology in Action*. London: Methuen.

Nixon, H. (1925). Popular answers to some psychological questions. *American Journal of Psychology* **36**, 418–423.

Pastore, N. (1949). *The Nature–Nurture Controversy*. New York: Kings Crown.

Pervin, L. (1988). *Current Controversies and Issues in Personality*. New York: Wiley.

Ralya, L. (1945). Some surprising beliefs concerning human nature among pre-medical psychology students. *British Journal of Educational Psychology* **15**, 70–75.

Robson, C. (1994). *Real World Research*. Oxford: Blackwell.

Rokeach, M. (1973). *The Nature of Human Values*. New York: Free Press.

Rosnow, R. and Rosenthal, R. (1992). *Beginning Behavioural Research*. New York: Maxwell.

Sabini, J. (1995). *Social Psychology*. New York: Norton.

Scarr, S. and Weinberg, R. (1976). IQ test performances of black children adopted by white families. *American Psychologist* **31**, 726–739.

Scott, T. (1991). A personal view of the future of the psychology department. *American Psychologist* **46**, 975–976.

Shipstone, K. and Burt, S. (1973). Twenty-five years on: a replication of Flugel's (1947) work and lay popular views of intelligence and related topics. *British Journal of Educational Psychology* **56**, 183–187.

Skinner, B. (1972). *Beyond Freedom and Dignity*. London: Jonathan Cape.

Smith, J. (1975). Che sera sera: the future of psychology, 1975–2035. *Bulletin of the British Psychological Society* **28**, 1–9.

Smith, M., Glass, G. and Miller, T. (1980). *The Benefits of Psychotherapy*. Baltimore: Johns Hopkins University Press.

Smith, P., Ashton, P., Elliott, J., Freeland, C., Jones, W., McKennon, A., Simpson, S. and Stroy, R. (1969). Sixth–formers and psychology: a survey. *Bulletin of the BPS* **22**, 205–212.

Stafford-Clark, D. (1970). *What Freud Really Said*. Harmondsworth: Penguin.

Stagner, R. (1948). The gullibility of personnel managers. *Personnel Psychology* **50**, 145–149.

Sternberg, R. (1982). Who's intelligent? *Psychology Today*, 30–39.

Sternberg, R. (1985). *Beyond IQ*. Cambridge: Cambridge University Press.

Sternberg, R. (1990). *Metaphors of Mind*. Cambridge: Cambridge University Press.

Sternberg, R., Conway, B., Kelnan, J. and Bernstein, B. (1981). People's conceptions of intelligence. *Journal of Personality and Social Psychology* **41**, 37–55.

Tedeschi, J., Lindskold, S. and Rosenfeld, P. (1985). *Instructors' Manual to accompany Social Psychology*. St Paul: West.

Terman, L. (1916). *The Measurement of Intelligence*. Boston: Houghton Mufflin.

Thorndike et al. (1921). Intelligence and its measurement. *Journal of Educational Psychology* **12,** 41–50.

Thurston, L. (1928). Attitudes can be measured. *American Journal of Sociology* **33**, 529–554.

Tolman, E. (1959). Principles of purposive behaviour. In S. Koch (Ed.), *Psychology: A Study of Science*. New York: McGraw Hill.

Tupper, V. and Williams, R. (1986). Unsubstantiated beliefs among beginning psychology students: 1925, 1952, 1983. *Psychological Reports* **58**, 383–388.

Wade, C. and Tavis, C. (1990). *Psychology*. New York: HarperCollins.

Wilson, E. (1978). *Sociobiology: The New Synthesis*. Cambridge: Belknap.

Wilson, M. (1973). *The Psychology of Conservation*. London: Academic Press.

Wober, M. (1972). Distinguishing centri-cultural from cross-cultural tests and research. *Perceptual and Motor Skills* **28**, 488.

Wober, M. (1973). East African undergraduates' attitudes concerning the concept of intelligence. *British Journal of Social and Clinical Psychology* **12**, 431–432.

Zimbardo, P. (1975). Transforming experimental research into advocay for social change. In M.Deutsch and H. Hornstein (Eds), *Applying Social Psychology*. Hillsdale, NJ: Erlbaum.

Index

academic psychologists 73–6, 124,
   247–52, 253
   research 89–94, 95, 96–8
advertising 202
affect vs. cognition 70–1, 72
Africa 170
age and happiness 12
aggrandising self-disclosure 150
aggression 75, 230
   Freud 118, 123
   psychoanalysis 59, 62–3
   sex differences 180, 182–7, 189, 191
Aiken, L 80–1
Albee, G 195, 196
alcohol
   myths 11, 14,15–16, 55
   prognosis for addiction 161
   unobtrusive research 108–9
   unresponsive bystander 228, 230
altruism 59, 73, 77, 202, 226
   field experiments 99
   unresponsive bystander 227–31
   see also helping behaviour
ambiguity of emergencies 228
American Psychological Association
   72, 245, 246
anal stage (Freud) 121
animal psychologists 109
anorexia 1, 75, 161, 200
anxiety 3, 75, 100, 107
   altruism 230–1

Freud 116, 119
nature/nurture 195
therapy 156, 157, 158, 161
applied psychology 152, 242–4 253,
   254
   research 89–94
   see also scientific psychology
appraisal of employees 127, 128,
   144–6
aptitude 58, 108, 131
archival research 102–3
Arnold, J, Robertson, I and Cooper, C
   128
Association for Behavioural Modification with Children 20
astrology 10–11, 41, 44, 46, 47, 49–50,
   55–6
attitude surveys 128–9, 134
aversion therapy 157
Azuma, H and Kashiwagi, K 170

Barnum Effect 44, 46, 47, 48
Baron, R 127
Baron, R and Byrne, D 202
Barrass, R 80
Beck, Aaron 156
behaviour 1–2, 55–6, 57, 77, 242–3,
   253
   academic psychology 73–6
   addicts 15
   assumptions of science 78

cognitivists 61
corporal punishment 21–2
degree of lawfulness 66, 72
factors leading to action 70–1
Freud 115, 118–25
generality of laws 69, 72
graphology 42, 50
Hawthorne studies 134–6
helping 182, 184–5, 201, 202,
    227–31
humanistic 60, 71–2
intelligence 168, 174
level of analysis 70, 72
modification 20, 246
nature/nurture 68–9, 195–200
neurobiology 61
obedience 231–7
organisms 71
prison study 238–41
psychoanalysis 59, 60, 62
research 78–87, 90, 96–112
sex differences 180–93
sexual 59, 62, 118–9, 121–3, 155,
    187–8, 193, 202
social psychology 202, 226
temporal aspects of lawfulness 68,
    72
therapy 154, 156–7, 159, 161–5
work-related 127, 129, 152
behaviour therapies 154, 156–7, 159,
    162, 164, 165
behavioural psychology 59, 60, 73, 75,
    246
alcohol 16
memory failure 62
beliefs 2–3, 105, 107, 194, 246
addicts 15
human nature test 4–7
lay people vs psychotherapists 160
sex differences 181
therapy 156, 159, 160, 163–4
bell curve of intelligence 176–7,
    179–80
Ben-Shaktar, G, Bar-Hellel, M, Belen,
    F, Ben-Abba, B and Fling, A 42,
    43
Beyerstein, B and Beyerstein, D 42
bias 245–6
appraisal of employees 127

interviews 105, 106
research 82, 98, 105
tests 108, 173
therapy 165, 166
Binet, Alfred 170–1
biofeedback training 157
biological determinism 180, 195
biological theories
alcohol 15–16
sex differences 186–7, 188–9, 193
biomedical therapy 154, 157–8
biopsychology 64, 65, 74
black box psychology 59
Block, Jack 181
blue-sky research 89
body language 75, 184, 202
Clever Hans 85
Bouchard, T and McGue, M 197
brain 1, 74, 76, 247
ECT 158
intelligence 177
neurobiology 61, 63
sex differences 185, 187, 193
brainstorming 139–42
British Psychological Society 243, 244
corporal punishment 19–20
Brown, R and Brown, N 73

catharsis 155
Cattell, Raymond 174
character and characteristics
intelligence 167, 176
nature/nurture 192
reading 52–5
researchers 78–80, 95
sex differences 181–3
victims 230
see also human nature; personality
children
corporal punishment 17–21
Freud 118, 120, 121, 122–3
happiness 13
nature/nurture 197–200
noisy 142–3
sex differences 185–91
sexual abuse 123
Clare, A 15
Clever Hans (horse) 83–7
client-centred therapy 154, 156, 159

clinical psychologists 58, 65, 115, 244,
    248, 254
  therapy efficacy 163
cognition vs affect 70–1, 72
cognitive psychology 59, 60–1, 64,
    242, 253, 254
  memory failure 63
  sex differences 190–1, 193
cognitive science 76
cognitive therapies 75, 154, 156, 159,
    162
Coleman, J, Butcher, J and Carson, R
    14
Colman, A 57
common sense 1, 22–9, 55–6, 79, 242,
    253
  battery of quotes 28–9
  intelligence 168
  management 22, 127–33
  psychological quiz (1) 203–13
  psychological quiz (2) 213–21
  psychological quiz (3) 221–6
  tests 23–6, 130–1
communication 127, 245
  meetings 137
  non-verbal 202
  researchers 80, 88, 94
community psychologists 65
compliance 202, 231
  prison study 240
confidence 52, 79
conformity 202, 231, 236
  prison study 240–1
  sex difference 182, 185
Conklin, E 3
conservation of energy (Freud) 117–18
consistency and care (researcher)
    79–80
constructionist theory 191–2
consultants
  bogus feedback 47
  CVs 146
  research 92–4, 95
  training 148, 149
contextualism 69, 72
Conway, J 247, 254
Cook, M 110
corporal punishment 17–22
  arguments against 18–19

  arguments for 17–18
correlation 247, 250
  research 81, 82, 83, 111
counselling psychologists 64, 65, 245
creativity 71, 72
  brainstorming 139–42
  intelligence 168–9, 176
  meetings 139
  research 79, 103
crime 22, 59, 60
  myths 11, 16–22, 55
crystallised intelligence 174
culture 3, 71, 136, 245
  corporate 148, 149
  intelligence 169, 170, 175, 176–7,
    200
  obedience 236
  projection 119
  research 94, 103
  sex differences 180–1, 185, 186–7,
    191, 193
curriculum vitae 146–7

Darley, J and Batson, C 228
deception 97
defence mechanisms 113–15, 119–20,
    123, 230
degradation 238, 239–40
de-individuation 229
demand characteristics 98, 103, 104,
    237
dementia 158, 161
denial 113, 114, 120
dependent variables 96, 99, 100–1,
    106
depression 1–2, 11, 12, 75
  memory failure 62, 63
  prison study 239
  therapy 154, 156, 158, 161, 162
design
  experiments 247
  questionnaires 104–5
  research 81–2, 88, 91
  work 128, 134, 135, 152
developmental psychologists 65, 109
deviation IQ 171
diffusion of responsibility 137, 229
disability 12, 13
displacement 113, 114, 115, 118, 120

Dole, A, Levitt, D, Baggaley, A and
    Stewart, B 244
Donald, J 253
dreams 74, 89
    psychoanalysis 116–17
    therapy 155, 159, 165
drugs 14, 15
    biomedical therapy 154, 157–8
    see also alcohol

education 3, 110, 120
    human nature 192, 193, 200
    intelligence 166, 167, 177, 178
educational psychology 65, 244, 254
ego 116–17, 118–20, 121, 123
Electra complex 121
electroconvulsive therapy (ECT) 158
Ellis, Albert 156
emergencies 184–5, 227–31
Emler, N, Renwick, S and Malone, B
    194
emotion 12, 73, 75, 226
    Freud 120, 123
    sex differences 180, 184, 185–8, 193
    therapy 156, 163
    vs cognition 70–1, 72
employment
    in psychology 73, 244–5, 253, 254
    selection 41–2, 110, 128, 144, 152
enthusiasm (researcher) 78–9
enuresis 158, 161
environment
    behaviourism 59
    Clever Hans 86
    cognitivists 61
    effect on performance 201–2
    Hawthorne Effect 135
    humanists 60, 63
    id 118
    intelligence 166, 167, 178–80
    nature/nurture 68–9, 72, 192–200
    research 88, 101
    sex differences 181, 189–90
environmental psychology 65, 73
equal opportunities 128
ergonomics 65, 128, 152
ethics
    obedience study 232, 234–5
    research 97, 98, 99–100, 109

    therapy 165
ethological psychology 61
evaluation apprehension 98, 103, 104
    meetings 138
    obedience study 235–6
evolutionary psychology 61–2
experiments 2, 78, 202
    Clever Hans 84, 86
    common sense 26
    design 247
    field 98–100, 101, 102
    illumination 133–4
    obedience study 231–7
    prison study 238–41
    quasi 100–1
    research 86–7, 88, 96–101, 104,
        109, 111
    vs correlation 247, 250
experimental psychology 64, 65, 73,
    109, 245
experimental realism 97
external validity 97, 99
extrasensory perception (ESP) 50, 58,
    200
extroverts 27, 42
    consultants 94, 95
Eysenck, H 27, 161–2, 195, 196
Eysenck and Gudjonsson 42
Eysenck, M 12

facial expressions 75
feedback
    behavioural therapy 157
    employee appraisal 144–6
    management training 149
    personality 44–9
    tests 108
field experiments 98–100
    compared with field study 102
    compared with quasi-experiments
        101
field study 81, 89–90, 101–2
    compared with laboratory 67–8, 72,
        102
    unresponsive bystanders 228
Fletcher, C, Rose, D and Radford, J
    245
flooding (therapy) 157
Flugel, J 166, 167

fluid intelligence 174
folk wisdom 23
Forsyth, D 239
Forsyth, D, Kelley, K and Nye, J 202
fortune telling 9, 49, 50, 51–4
   see also astrology
Franklin, Benjamin 92
fraud 80, 115
free association 116–17, 155, 159
Freud, Anna 119
Freud, Sigmund 49, 58, 59–60,
   113–26
   sex differences 187–8
   therapy 154, 155, 165
Furnham, A 29, 42, 46, 242, 247
Furnham, A, Johnson, C and Rawles,
   R 195, 196
Furnahm, A and Oakley, D 23, 28, 29,
   62, 73–4, 96
Furnham, A and Pendleton, D 92
Furnham, A, Wardley, S and Lillie, F
   158

Galton, F 195, 197
garbology 108–9
Gardner, Howard 175
gender *see* sex differences
generalisation 124, 164
   CVs 147
   meetings 139
   research 88, 97
General Measure Aptitude Tests
   (GMATs) 108
general mental ability 172, 174
genetics 253, 254
   intelligence 167, 178–80
   sex differences 181
   see also heredity
genital stage (Freud) 122
Genovese, Catherine (attack victim)
   227, 228
ghosts 7
graphology 41, 42–4, 49–50, 51, 55
Gregory, C 3
groups 244
   brainstorming 139–42
   conformity and obedience 231
   Hawthorne Effect 134, 135, 136
   intelligence 177–80

meetings 137–9
   sex differences 182, 185
group therapy 157

Hall, J 78
halo effect 82
Haney, C, Banks, C and Zimbardo, P
   238
happiness 1, 202
   myths 11–15, 55
Hawthorne Effect 82, 133–7
helping behaviour 201, 202
   bad Samaritan 227–31
   sex differences 182, 184–5
   see also altruism
heredity 74, 75
   nature/nurture 68–9, 72, 192–200
   see also genetics
Hogan, R and Schroeder, D 73
Horney 123
honesty (researcher) 80
hormones 186–7, 193
horse (Clever Hans) 83–7
human nature 253
   nature/nurture 192–200
   test 4–7
   twins, siblings and adopted children
     197–200
   see also character and characteristics;
     personality
humanistic psychology 59, 60, 61, 76,
   242, 245–7, 253
   compared with scientific 71–2, 73
   memory failure 63
   therapy 156
   values 64, 66
Huxley, T 27
Hyman, R 51
hypnosis 123, 154
hypotheses 1, 187
   Freud 123, 125–6
   research 81, 82, 86–8, 91, 98–9,
     103
hypothetical constructs 69–70, 72

id 59, 116–17, 118–19, 120
identification (Freud) 122
illumination experiment 133–4
implosive therapy 157

impotence 158, 161
impression management 94, 146, 150
independent variables 96, 99, 100–1,
    106
industrial psychologists 65
inkblot tests 46
intellectual deficits 247
intellectualisation 120
＊intelligence 2, 75, 166–80
    facts 171–3
    ＊happiness 12–13
    nature/nurture 192, 195 197–200
    sex differences 167, 170, 173, 180
    tests 106, 108, 167, 168, 170–3,
        176–7, 200
intelligence quotient (IQ) 58, 172,
    176–80
    constancy 167
    nature/nurture 197–9
    tests 106, 168, 170–1, 173, 177
interpersonal competence 75, 128, 169
interpretation 82–3
    therapy 155, 156, 159
intervening variables 70, 72
interviews
    attitude surveys 134
    bias 105, 106
    research 104–6, 109, 112
    selection 110
introverts 94, 95
intuitions 67, 72
inventiveness (researcher) 79

Jahoda, G 7, 8
Jaks, Dr Stanley 52
Japan 170, 173
job satisfaction 127–8, 142–3, 152

Kalat, J 64, 83, 87, 110, 113, 175
Keehn, J and Prothero, E 170
Kimble, G 64, 71, 72, 245–6, 247, 253,
    254
Klein, P 116, 124
Klimoski and Rafael 43
knowledge
    assumptions 78
    intelligence 166–7
    of psychology (test) 29–41
    sources 66–7, 72

Krasner, L and Houts, A 73, 246

laboratory research 81, 89–90, 96–8,
    104, 109
    bias 98, 105
    compared with field experiments
        98–100
    compared with field study 67–8, 72,
        102
    compared with quasi-experiments
        101
    obedience study 231–7
language 1–2, 67, 74, 83
    Stroop technique 77
    tests 107, 108
    training 148, 149
Latane, Bob 138
latency stage (Freud) 122
latent content 155
leadership 183, 185
learning theory 246–7, 253
Lebanon 170
Lester, McLaughlin and Nosal 42
Levitt, E 3, 8
Lippa, R 182, 186, 193
love 202
luck 9–10
lumpers 172

Maccoby, E and Jacklin, C 181–2
management
    ability test 131–3
    appraisals 144–5
    brainstorming 141–2
    common sense 22, 127–33
    common sense test 130–1
    meeting 137–9
    rewards 142
    training 147–50
manifest content 155
manipulation check 96–7
Marks, D and Kammann, R 50, 51
marriage 11, 14, 16
Marxism 195, 196
Marzillier, J 163
mathematics 2, 172
    sex differences 182, 183, 184, 185
McClutcheon 29
McKeachie, W and Doyle, C 22–3

Medawar, P 115–16
meetings 137–9
memory 74, 119, 124–5
    failure 62–4
    intelligence 170, 173
mental illness 58, 247, 248
    therapy 154, 158
meta-analysis 162, 182–3
methodology 67, 72, 243
    Hawthorne Effect 135
    research 74, 81, 86, 88–9, 91, 94,
        96–112, 242
Milgram, Stanley 231–7
money and happiness 13, 15
moral drift 240
motivation 75, 142–4
multiple intelligence 175
mundane realism 97
myths 11–22, 55, 242

Nachmias, C and Nachmias, D 78,
    104
nature/nurture issue 68–9, 72,
    192–200
Nederhof, A and Zwier, A 254
neurobiological psychology 59, 61–2
    memory failure 63–4
neuropsychology 246, 254
neurosis 158, 161, 230–1
neutrality of science 246
Nicholson, J and Lucas, M 16
Nixon, H 2, 3, 8
non-behavioural psychology 73
non-verbal behaviour 85
    communication 202
    sex differences 182, 184
    see also body language
non-verbal tests 167, 177
norms 240–1
numerical ability 172
    see also mathematics
nurture/nature issue 68–9, 72,
    192–200

obedience 202, 231–7
    electric shock 231–7
objectivism 66–7, 72
observation 2, 67, 78, 123, 202
    Clever Hans 84, 86

common sense 26
field study 101–2
Freud 125
interviews 105
research 78, 80, 86–7, 88, 109, 111
scientific criteria 78
sex differences 184, 186, 189, 193
occupational psychology 65, 127,
    128–9, 136, 244, 254
    seven applications 137–52
Oedipus complex 115, 121–2, 188
open mindedness (researcher) 79
oral stage (Freud) 121
organisational change 128, 134
organisational psychology see occupa-
    tional psychology

parapsychology 58
Pastore, N 195
penis envy 122, 123, 188
perceptual ability 173
personality 2, 3, 75, 117–23, 192, 200
    alcohol 15–16
    assessment 42–9, 73
    character reading 52–5
    development 117, 121–3
    dynamics 117–18
    Freud 117–23
    graphology 42, 43–4
    happiness 14
    human nature 194, 196–7
    intelligence 170, 176, 178
    management 131
    obedience 236
    psychometrics 58
    researchers 65, 94, 95, 119
    selection tests 110
    sex differences 180
    structure 117, 118–20
    tests 106–8, 166, 253
    therapy 154
    see also character and characteristics
Pervin, L 230
phallic stage (Freud) 121–2
phenomenological psychology 59, 60,
    64
    memory failure 63
phobias 75
    therapy 154, 157, 158, 161, 162

phrenology 3
physiognomy 3
pluralistic ignorance 228–9, 240
political ideology 27, 194–7
Pollyanna Principle 49
Popper 125
prejudice 27, 131, 202
primary mental abilities 172–3
prison study 238–41
problem solving 27, 60, 74, 75, 92
  brainstorming 142
  intelligence 168, 169, 171, 176, 178
  meetings 139
productivity 127, 152
  Hawthorne Effect 133–4
prognosis 158, 161, 164
projection (Freud) 113, 114, 115, 119
propaganda 202
psychiatry 58
  Freud 113, 115
psychic phenomena 50–1, 58, 200
psychoanalysis 58, 59–60, 75, 242
  alcohol 16
  altruism 230
  Freud 115–19, 120, 121, 123–6
  memory failure 62–3
  sex differences 187–8, 193
  therapy 155, 159, 163–4
psychodynamic therapy 75, 154, 155
  Freud 117–18
psychokinesis 50, 58
psychological development 74–5
psychometrics 58, 65, 125
  tests 42, 169, 174
psychosexual development 121–3
psychotherapy see therapy
puberty 122

quantification (Freud) 125
quasi-experimental research 100–1
questionnaires 3, 104–6, 109, 245–7
  academic psychologists 248–52, 253
  efficacy of therapy 164
  lying 150–2
quiz
  psychological common sense (1)
    203–13
  psychological common sense (2)
    213–21

psychological common sense (3)
  221–6

race 7
  intelligence 173, 176–7, 179–80
Ralya, L 3, 8
  human nature test 4–7
randomisation 96
rational-emotive therapy 156
rationalisation (Freud) 113, 114, 120
reaction formation 230
  Freud 113, 114, 115, 119
reactivity 71, 72, 99
reading difficulties 247, 249
realism 97, 102
reasoning 60, 74, 172
regression (Freud) 113, 114, 115, 119–20
reliability 101–2
repression 155
  Freud 113, 114, 119, 125
research 78–94, 106–8, 243, 247
  analysing 82
  archival 102–3
  field experiments 98–100
  field study 101–2
  implementation 81–2
  intelligence 167
  interpreting 82–3
  interviews 104–6, 109, 112
  methodology 74, 81, 86, 88–9, 91, 94, 96–112, 242
  obedience study 231–7
  planning 80–1
  prison study 238–41
  process 87–9
  pure compared with applied 89–94, 95, 244
  quasi-experimental 100–1
  questionnaires 104–6
  reporting 83
  role play 103–4
  sex differences 183
  social psychology 227–8, 231
  therapy 163–6
  unobtrusive 108–9
  unresponsive bystander 228, 231
  see also laboratory research
researchers 73, 74–6

characteristics 78–80, 95
   Hawthorne Effect 134, 135–6
   personality 65, 94, 95, 119
   recommendations 80–3
resistance 155
responsibility diffusion 137, 229
Ringleman 138
Robson, C 89–90
Rogers, Carl 156
Rokeach, M 194
role play 103–4
   prison study 238–41
role-taking ability (researcher) 79
Rosenthal, A M 227
Rosenthal and Lines 42
Rosnow, R and Rosenthal, R 100
Rutherford 195

Sabini, J 228
sampling 105, 124, 125
Scarr, S and Weinberg, R 198
schizophrenia 75, 161, 162, 200
school psychologists 65, 244, 254
scientific psychology 76
   compared with humanistic 71–2, 73
   see also applied psychology
Scott, T 247
selection for employment 41–2, 128, 152
   tests 110, 128, 144
self-disclosure 183, 184, 185
   aggrandising 150
self-fulfilling prophecies 11, 50, 243
   therapy 158, 161
self-presentation theory 191–2, 193
self-reports 77, 81, 105–6
   efficacy of therapy 164
   knowledge 66–7, 72
   sex differences 184, 186
sex differences 75, 180–92, 193
   happiness 13
   intelligence 167, 170, 173, 180
   management 127
   obedience 236
   susceptibility 47
sexual abuse 123
sexual behaviour 155, 202
   Freud 118, 119, 121–3
   psychoanalysis 59, 62, 187–8, 193

Shipstone, K and Burt, S 167
simulation research 103–4
Skinner, B 27, 80
sleep 74, 158, 161
Sloan, Alfred P 139
Smith, J 246, 253, 254
Smith, M, Class, G and Miller, T 162
social embarrassment 229
social learning theory 189, 193
social loafing 138
social psychology 65, 75, 109, 201–2, 226–7, 245
   bad Samaritan 227–31
   nature/nurture 192
   obedience study 235–7
spatial location 180
spatial visualisation 172–2
   sex differences 182, 183, 185, 187, 189
Spearman, Charles 172, 174
splitters 172
Stafford-Clark, D 113
Stagner, R 44
Stanford-Binet test 171
statistics 81, 82–3, 125, 243, 253
Stern 171
Sternberg, Robert 168–70, 172, 174
Sternberg, R, Conway, B, Kelnan, J and Bernstein, B 168
stereotypes 202
   sexual 170, 181, 190, 191, 193
stress 12, 15, 75, 120, 129, 245
Stroop technique 77
subject roles 236–7
sublimation (Freud) 113, 114, 115, 118
superego 117, 118, 120, 122
superstition 2–11, 55, 90, 242
   human nature test 4–7
synergy effect 137
synthesis 244
systematic desensitisation 156–7

Tedeschi, J, Lindskold, S and Rosen-feld, P 202
television 100, 189–90
Terman, Lewis 171
tests
   bias 108, 173
   common sense 23–6, 130–1

human nature 4–7
intelligence 106, 108, 167, 168,
    170–3, 176–7, 200
IQ 106, 168, 170–1, 173, 177
knowledge of psychology 29–41
management 130–3
non-verbal 167, 177
personality 106–8, 166, 253
psychometric 42, 169, 174
selection 110, 128, 144
validity 108, 110, 112
textbooks 73, 75, 202
therapeutic alliance 162–3
therapy 58, 75, 153–66, 245
    efficacy 161–6
    psychoanalysis 116, 126
    psychodynamic 75, 117–18, 154,
    155
Thorndike *et al* 166
Thurstone, L L 172
token economies 157
Tolman, E 79
training 127, 128, 129, 157
    management 147–50
transference 155, 157
triarchic theory 174
trichosis diagnosis 46–7
Triplett 201–2
Tupper, V and Williams, R 3
twins 197–9

unconscious 58, 59–60, 62
    Freud 116–17, 119, 124

therapy 154, 155, 159
universalism 69, 72
unobtrusive research 108–9
unresponsive bystanders 227–31

validity 87, 97, 99
    tests 108, 110, 112
values 94, 246
    addicts 15
    human nature 194, 195
    most important 64, 66, 72
verbal abilities 172
    sex differences 182, 183, 185, 187
Vestewig, Santee and Moss 42
visual-spatial ability 172–3
    sex differences 182, 183, 185, 187,
    189

Wade, C and Tavis, C 114
Warburton 8
Wechsler tests 171
Whitehead 27
Wilson, E 189
Wilson, M 194, 195
wisdom 168–9
    folk 23
wish fulfilment 243
Wober, M 170
womb envy 123
work psychologists 128–9, 136
    see also occupational psychology

Zimbardo, P 238–41